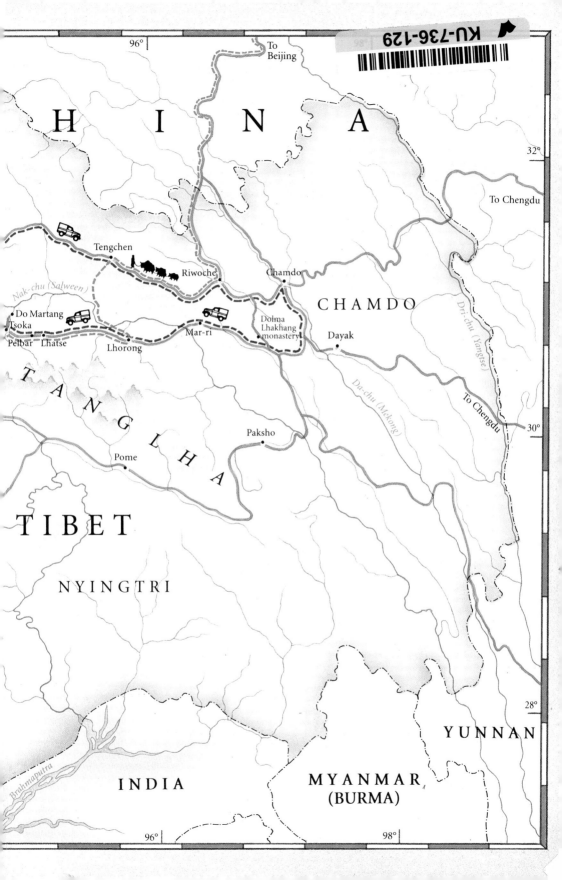

TIBET'S
SECRET MOUNTAIN

By Chris Bonington

I Chose to Climb
Annapurna: South Face
The Next Horizon
Everest: South West Face
Everest the Hard Way
Quest for Adventure
Kongur: China's Elusive Summit
The Everest Years
Mountaineer
The Climbers: A History of Mountaineering
Sea, Ice and Rock (with Robin Knox-Johnston)

By Chris Bonington and Charles Clarke

Everest: the Unclimbed Ridge

By Charles Clarke

Everest

TIBET'S SECRET MOUNTAIN

The Triumph of Sepu Kangri

Chris Bonington & Charles Clarke

Weidenfeld & Nicolson

LONDON

First published in Great Britain in 1999
by Weidenfeld & Nicolson

A CIP catalogue record for this book
is available from the British Library.

ISBN 0 297 819844

Typeset by Selwood Systems, Midsomer Norton
Set in Minion
Printed in Great Britain by Butler & Tanner Ltd, Frome and London

Weidenfeld & Nicolson

The Orion Publishing Group Ltd
Orion House
5 Upper Saint Martin's Lane
London, WC2H 9EA

For Wendy and Ruth

Contents

Illustrations and maps

The retreat from Moscow.[3]
High tech communications at camp I – Chris using the BT Mobiq.[1]

Between pages 114 and 115

Charlie with solar panels rigged across his rucksack.[5]
Charlie exploring the eastern approaches to Sepu Kangri.[5]
The small caravan of Charlie, Elliot and Pasang in the Tashi Lung.[5]
Charlie with Puh and Jayang leaving the Tanglung Valley.[5]
Charlie calling Chris's press conference at the Royal Geographical Society.[5]
Interior of Nima's *ba*.[2]
Charlie, Pasang and Elliot, the great explorers.[1]
The climbing team reaches the roadhead at Khinda.[1]
The bridge from the roadhead to the little village of Khinda.[1]
Charlie crossing the river by wire.[1]
Harvest time.[6]
The Bon monastery at Samda.[1]
Members of the team resting on their way up to Samda.[1]
The annual dance festival at Samda monastery.[2]
The white clown frightening the audience.[2]
Wherever Charlie went, people came for treatment.[5]
Some of the monks.[2]
A noviciate monk.[7]
The entire team and our neighbours.[1]
Pala and Tambu with home-made toys made from reels of the fixed rope.[1]
Base camp and Sepu Kangri reflected in the Sam Tso Taring.[1]
Afternoon matinee.[1]
Chris reporting for ITN.[1]
Scott repairing a wind generator.[1]
Orsa, Tsini, Jambu, Karteh and Tsering Sonam.[1]
Puh, Kokor and their children.[1]
At the end of the expedition we gave our neighbours food and equipment we no longer needed.[7]
Dorbe and his family.[1]
Sepu Kangri and Sam Tso Taring.[1]
The north face of Sepu Kangri.[1]
A view from the hermit's house, looking towards base camp.[7]
Scott Muir playing Atlas.[7]
Scott Muir on the summit of Thaga Ri.[8]
Victor showing Elliot how to shorten a rope at camp I.[1]
Scott and Elliot at camp I.[9]

Sources

[1] Chris Bonington

[2] Charles Clarke

[3] John Porter

[4] Jim Lowther

[5] Elliot Robertson

[6] Jim Curran

[7] Graham Little

[8] Scott Muir

[9] Victor Saunders

[10] Régis-Evariste Huc, *Travels in Tartary Tibet and China* (1852 edition translated by William Hazlitt)

Dr Akong Tulku Rinpoché

Sir Chris Bonington and Dr Charles Clarke, the two authors of *Tibet's Secret Mountain,* are friends of Samye Ling. In 1998 Charles Clarke and Elliot Robertson were among the first visitors to my monastery, Dolma Lhakhang in Kham, eastern Tibet. This made me very happy.

The members of these three expeditions wish to preserve the natural beauty of this land. Their illustrated account of this remote region will, I am sure, interest readers and I wish them every success in this venture.

Dr Akong Tulku Rinpoche

Kagyu Samyé Ling Tibetan Centre, Eskdalemuir, Dumfriesshire DG13 0QL, UK

Authors' Note

These three expeditions came to fruition only with the help of many people, in Britain, in Nepal and in Tibet itself. We thank all those who helped us, in particular National Express, without whose generous financial assistance the 1998 trip would have been difficult, if not impossible.

The expeditions were very much team efforts and we would like to record here our thanks to all our fellow members for their single-minded resolve on the mountain, for their contributions to the text and for making their photographs available. Graham Little and Victor Saunders drafted the sketch maps of the Sepu Kangri region. We would also like to thank Frances Daltrey who runs Chris's picture library for organising and keeping track of the thousands of transparencies taken by expedition members. We also appreciated the detailed first-line editing carried out by Louise Wilson, Chris's secretary.

We also owe thanks to our patient and ever-effective editor, Margaret Body. At Weidenfeld & Nicolson thanks also to Ion Trewin and Rachel Leyshon and to Bryony Newhouse who designed the book. John Gilkes drew and corrected with painstaking care the maps of Tibet.

Our most enduring memories are of the hardy people of the Sepu Kangri region, whose kindness, honesty and humour made these journeys so worthwhile.

Chris Bonington
Charles Clarke

February 1999

1 The White Snow God

1982 – 1986

CHRIS BONINGTON

There were jagged peaks, sinuous ridges and glaciers stretching into the far distance to the northern horizon. We peered through the scratched, slightly bleared windows of the old Russian turbo-prop, jockeying for position, climbing over each other to get a view and photographs of this mountain feast. It was March 1982 and we were on our way to the north-east ridge of Everest. Before dawn that morning we had boarded the plane bound for Lhasa at Chengdu, in south-west China. Barely half an hour airborne, we had started flying over this huge mountain range. We were somewhere in Tibet to the north and east of Lhasa. There were six of us on the 1982 Everest expedition. Peter Boardman, Joe Tasker, Dick Renshaw and I were going to make the first attempt on the ridge, while Charlie Clarke, our doctor, and Adrian Gordon were in support. We also had with us a trekking group from our sponsors, Jardine Matheson. The trekkers, more restrained, remained in their seats, but as climbers we were too excited by this intriguing, unexpected range of mountains. There were cries of, 'They must be at least 6000 metres.'

'Look at that peak over there. It could be even higher.'

'I wonder if anyone has ever been into them?'

'Where on earth are they?'

But then the peaks became smaller and soon we were losing height to land at Lhasa airport. The fascination of that ancient city and the challenge of the north-east ridge of Everest filled our minds and the vision of those endless peaks receded.

Two years later I received an intriguing letter from an armchair traveller and map enthusiast called Frank Boothman. He was fascinated by the geography of Tibet and had noticed on the US Air Force pilotage charts a range of peaks of over 7000 metres to the north-east of Lhasa, the highest being shown as 7350 metres, which would make it the highest point on the Tibetan plateau. He very kindly sent me the air charts and examination showed that this peak could well be the mountain that seemed to dominate all around it, the very one that we had seen from the plane from Chengdu to Lhasa. At the same time he warned me that the altitudes given were not over accurate and would almost certainly err on the high side.

At the time I had other projects to which I gave a higher priority. Yet the thought of those mysterious mountains in eastern Tibet remained in the back of my mind. Frank Boothman kept the spark alight with the occasional fresh piece of information and in 1987 the Royal Geographical Society published a map and gazetteer of the mountains of Central Asia. Sure enough, our mountain was there at 30.91°N, 93.78°E, and 7350 metres high but this hardly confirmed its true height since the RGS map had used existing material largely from the USAF flight charts. But the gazetteer served to focus my interest and I enthused about it to Jim Fotheringham, a regular climbing mate of mine with whom I had shared local climbs in the Lakes, sorties up to Scotland, a lightning trip to Shivling in the Gangotri Himalaya in 1983 and an attempt in 1987 on Menlungtse in southern Tibet. Our trip to Shivling had been one of the best I had ever undertaken. With just two of us the organisation and decision-making process had been so wonderfully simple. The climb had been committing, for, once at the mountain, we changed our objective from the one we had researched. We climbed the west summit (6500 metres) of Shivling on sight, making the first ascent alpine-style, taking four days for the climb and then descending in one day down the north-west side – because we thought the line of our ascent was too dangerous to reverse. We talked of using the same tactics on this mysterious mountain in eastern Tibet.

But in trying to reach our mountain in 1989 or even find its name I was to draw a blank. We had experienced problems with the Chinese Mountaineering Association the previous year on our second trip to Menlungtse. On that occasion we had been delayed in Kathmandu for a fortnight whilst another organisation, the Tibet Mountaineering Association, disputed the right of the Chinese to give us permission for a mountain that was not on their original list. This time, after numerous enquiries, I eventually made contact with a travel agent in Hong Kong who assured me he could get us permission through the Tibet Mountaineering Association. We were a week from setting out. Jim and I had bought our air tickets to Hong Kong, found sponsorship and had our bags packed. We then received a fax from the TMA. It told us they were very sorry they could not give us permission for this area, but that we could apply through the Chinese Mountaineering Association for another mountain. We considered the peaks on offer, but none had the fascination of the unknown centre of Tibet. Disillusioned, we gave up all thoughts of Tibet and used the time to go climbing in the far north of Scotland.

I put Tibet to the back of my mind for a few years and became immersed in other projects. In 1991 I sailed to Greenland with Robin Knox-Johnston with the aim of taking him up an unclimbed peak on the east coast. It was through this expedition that I came to know Jim Lowther, a twenty-five-year-old Lakeland climber who had extensive experience of travelling in Greenland. He came with us and as a result became a good friend, sharing in other adventures. In 1992 I went to the Panch Chuli massif in India with a joint Indian/British expedition, then back to Greenland in 1993 to climb more of the wonderful granite needles we had seen in 1991. An exploratory expedition to Kinnaur in northern India followed in 1994, once again with Harish Kapadia who had been co-leader of our Panch Chuli expedition. 1995 was the tenth anniversary of the successful Norwegian Everest expedition and we were all reunited to attempt the first ascent of Drangnag Ri, a shapely unclimbed peak of 6801 metres about fifteen miles east of Everest in Nepal. I seemed to go strongly and was a member of the summit team.

I found it almost a shock that I was now sixty. Yet my enthusiasm for climbing remained the same as when I was in my twenties. I had discovered a pattern and style of climbing that I loved, going to little known places off the beaten track to attempt unclimbed peaks with small groups of friends whose company I enjoyed. I have often been asked if climbs I have done after reaching the top of Everest have not been an anticlimax. The very reverse has been true. I really did need to reach the top of Everest and will always be grateful to Arne Næss, leader of the Norwegian Everest expedition, for making it possible. I don't think I realised how much I needed to climb Everest until I stood there in 1985. I find it difficult to define just what it meant to me. I was making neither a first ascent nor a new route. I was climbing it by the easiest possible route, via the South Col, with a strong team of Sherpas and masses of oxygen. I think I was the 236th person to get there. Yet reaching the summit was more than just the satisfaction of ego, though there was undoubtedly some of that. It was a milestone which marked the end of a chapter that had been full of challenges, uncertainty and also sorrow, of lost friends and difficult decisions. It had also been a time of tremendous stimulus and enjoyment. Friends have commented on the fact that after reaching the top of Everest I became much more relaxed.

The ascent certainly gave me the freedom to pursue the kind of climbing that really attracted me.

At the Norwegian Everest reunion in 1995 I had already been thinking once more of that mysterious mountain in Tibet. You need to be one expedition ahead of yourself at all times if you want an annual trip to interesting places so I started making enquiries in early 1995. I heard that the Tibet International Sports Travel (TIST), a trekking company in Lhasa, part owned by the Tibetan local government, were reliable and effective. I was agreeably surprised when they replied promptly to my faxes and told me that there would be no problem at all in organising our trip to the area I indicated on a map. They offered a fixed price for organising the entire expedition in the spring of 1996. It all seemed too easy.

And so to forming a team for 1996. This too seemed easy, at first. I decided to stick with a formula that had worked well in the past, inviting Jim Fotheringham with whom I had had so many good times in the hills. I also asked Jim Lowther and Graham Little, both of whom had been with me on three separate occasions. All four of us had been on the Kinnaur expedition in 1994. Charlie Clarke would join us as doctor. After some discussion we decided we would like to make a film of our trip and asked Jim Curran to come. He is a climbing film-maker and good friend who once again had been with me on several expeditions. I also invited Paul Nunn, whom both Jim Curran and I had known for many years.

In the summer of 1995, after returning from Drangnag Ri, life became more complicated. I was invited to join an intriguing Norwegian expedition to Antarctica to attempt a formidable rock pinnacle jutting a thousand metres out of the ice cap. This trip was scheduled for November 1996 so I thought I'd be able to go on both expeditions, but I became heavily committed in the search for sponsorship for the Antarctic. I also realised that I would have to start training for high standard technical climbing if I was to be more than a passenger on the Antarctic climb. In addition, the Tibet trip was beginning to look less simple. In the summer of 1995 I learned that Tibet International Sports Travel were in conflict with the China Tibet Mountaineering Association which claimed they were the only body allowed to handle mountaineering expeditions. I had become a little worried when our contact with TIST had urged us not to mention we wanted to climb mountains in any of our applications. They then stopped answering my faxes. Things were obviously becoming difficult.

After much agonising I decided I could not possibly do justice to both expeditions and decided to give priority to the Antarctic venture. My colleagues continued trying to get the Tibet expedition off the ground, but had difficulty both in raising sponsorship and securing permission. They finally decided to postpone the trip until the following year. I also had been having a hard time. I became increasingly aware that, although the thought of an unexplored mountain range in Antarctica was fascinating, that of spending up to twenty days on a featureless rock tower, living on a porta-ledge with people I did not know at all well was less appealing. After much soul searching I decided to pull out.

I invited Jim Fotheringham, Jim Lowther and Graham Little out to dinner to see if they would have me back in the team and whether we could focus once again on our expedition to Tibet for the following year, 1997. It was a delightful evening and brought home to me how important it is to work with friends whom one knows and trusts. But I was left without an expedition for 1996. I began to consider whether it would be possible to organise a reconnaisance of this remote Tibetan region. This would be very useful not only to help us find the mountain and the best approach for climbing it, but it would also enable us to negotiate directly with the China Tibet Mountaineering Association. Charlie was the only member of the team who could get away, so we decided to go out as a pair, at short notice, early in August 1996. After a few phone calls I was given the name of a Tibetan based on Kathmandu, Mr Tse Dorje, who was a good fixer with the right connections. He told us he could provide a jeep, guide, cook and driver for $5,000 a head. Charlie and I bought our airline tickets and decided to risk a journey into the unknown.

We also learnt a little more about our mountain from an unexpected source. Ian McNaught Davis, an old friend of mine, had recently become President of the UIAA (the international body representing all national mountaineering associations). He had just come back from a meeting in Seoul in Korea and had been given a book of photographs of Tibetan mountains. It was a wonderful book with page after page of peaks most of which were unclimbed and had never before been visited or photographed, some which were great featureless hummocks jutting out of arid plateau, and others which were icy towers and jagged rocky pinnacles. Enough unclimbed peaks to keep anyone occupied for several lifetimes. And our mountain was there. The book was very well documented with not only the co-ordinates of each mountain photographed but also the direction from which the picture had been taken. It meant that we could identify our mountain as a peak named Sepu Kangri. It even gave its height as 6956 metres, and there was a map of the massif itself. The peak was the highest in the eastern section of a range called the Nyenchen Tanglha which stretched across central Tibet.

My reaction to this information was mixed. It was reassuring to see a picture of at least one aspect of the mountain, and to know that, though it appeared to be a complex snow peak, guarded by séracs, it looked climbable. But publication did take away some of the magic of being totally unknown. Still, the photographers, who had been from the Chinese Mountaineering Association, were probably the only outsiders who had ventured into the region. Theirs had been a fleeting visit. Certainly, no non-Chinese climber seemed to have been anywhere near the mountain. It remained a challenge that there was a range of 5000–7000-metre peaks, comparable in length to the entire Swiss Alps, that was still completely unknown.

This book is the story of three expeditions; our reconnaissance to the Sepu Kangri region in 1996, and two subsequent expeditions in 1997 and 1998. It is also a story about people; about our own relations as small teams during these trips; and about the people who lived below this great mountain, their families, their lives and problems. Sepu Kangri had a special significance for them, embodied in the translation of its local name, the White Snow God.

Before leaving for Tibet in 1996 I started to attempt to trace the early European travellers who might have visited neighbouring regions. Charlie continued this research and discovered that, whilst several European travellers had passed close by Sepu Kangri, this peak remained elusive, unseen and unknown to the outside world.

2　Missionaries, Map-makers and the Military

1160 – 1940

CHARLES CLARKE

Interest in terrestrial exploration of the remote areas of Asia has become a little unfashionable these days. Partly this is because many past claims of travel 'where no man had gone before' have proved either specious, exaggerated, or referred exclusively to the white man, or more particularly, the journeys of 'Englishmen'. We must remember that since mediaeval times vast areas said to be unknown and uncharted had been the arteries of trade between Tibet and its neighbours – China, India, Nepal and Bhutan; and if not mapped in any conventional way, these routes, across high passes and through gorges were known intimately to the yak caravans and horsemen of the plateau, the armies of China, and to traders on the great highway between Peking and Lhasa, known as the Gya Lam, meaning simply, The Road. This yak route runs along the southern border of the Nyenchen Tanglha, or Tangla Mountains of older maps. It would be all too easy to claim that what is now called the eastern Nyenchen Tanglha was unknown when, in reality, Tibetans and Chinese had been travelling through these mountains at least since the time of the Armada. Perhaps another reason for waning interest is that filming and photography, especially of mountain areas, portray vivid yet similar landscapes, regardless of remoteness. It becomes difficult to interest a contemporary audience. The view of such-and-such a range, or this-and-that pass which has never before been crossed somehow seems banal when captured on film. Are these places, the camera asks, so very different from the Himalaya, now often a land of package tours? The woodcut, and the aquatint were better media for creating that aura of mystery.

Such a view had not always been so. The fascination with central Asian travel, and Tibet in particular, rose to a crescendo in the early 1900s, during a time of increasing imperial control and travel within India, which boasted a comprehensive network of railways. The Survey of India had already produced an accurate series of quarter-inch maps, being second only in quality to those of the Ordnance Survey in Britain. By contrast, at that time, Tibet, that unruly nation state on the northern border of the empire, was almost uncharted. A historian writing in 1904 tells us that 'the last and first Englishman to reach Lhasa was Thomas Manning in 1811–12; the latest European visitors to the capital were the French missionaries Huc and Gabet in 1846. Since then, during a lapse of nearly sixty years, none but Asiatics have gained this goal of ambition of all modern explorers.'

The British expeditionary force led by Colonel Francis Younghusband that marched towards Lhasa in September 1904 attempted to change this state of affairs. This was one of Britain's last imperial forays and the only time British troops entered Tibet, other than in border skirmishes. This military action seems to have galvanised Tibetan scholar Graham Sandberg into publishing a seminal work on early Tibetan travellers, comprehensively titled *The Exploration of Tibet, its History of Particulars from 1623 to 1904*. The author doubtless captured a broad audience because he added an up-to-the-minute account of Younghusband's exploits. Sandberg had graduated at Trinity College, Dublin in 1870, and practised briefly as a barrister before taking holy orders in 1879. For the rest of his life he held chaplaincies in India; a post in Darjeeling inspired an interest in Tibet which was later to dominate his life.

The Exploration of Tibet is of interest for several reasons. First, it provides an accurate historical record of those who had travelled there. Secondly, and perhaps without realising it, like many publications by the imperial masters of India, the book is a mine of information, unfettered by current political correctness, about prevailing attitudes towards Tibet and Tibetans, demonstrating in general little sympathy towards this land which fascinates the west so much today. Also, in this rare book there are two maps; one is an accurate street map of Lhasa as it was in 1904. The second map is of the entire Tibetan plateau; this is vague and sometimes fanciful. Neither mountain ranges nor rivers are portrayed with much accuracy. Whether this was because better maps of the Survey of India were classified as secret, or whether no such maps existed is difficult to know; certainly at that time the great majority of Tibet had had no surveys, and those that existed had been surreptitious, at the hands of the *pundits*, the secret surveyor-spies of the Raj.

The study of previous travellers has provided a cultural and geographical backcloth to the areas we have visited and, whilst it is sometimes hard to follow precise routes, the accounts of some, at least, of the early journeys enrich our knowledge and in themselves are enthralling. It is a matter of some irony that the recorded history of the travel within Tibet comes from European sources; certainly, in part this is because of the difficulty we have locating and understanding Tibetan and Chinese texts. There are many stories here from our own imperial legacy, intrigues between opposing Christian sects battling for supremacy within Tibet, and descriptions of local customs and clothing, many of which survive today. Furthermore we can learn at first hand of the historical inter-relation between Tibet and imperial China which, with varying intensity, regarded Tibet as a fiefdom – a state of affairs rarely reciprocated by the Tibetans themselves. There are accounts of great hardship and legends of mystery travellers whose very exploits remain in doubt. For some of these men and women, death from natural causes far from home, or murder at the hands of the local inhabitants marked the end of a lifetime's endeavour.

Graham Sandberg, in this first compendium of travellers to Tibet, felt nevertheless that he could describe the Tibetan race as 'a weak and cowardly people, their very pusillanimity rendering them readily submissive', though in a hastily tipped-in note to the introduction of *The Exploration of Tibet*, he felt he could argue for their 'want of discipline and military inexperience'. This was despite a deep and genuine interest – he had written *The Handbook of Colloquial Tibetan, A Descriptive Itinerary of the Route from Sikkim to Lhasa*, and later, *Tibet and the Tibetans*, which was published posthumously. He died, it is said of tuberculous laryngitis, in June 1904. As far as one can gather, he never visited the country himself. In one sense however he was unprejudiced – he ladled criticism readily on those travellers who, in his eyes, failed to meet his own exacting standards of route descriptions – though it did seem a disadvantage to be heathen.

Sandberg began his record of foreign visitors to Tibet in mediaeval times. He had no time at all for the Rabbi Benjamin of Tudela who might have crossed the Tibetan border around 1160: 'the absurd geographical blunders indicate a man who writes rather from faulty hearsay,' and 'his main purpose was to describe the various centres where Jews had settled in any large number . . .' A second putative visitor was the Franciscan friar Jean de Plano Carpini despatched by the Pope in 1243 to visit the Mongol princes; he probably stopped west of the Karakoram. Another Franciscan, William de Rubriquis (also know as Wilhelm van Ruysbroeck) set out from Brussels in 1253. He too failed to enter Tibet, but he was the first to describe the

Tibetans as a distinct mountain people living to the east of the Karakoram. They had, he wrote, 'the custom of eating the flesh of their parents when dead from a motive of piety' and 'they still made offering bowls and drinking cups of skulls.' These bowls are still on sale in the Lhasa markets today. De Rubriquis was the first to record the yak as a peculiarly Tibetan creature. Marco Polo (1271) also mentioned the Tibetans but never crossed the border; he perhaps visited Sining, in western China. In 1288 Pope Nicholas IV despatched a Minorite monk, Giovanni da Montecorvino to preach the faith in China, and later declared him Archbishop of Cambalee (Beijing); it is just possible that Montecorvino travelled across Tibet en route from India. Tibet then disappears from European writings until the seventeenth century, though before this the Society of Jesus had developed an interest in China, sending the first Jesuit missionaries there in the 1580s.

The first certain foreign visitor to enter and cross Tibet was a Portuguese Jesuit, Antonio de Andrada in 1626, though his route is unclear. Andrada probably visited Lake Manasorowar, in western Tibet, and travelled through to China. He wrote to his superior on 15th August 1626 from 'The Court of the Great King at Chaparangue', probably Tsaparang, a town on the Sutlej in Gartok, western Tibet. The Jesuits in China then attempted to extend their influence west in the mid-seventeenth century. The priests Johann Grueber and Albert d'Orville reached Lhasa via Macao and Peking in 1661, taking the caravan route via Sining. They probably passed through Nakchu, and recorded a visit to the monastery of Radeng, a week or so north of Lhasa. They finally entered the Holy City, which they knew as Barantola, where they stayed for several weeks. Their drawings, subsequently engraved, depict costumes and buildings, including the Potala Palace, called then the Bietala; these were published later by Father Athanasius Kircher in *La Chine Illustrée*. The priests were not able to see the Dalai Lama because they had made it known that they would refuse to prostrate themselves before him, or so it said. The pair continued on their remarkable journey south, eventually reaching Kathmandu and the neighbouring city of Patan. Their geographical observations were detailed – they placed Sining and Lhasa with some accuracy, the latter at latitude 29°62' N, only around half a degree out.

The next European incursion came from the south, in the form of four Capuchin friars, Domenico da Fano, Guiseppe da Ascoli, Francis Maria da Tours and Francesco Olivero Orazio della Penna. They travelled from Kathmandu in 1708, intent upon reaching Lhasa, where they were received favourably and stayed for some three or four years before their masters in

Italy, having felt their expenses were too high, forced them to abandon the Lhasa mission and retreat to India. The Financial Commission in Rome of 1713 noted that for the entire series of Capuchin mission stations extending from northern India through Nepal to Lhasa, 'A sum of 5200 scudi [an estimated £1125] had been spent', and fifteen priests at various times had 'in ten years succoured 380 dying infants and had administered Holy Baptism to two adults making them the children of God' – a harsh reminder that the world of audit and value for money is nothing new, even in the pursuit of souls. A personal remonstration in Rome by one of the four Capuchins, Domenico da Fano, reversed the financial stringency: the Order was soon re-established. Orazio della Penna, as leader of the Lhasa Capuchin community, became involved in an amicable religious dialogue with the Dalai Lama, which ended with a document empowering the Capuchins to build 'a monastery or hospice, and a public church to be used for the free and unhindered exercise of the Christian religion'. Presumably translating the Dalai Lama somewhat freely, della Penna added 'because the Capuchins live in Tibet for no other purpose than to help other people and do good for all'.

Such peace for the Lhasa Capuchins was to be short-lived. A massive flood which engulfed the city in 1725 was blamed on the Christians, who were beset by riotous mobs. Delicate negotiations between the visitors, the Mongol ruler of Lhasa, Gyalpo Telchen Batur, and the High Lama of the Samye monastery ended with the blame being shifted neatly to misdeeds of the Tibetans themselves; it even became a penal offence to molest the Capuchins. The only church in Lhasa, its site now unknown, was built. Trouble was however far from over, and came from several quarters. The Jesuits in Rome, questioning their Christian brethren's rights to be in Tibet at all, and noting their failure to procure conversions, demanded again that the Capuchin allowances be reduced. There were also intermittent conflicts with the Tibetans, and della Penna's health failed. He left Lhasa in April 1733 for Kathmandu, where he was promptly, if briefly, imprisoned; his remaining colleague left Lhasa later that year.

Between 1733 and 1740 the Capuchin Lhasa mission lay abandoned. However Orazio della Penna, his health restored, was a man of iron resolve. He argued the case in Rome and secured further funds, gaining sanction from the Pope to return to Lhasa in October 1738. The party's departure was delayed by, amongst other matters, surgery for della Penna's lachrymal fistula – his tear duct – until March 1739. This was perhaps a wise precaution for the cold dry climate of the Tibetan plateau. Particular interest surrounds this enterprise because it was recorded in minute detail by Cassiano Belligati, one of the priests in the Capuchin team. Like their precedessors, the priests travelled through Nepal, crossing the border at Nyalam, close to the present customs posts at the Friendship Bridge, where they complained of the high tolls exacted by the *jong-pon*, the government officer. Belligati's narrative describes day to day life, with the diet of *tsampa*, tea, raw and dried meats with which we would become all too familiar. The yak caravan of 1740, with attention to the details of collecting dry yak dung for fuel, attaching loads and the method of tethering yaks at night emphasises just how little a traveller's life has changed in 250 years.

Once in Lhasa, the Capuchins moved back into their former house: the church was as it had been left, and for some months all seemed well. Belligati recorded, it appears, almost every meeting between members of the Order, Tibetan notables and the Chinese governors, and gave graphic accounts of religious celebrations. He and his colleagues clearly befriended some of the ruling class, as they had done on their first visit. However, before long, factions of Tibetan priesthood became hostile and friendships established with the Dalai Lama's father, amongst others, soured. First Belligati left Lhasa, and finally, on 20th April 1745, the ailing and disappointed della Penna followed with the remaining members of the Order. He died shortly afterwards and was buried in Patan, Nepal, on 20th July 1745, in a grave whose site has become lost. Shortly after della Penna's death, news came from Lhasa that the 'whole of the mission premises had been levelled to the ground'. Not a trace of the Capuchins remains today.

During the Capuchin era, the Jesuits, despite an absence from Tibet of nearly a century, clung to the tenuous historical concept that they had a prior claim to work there following Antonio de Andrada's visit in 1626. To attempt to assert this right and to report on the Capuchin endeavours, the Jesuit priest Ipolloto Desiderati had visited Lhasa in 1716, staying some five years, before being recalled by Pope Clement himself in 1721. In 1728 Desiderati presented a sixty-eight page legal diatribe promoting the Jesuit claim. The case was finally thrown out in favour of the Capuchins by a judgement from the Congregation of the Propagation of the Faith in 1732. His cause defeated, Desiderati died in April 1733. It is bizarre to think that a formal court case had taken place in Rome over 250 years ago regarding the right to attempt to convert Tibetans. In the event, the spread of Christianity within Tibet was a spectacular failure. Had the Jesuits themselves been successful, perhaps a fate similar to that of the Incas might have befallen the culture of the Tibetans. We shall never know.

Geographically, however, these tales from the distant past were, by and large, of little direct relevance to ourselves. None of these travellers seemed to have ventured close to our mountains north-east of Lhasa. But one hundred years later, it would be another party of Christian priests, also expelled from Lhasa, who would become the first to walk close by the Sepu Kangri massif. Before mentioning this last intriguing journey, the Englishman's race for Lhasa dominates the scene.

Some thirty years elapsed after 1745 before Tibet was visited again by Europeans, culminating in the first entry into Lhasa by an Englishman, Thomas Manning in 1811. There had however been one earlier traveller at the time of the Capuchins, the Dutchman Samuel van der Putte; his journeys across Tibet are of some interest. He probably visited Nakchu, and then travelled eastwards to China. Unfortunately, as he lay dying in Java in 1737, he burnt his diaries. We are thus dependent upon others, principally Belligati, for the record of this journey, and the 'rude yet not greatly inaccurate map of Tibet' preserved in a museum in the Hague. Van der Putte crossed Tibet from Ladakh in 1728, reached Lhasa and met the Capuchins. The following year he went north-north-east of Lhasa, via Dam, a town south of Nakchu, and then north-east to the Di-chu, the Tibetan name for the main tributary of the Yangtse north of Chamdo. He ended his outward journey in Mongolia, before returning by the same route to Lhasa, to be the guest of the Capuchins again in 1732. His precise route is unknown, but he must have crossed, or passed nearby the Nyenchen Tanglha mountains.

From 1745 for some seventy-five years Tibetan travel remained the sole privilege of the British, or Englishmen, as they were termed. Only four parties travelled within the interior. In 1774 Warren Hastings, the first Governor-General of India selected a twenty-seven-year-old East India Company writer, George Bogle, and a surgeon Alexander Hamilton (both were Scots) to go to Shigatse to visit the Panchen Lama, the ruler of the southern Tibetan counties bordering India. Legendary wealth, particularly gold, was in part the reason for this journey. Bogle travelled through Bhutan, where he is said to have introduced the potato, and passed close to Chomolhari (7326m). Reaching Shigatse in November 1774, he found the Panchen Lama had been elsewhere for some three years because of smallpox in the town. The party travelled north into Lhasa county to meet the Panchen, crossing the Yarlung Tsangpo, a river 'about the breadth of the Thames at Putney'. Relations between Bogle and the Panchen were cordial and there was a subsequent exchange of presents. In due course a Buddhist monastery was even established in Calcutta. This shrine, the Bhot

Magan contained artefacts and books from the Tashilumpo monastery in Shigatse; it was a place Tibetan traders could visit during their journeys to India. These trips usually took place in winter to escape the cold of the northern highlands. The Panchen Lama died in 1777, and Bogle a few weeks later, severing this earthly relationship.

A second politically motivated trip took place in 1783. Lieutenant Samuel Turner, a cousin of Hastings, was accompanied by a surgeon, Thomas Saunders, and another, Lieutenant Davis (also a Scot). They followed Bogle's route to Shigatse to meet the new Panchen Lama, then a child of eighteen months and his Regent, continuing, apparently in the mistaken belief that Shigatse was the genuine seat of power in Tibet, though it was the Dalai Lama in Lhasa, with the Chinese *ambans*, the resident imperial representatives, who held the upper hand. Turner described the Tashilumpo in detail, calculated fairly accurately its position (29° 4' 20'N, 89°7'E), and published an illustrated account of his travels shortly before he died, nearly twenty years later. After Tibet, Turner took part in the seige of Seringapatam (Srirangapatna, near Mysore), and apparently made a fortune there. His end was less salubrious: 'seized ... with a fit of apoplexy in a low street in London ... he was conveyed to a workhouse in Holborn.' He died ten days later but was buried in somewhat finer style, at St James's church, Piccadilly.

Thereafter the focus of attention is upon the first Englishman to reach Lhasa. While this illusory prize went to Thomas Manning in 1811, the two extraordinary trips of Thomas Moorcroft, in 1812 and 1819 stand out as tales of mystery and still leave unanswered questions.

Manning sounds an unusual man. He was part of a small literary circle at the centre of which was Charles Lamb. He travelled to Canton in 1807, and lived in the centre of the Chinese community, a highly eccentric departure for a European. By 1810, when Manning visited Calcutta, he had a flowing beard and wore Chinese costume, which did little to further his application to enter Tibet on a British governmental mission. Instead, he pressed on alone to Bhutan and there by chance met a Chinese general on his way to Gyangtse. Manning had learnt not only Chinese and Tibetan, but had studied traditional medicine. He treated some of the general's troops, was invited to travel with them to Gyangtse, and reached Lhasa on 9th December 1811. We would learn on our own journeys in the Nyenchen Tanglha to value medical practice as a passport to friendly relations. Manning sought and was granted an audience with the Dalai Lama, perhaps because he adopted so many of the habits of those with whom he lived and travelled – the very reason the British authorities had cold-shouldered him. He spent a pleasant four months in the capital, unlike Turner, dying in his own bed, aged sixty-eight, in 1840.

Thomas Moorcroft was from a different school. He is described variously as 'superintendent of the East India Company's stud farm' or a British 'officer of the Indian Civil Service'. He obtained government permission (British Indian, that is) to travel into western Tibet in 1812, and hired a *pundit* as a companion 'with the stipulation that he should make every stride precisely four feet in length'. It is salutary to attempt this nearly impossible task on level ground, even if one is six feet tall. His public motive was trade. On this first journey Moorcroft reached Lake Manasorowar in the far west, before returning to Almora in the foothills of the Indian Himalaya. Moorcroft was to travel again in this region, at least to the Tibetan borders, and presumably when he first left India in 1812 he been unaware of Thomas Manning's journey to Lhasa the year before.

Thomas Moorcroft's second trip was more mysterious, though less fortunate. In 1819 Moorcroft set out again from India on a lengthy journey which was to last six years – or seven, or nineteen years, depending upon the version you choose. By 1824 he was at Kashgar in Turkestan (now Xinjiang), rather than in western Tibet, once again under the guise of trade. The following year one of his companions sent word home that Moorcroft had died of fever, on 27th August 1825, on the road between Bokhara and Balkh. The East India Company recorded the date of his demise as being a year later, in 1826. A subsequent traveller and writer, Abbé Huc, will tell a very different story.

Régis-Evariste Huc and Joseph Gabet were two Lazarist priests who reached Lhasa in January 1846. Whether they had heard of Thomas Manning (whose own record was published long after Huc's), is open to doubt and until Huc arrived in Lhasa he had not known of Moorcroft. Huc described a visitor more recent than Manning, who left in 1812, and recorded with some certainty that it had been Thomas Moorcroft himself. The story Huc related was that Moorcroft had arrived in Lhasa in 1826. He checked his sources carefully with the Dalai Lama's Regent, with a man named Nisan whom he believed had been Moorcroft's servant, and with the leader of the Lhasa Muslims. Huc was told that a man named Moorcroft used to dress as a Muslim and did not speak much Tibetan, conversing instead in Persian. He would thus talk only with Lhasa Muslims, an old community, and with Kashmiri traders, among whom his features would blend in. Huc had also been told that Moorcroft had then lived in Lhasa for twelve years and had been murdered on his return journey towards Ladakh in 1838. The authorities had recovered some of his belongings, amongst them maps. Turning to another source, less first-hand than Huc, in my own copy of Sandberg, in an anonymous pencilled note alongside the author's account, which leaves the Moorcroft affair open, are these forceful words: 'The man referred to erroneously as Moorcroft by Huc was SOMEONE ELSE. Moorcroft died in 1825.' I must leave the latter as sheer conjecture, but remain rather convinced by Huc. I have no difficulty picturing an eccentric Englishman settled, until the age of sixty, near the mosque in the Lhasa Muslim quarter just behind our own lodgings in Lhasa.

With the arrival of Huc and Gabet, and those who may or may not have reached the capital, there began a trickle of travellers who passed through or nearby the regions we visited in 1996, 1997 and 1998. These two priests were the first foreigners we can identify to pass through the Nyenchen Tanglha itself. They had first travelled to Lhasa and in inimitable style recorded their visit, with detailed descriptions of their encounters with living personalities, rather than a dry record of the place itself. Huc had an impish sense of humour. Early during their stay the two Lazarists were careful to emphasise their origins as French, rather than British. It is with obvious delight that Huc records the views of the leader of the long-established Muslim community: 'Pelings [a word meaning foreigners, but here, British] are the most cunning of men. They are getting control of all parts of India, but it is always by trickery rather than by open force. Instead of overturning the authorities, they cleverly try to win them over to their side and share the spoils with them. In Kashmir [his own homeland] there is a saying: The world is Allah's, the land is the Pasha's, but the East India Company rules.'

Sadly for them, the wishes of the two French 'Lamas of the Western Heavens' to remain in Lhasa and found a mission there were at odds with the views of the Chinese *kachin*, the governor. After little more than a month they were expelled, but were granted permission to travel east with an escort, via a route unknown to them which would lead to Tsiamdo (Chamdo), the provincial capital of Kham. Although placenames differ, and sometimes cause us difficulty, their journey can be followed along the southern extent of the eastern Nyenchen Tanglha, through the towns of Alan-to (Alando), thence crossing the Shargang La to Pelbar and Lha Dze (Lhatse).

There are several striking features of their account. First, the priests seemed to enjoy themselves, despite the hardships of their journey. Secondly, at that time, it is apparent, even in the smaller towns, there was a strong Chinese presence, civil and military, and Chinese merchants. This charming and vivid narrative must rank as one of the most readable books on Tibet, or of travel anywhere. At the time of its first publication in Paris in 1851, it was a bestseller. They followed the Gya Lam, the great yak highway from Lhasa to Peking towards Lhari (Lharigo, or Jiali, as it is now known). On the way they described the unicorn which 'long regarded as a fabulous beast really exists in Tibet'. (Sir Joseph Hooker was later to disappoint the public with news that this fabled creature was the two-horned *antelope hodsonii*.)

Moving east towards Lhari, they mentioned their first obstacle, the Mountain of the Spirits,

> whose summits rise up sheer. The ice and snow do not melt at any season. Its cliffs are as steep as the cliffs by the sea, often the wind fills them with snow. The paths are almost impassable, so steep and slippery is the descent.

Once surmounted, whether pass or peak is difficult to say, the priests glissaded down.

> We sat cautiously down on the edge of the glacier, holding our heels together and pressing them hard on the ice. Then using the whip as a rudder we sailed off over the frozen waters with the speed of a train. A sailor would have said we were making at least twelve knots. In our long and numerous journeys we have never encountered a method of travel so comfortable, so speedy and above all refreshing. At the bottom of the glacier, each man retrieved his own horse as best he could, and we continued on our way in common fashion.

Along this trail to the east they recounted numerous adventures, of other passes, narrow gorges and noted:

> along that whole great distance there are continuous vast chains of mountains, divided by cataracts, deep ravines and narrow defiles. Sometimes the mountains are piled and jumbled together in monstrous shapes; at others they follow one another in a regular progression like the teeth of a monstrous saw.

The final hurdle on the route to Lhay Dze was the Tanda Mountain, almost certainly the Shargang La of my own 1998 journey. They were first told that it was impassable, leading Huc to argue with a local Tibetan noble.

'We managed to cross the Chor-Kou-La, so why not the Tanda?'
'What is the Chor-Kou-La to the Tanda?' [the Tibetan had replied.]
'These mountains cannot be compared. Yesterday three men from the Tanda district wanted to try the mountain and two of them disappeared in the snow; the third arrived here this morning, alone and on foot, for his horse was also buried. Of course, you can leave when you want ... but you will have to pay for any yaks or horses which die on the journey.'

After delivering this grim ultimatum, the Tibetan had put out his tongue in salutation, scratched his ear and turned to leave.

Chastened, yet one suspects disbelieving, Abbé Huc took his Chinese guidebook, perhaps like many of us a little late in the day, to find the route description even worse than anticipated. Three mornings later, with the sky overcast and in strong winds:

we reached the foot of the Tanda, we could see a long dark trail, like a huge caterpillar, winding its way up the slopes ... a party of monks returning from a pilgrimage ... Before we reached the summit the wind began to blow with fury and take the snow with it; the whole mountain seemed to be disintegrating. The climb was so steep that it was too much for man or beast. The horses fell repeatedly and had they not been stopped by great piles of snow, would have rolled down as far as the valley we had just left. Father Gabet, who had never really revcovered from the illness caused by our first journey, nearly failed to reach the top of the Tanda; when his strength failed and he was no longer able to hang on to the tail of his horse, he fell exhausted and was almost buried in the snow. The men of the Tibetan escort went to his assistance and after long and painful efforts managed to hoist him as far as the summit. He was more dead than alive; he was ghastly pale, and panted with a noise like a death-rattle.

Huc and Gabet had travelled along the southern boundary of the Nyen-chen Tanglha, immediately below the south face of Sepu Kangri. Some 120 years later, Chris Bonington and I would see those saw-toothed summits, while Elliot Robertson, Pasang and I would cross the Shargang La.

It is worth considering briefly why these journeys were described as being so difficult, whereas today it would be a gross exaggeration to describe them as arduous; we would not claim to be stronger, or fitter than these travellers, who were frequently recording twenty or thirty miles on foot a day. First, the memories of the writer may have been amplified; Huc's journal was written several years after the event. Secondly, in bad weather, that can arrive unannounced within minutes, a gentle walk can become a nightmare. But the crux of the matter is that it *was* genuinely colder by several degrees, the glaciers were larger, and these journeys more demanding than they are today. Also, Huc and Gabet were travelling in March and April; the winter snows were unmelted. Spring comes late in Tibet. Theirs was a considerable achievement. The party reached Chamdo after thirty-six days from Lhasa, and made for western China. Neither was to survive for long afterwards. Gabet was to die of yellow fever in Rio de Janiero in 1853, and Huc in France in 1860 at the age of forty-seven.

After this personal quest for the first Europeans to visit the region which entranced us, I read many more travellers' tales. None gave us more information, though several highlighted the dangers and difficulties of these parts of Tibet. One that deserves mention is Brigadier-General George Pereira, who wrote little other than his own meticulous diaries. His journeys in the 1920s were little known until Sir Francis Younghusband, some twenty years after his own invasion of Lhasa, published an account of Pereira's journey there in 1921–22 from Sechuan, western China. Pereira had followed Huc and Gabet's route in reverse along the Gya Lam. He travelled alone, in the company of his Chinese 'boy' and recruited local Tibetans as guides. Reaching 'the dirty little village' of Chamdo in September 1922, he travelled west to Tengchen (also Dingchen), and then south towards the Shargang La, crossed by Huc and Gabet some seventy years earlier. Younghusband's terse, boy-scoutish and soldierly account of this journey, dwelling incessantly on distances and placenames that are difficult to identify, becomes coupled with Pereira's vitriol against the Tibetans, the Chinese, and worst of all 'the students'. This gives us an unencumbered account of attitudes towards races that were felt inferior to the British imperial masters of the east.

'The student [in China]', Pereira wrote, 'usually a wretched half-baked creature who argues like a small child without fear of correction, has no solid basis of education to help him. He picks up a smattering of foreign learning, which enables him to pose without difficulty amongst his own people ... If students were under a strong foreigner, not afraid of them ...

Huc's defile of Alan-to on the Gya Lam.

the student would no doubt benefit ...' While Pereira wrote his diary, little did he know that one Sechuan student, Deng Xiaoping, had already completed his studies nearby, latterly under the guidance of the revolutionary Wu Yuzhang in Chongqing; by 1920 Deng had already left for France. He would soon become a distinguished military commander and later Chairman of the People's Republic of China. Deng's predecessor in this latter role was a less scholarly figure, Mao Dzedong, from Hunan, further west. He was already thirty. It would not be long before the British empire Pereira knew would have vanished. His 'Tentative Proposal', a solution for China, is published as an appendix in Younghusband's book: 'The best thing would be to raise a small model army under young and energetic foreign officers, starting in some isolated place ...' It is almost redolent of Jonathan Swift's 'Modest Proposal for Preventing the Children of Ireland from being a Burden to their Parents' (namely, eating them). Pereira ends with the comment: 'as an outsider, who after twenty four years experience of the country, is thoroughly disgusted with China, and determined never again to revisit under any circumstances'. Pereira died, probably of a perforated gastric ulcer, on the Chinese border of Tibet in 1923. It is easy to digress and to become irritated by this account, and miss his real legacy, a 1:2,500,000 map. This was painstakingly assembled from his observations and published by the War Office in 1925. North-west of the Shargang La is marked, unnamed, a range rising above the 6000-metre contour in the very position of Sepu Kangri, though there is almost no description of these mountains in his text.

Another goal drew expeditions to eastern Tibet, the sources of great rivers. Throughout the latter part of the nineteenth century doubt had surrounded the eastern route of the Tsangpo. Having risen in Tibet, the river courses south through the Himalaya into Assam to become the Brahmaputra. There had been speculation that it might have continued east and have flowed into the Irrawady. In the twentieth century the focus shifted to the sources of the Salween and the Mekong. In 1935 two British explorers, Ronald Kaulback and John Hanbury-Tracy walked from Burma into eastern Tibet, mapping and tracing the Salween gorge. They reached the town of Diru (also Biru, Nakchubiru), to be told by the Tibetan authorities that their proposed journey west and on to Lhasa was out of the question because of robber bands. They walked back to Fort Hertz, in Burma, ending this marathon in 1937. Whilst they had passed close to the northern side of the Nyenchen Tanglha, and within two days of Sepu Kangri, we later came to understand why they had not seen the massive range just to the south. From the north Sepu Kangri remains hidden in a maze of valleys until one is directly beneath it.

As a finale to these European travellers' tales, there is story of Guibaut and Liotard in 1940. André Guibaut was the Free French envoy in China during the Second World War. He and his friend Louis Liotard were exploring the upper Mekong and Salween gorges when they were attacked by bandits. Liotard was shot dead, and Guibaut lucky to escape. Liotard was awarded a posthumous Legion d'Honneur by de Gaulle after the war, while Guibaut went on to become French Consul-General in Singapore, Casablanca and Cambodia before his death in 1966. There was thus a somewhat ominous history of European travel in this region.

Early Tibetan and Chinese sources proved more difficult to locate than those of Europeans, and even now we have but a sparse selection of data. We will, I think, never know the detailed Chinese guidebook used by Abbé Huc. There is however a slim paperback by a Chinese woman, Ma Lihua, who was born in 1953 and later became vice-chair of Writers' Association of Tibet. She clearly loved this landscape and the people, and tells in glowing terms of her seven journeys to northern Tibet. The topography is sometimes hard to follow. She writes about the quelling of nomadic robber gangs and warlords of eastern Tibet after 'Liberation', and the monasteries, local legends and customs in the aftermath of the Cultural Revolution. The destruction and cruelty had affected even these remote areas. She mentions the Nagru and Tashi valleys, which are north-west of Sepu Kangri, as a former Hidden Kingdom, cut off from the outside world, lands of peace and plenty, where even wild animals were tame. She never reached these valleys herself. She also describes Mount Khamsun, nearby, which is probably another name for Sepu Kangri: 'Sadnam Dorje described it to me with the vision of a poet: all the mountains in Tibet are like nymphs in a supine posture, and Mount Khamsun stands on the left breast of a nymph. The nine snow-capped peaks are like a galloping horse's mane streaming in the wind and the nine lakes on these peaks are wrapped in cloud and mist. From the peaks big and small waterfalls cascade like white silk scarves when viewed from a distance.'

There the trail ended, at least until we reached Sepu Kangri itself. The reader may wonder whether we found the route to Sepu Kangri by carrying a small but valuable library of old books and a large folder of historical cartography. The reality was rather different. When Chris Bonington and I first reached Sepu in 1996 we were using a tourist map bought at the airport, an old photo which the local Diru postmistress had produced from her handbag and the Chinese book on mountains – and little else. Even the best research sometimes follows a discovery.

3   Mrs Donkar's Handbag

2nd – 13th August 1996

CHRIS BONINGTON

It was 2nd August 1996. I was standing outside the Wembley Conference Centre waiting for Charlie. It seemed a strange way to start an expedition. I had just finished making a motivational presentation describing my ascent of Everest to several thousand hyped up pyramid-sellers. We were due that night to fly to Delhi on the first leg of our journey to our secret mountain. Charlie's wife Ruth was going to deliver him to the conference centre, so that my son Rupert could drive us to Heathrow. Charlie was late. I'm always neurotic about flying – not afraid of the flying, but terrified of missing the plane. I like to be there in stacks of time.

A car pulled in and there was Charlie, looking rather plump but elegant in a faded almost effete kind of way, in a striped blazer and jeans – 'Useful for getting upgrades and seeing ambassadors,' he assured me. 'I bought the blazer at Oxfam.' In spite of greying hair, he has a youthful charm.

He packed yet more boxes and duffel bags into my already heavily laden estate car and we were off. We were on our holidays. I had a wonderful sense of freedom, anticipation and excitement. It was the snatched nature of our venture, the way we had grabbed the opportunity with the minimum of organisation or planning. I like small trips and Charlie is fun to be with. Oddly enough, although he had been with me on four expeditions since 1975 and we collaborated in the book on the 1982 Everest expedition, I still felt that I didn't really know him. There is an elusive quality about Charlie – urbane, worldly, with a delightful twinkling sense of humour. But there is a reserve as well, a door in his personality that seems firmly shut. Maybe it's the years of practising medicine, of remaining objective. I was looking forward to getting to know him better in the way that one does on any small trip in the mountains.

As Charlie and I sat in some luxury in the Executive Club lounge, having sneaked an upgrade to Business Class courtesy of British Airways, it began to dawn on both of us that we had almost no idea of where we were going. We made a list of things we did not know. We did not know how to approach Sepu Kangri from the north, south, east or west. We had little idea of the roads, no inkling of what the terrain was like, and no information about the weather, the availability of food, yaks or petrol. We were unaware whether we needed to take Chinese staff with us, or what permits were required, or whether or not we could visit monasteries – the list of blanks seemed endless. All we knew for certain was that the co-ordinates of Sepu Kangri were 30.91°N, 93.78°E, figures that recurred on several maps. I daydreamed about what the range might be like. Having been to Tibet several times I thought of barren hills, wide treeless valleys, the rolling wastes of the plateau with featureless peaks, many rising to over 6000 metres. Perhaps the country around Sepu would be like that: I simply did not know.

We flew into Kathmandu, failed to meet the mysterious Tse Dorje, our Tibetan Mr Fixit, who was to arrange everything with the authorities in Tibet. 'He's gone to Lhasa', we heard. Visas were however ready at the Chinese embassy; we caught the Lhasa flight on 5th August, seeing little of Everest or the Himalaya, since they were clad in monsoon clouds. We wondered if we were going to be met, or whether any arrangements at all had been made. The plane was a big new Boeing 757, crammed with tourists from many different countries and just a few Tibetans, some of them in the saffron robes of monks. We got through immigration and customs more quickly and easily than we had a few days earlier when passing through Kathmandu and to our immense relief on the other side of the barrier stood a young Tibetan bearing a notice with 'BONINGTON' written on it. He introduced himself as Pasang and told us that he was our guide. We were to get to know him well in the coming weeks.

It is a two-hour drive from Gonkar airport to the city of Lhasa. Tibetan villages give way to sprawling outskirts: at first the capital seems much like any other enlarging Chinese city. Trees are being felled to make the roads yet wider. But the military presence is immediately striking. Army convoys are often on the highway. There are many barracks. Armed sentries, immaculately turned out, stand to attention outside the ornate gates of the military compounds.

We were booked into the Lhasa Holiday Inn, a complex of interlinked concrete blocks just outside old Lhasa. How the city had changed since the drab days of 1982, my first visit, when we had had that glimpse of the mountains that were now luring us back. I had visited Tibet several times since then, but had spent only one night in Lhasa on our return from Menlungtse in 1988, on the way to Beijing. We had stayed in the Holiday Inn on that occasion too and had come across Reinhold Messner, arguably the world's most famous mountaineer. Having become the first person to climb all fourteen of the world's 8000-metre peaks, he was directing his boundless energy in other directions, undertaking a series of long ice walks in polar regions and researching a book on the culture of mountain people around the world. He had just returned from a trip to eastern Tibet and was convinced that he had seen the yeti.

We had chosen the hotel's Tibetan restaurant for our evening meal and had it to ourselves. After we had been dressed in traditional Tibetan coats in the best tourist fashion, Charlie produced a bottle of champagne. I had almost forgotten that it was my birthday – it was the 6th August and I was sixty-two. The following day, Pasang came to collect us and we called at the office of TIST, Tibet International Sports Travel, who were looking after our journey. It emerged that they knew no more than we did about the area around Sepu Kangri. No one from their office had ever been there, but Mr Su Ping, their general manager, assured us that all our paperwork was in order and that Pasang would take good care of us.

The greatest difference that struck me at this stage, since my first visit in 1982, was the arrival of capitalism. Although TIST was a local Tibetan government organisation, it was obviously running on a strong market force base. Mr Su Ping was also managing director of a bottled water company and the big modern-looking hotel next door. Mobile phones were very much in evidence, but, more important, they really seemed to want to give us good service and value for money, something very different from previous mountaineering trips in China when we had been faced with endless negotiations and red tape.

We also found time to get an impression of the changes that had take place since our last visit. Charlie observes:

> Lhasa inspires many different emotions. Since 1980 the capital has had tens of thousands of European visitors. It is no longer the Forbidden City, no longer a place enshrined in, or perhaps imprisoned by the old religious culture. In one sense Lhasa epitomises many of the issues in Tibet, though change is faster and more pronounced here than elsewhere. Few visitors fail to have strong feelings about this city. Many views are divergent, but, perhaps curiously, affection for Lhasa remains

dominant. This affection is in contrast to a sense of increasing distaste
many regular visitors develop for Kathmandu. I am appalled by the
pollution of the Kathmandu valley, the poverty and the gradual drift
away from the charming, culturally distinct, idiosyncratic city it used
to be. This is despite, or because of a wealth of western aid.

Nearer the centre of town, there are little shops, car and truck
mechanics, eating houses, bars, pool tables and, most prominently,
prostitutes. There is nothing covert about prostitution in Lhasa; it is
open and, to the unspecialist eye, entirely Chinese. From tiny booths
the girls advertise their wares, with garish lipstick, plastered make-up,
skirts split thigh-high and seamed stockings. One even catches an
occasional glimpse of a suspender as they sit, legs slightly apart, waiting
for trade. Their appearance seems a caricature of sexual enticement. As
in Amsterdam, one soon becomes used to the sex industry. But there is
a dual irony here. This was the Holy City of a religion that celebrated
celibacy: it is like having brothels in the Vatican City. While in China
before Mao's accession prostitution was one of the hated hallmarks of
the old regime, that, together with opium and feudalism, had denigrated
the Chinese people. The word 'prostitution' was even banned from
conversation in the idealistic epicentre of the early Communist Party.

Today Lhasa has a population of 160,000, which includes an
immigrant Han Chinese population of nearly 50,000, increasing
annually, and encouraged by central government. The latter figure is
probably an underestimate. With such an influx there is economic
pressure; it clear that new Lhasa is a thriving, bustling, modern city.
New building, in the concrete, glass and the white tile of modern China,
is rife. Brash supermarkets, banks, department stores, fashion houses
and camera shops dominate the new city centre.

Sixteen years ago, in March 1982, on my first visit I had found a drab
place, and one still emerging from a period of depression and the
Cultural Revolution. At that time the Six Point Directive of Hu Yaobang,
Communist Party Secretary, had brought the first economic and cultural
concessions to Tibet and these were beginning to take effect. They were
accompanied by calls for refugees abroad to return home. In a later era
Hu Yaobang's death in 1989, with the apparent extinction of his liberal
views, led indirectly to the student demonstrations and the killings of
Tiananmen Square.

In 1982 the rebuilding of the monasteries had begun. There was
however little to see other than the ancient monuments of Lhasa, the

Potala, the Jokhang Temple and Lhasa's great surviving monasteries. The Barkhor, the old market surrounding the Jokhang, was dismal. Then, few Tibetans engaged us in conversation; there was none of the jostle, laughter or bartering of the present-day bazaar.

I found the lack of abject poverty in Lhasa striking. Of course, Lhasa has its beggars but they are few, and they are often beggars on religious grounds.

'They've destroyed most of the old city,' is a frequent warning to travellers. I showed Chris the map of Lhasa in Graham Sandberg's book, dated 1904. I found the old city limits almost identical today to what they were then and, whilst in surrounding new Lhasa the buildings are modern, and often to western eyes monstrous, in the old city rebuilding is with traditional granite blocks, the wooden window sills and architraves, which are so characteristic of Tibetan houses. I thought of the dreadful new buildings obscuring St Paul's cathedral in London.

The people in Lhasa seemed lively, reasonably prosperous and relaxed but our views, like that of any tourist, were superficial. Pasang felt sufficiently confident to invite us to his home, the first time either Chris or I had ever been invited to meet the family of a Chinese citizen. His small two-room flat was on the rooftop of a typical old Barkhor tenement. It opened onto an open veranda, filled with flowering pot plants, round a central courtyard. There was a cabinet full of religious artefacts down one wall, a big refrigerator and television – a combination of old and modern. We ate a superb Tibetan meal, washed down with beer and chatted with Pasang, while his wife, Yishi, looked after our needs with a quiet but friendly dignity.

There is, however, in Lhasa and throughout Tibet an aura of control that is Chinese. Public political dissent is likely to be punished with imprisonment. You could argue that the Chinese are consistent, treating people in Tibet no differently from the rest of their citizens but the fact remains, that whatever legal claims China might or might not have had on Tibet, they invaded a country in 1950 that had, in effect, been independent for over fifty years. The condition of occupation remains, already over a generation old. There can be little doubt that if a referendum were held tomorrow a substantial majority of Tibetans would vote for self-rule and the return of the Dalai Lama.

We were glad to leave the Holiday Inn on the morning of 8th August and drove proudly out in a Jinbei 2.8 diesel truck, a pick-up with a cabin, which seated five with ease. The kit bounced around in the open back. Our short stay in Lhasa had been smooth and uneventful. The mysterious Tse Dorje put in a brief appearance to slip $10,000 into his back pocket. Our team had assembled. Pasang Choephel was our guide, interpreter and, as would emerge, a determined and wily supporter of our enterprise. He was twenty-eight. He had learnt English in India, where he had fled in the 1980s, after an early training spent painting monastic *tangkhas*. But he had disliked living in an alien culture in northern India and returned to Lhasa in the late 1980s where he had married Yishi, an entrancingly beautiful woman.

Mingma was to be cook. His qualifications for this important task were never established. It soon became clear that he was simply Pasang's next-door neighbour who had been out of a job. Cheerful, energetic and helpful, Mingma's culinary skills were those of the average eighteen-year-old male: zero. Tsering was the driver, and owner of the Jinbei truck, which he had just bought; he was a careful, quiet and sober man. Throughout the expedition he wore a gabardine golfing jacket, a trilby hat and pair of black shoes with pointed toes, emphasising his city origins. We were soon to recognise his driving abilities and felt safe in his hands: a change from the white-knuckle rides which are so familiar in Asia.

Our principal map was simply the tourist sheet of Tibet bought at the airport. It was the best that we could find since the Chinese treated accurate large-scale maps of the area as state secrets. Our map marked most of the roads of Tibet and the town of Diru, north of Sepu Kangri. It would be a day's drive north of Lhasa to the city of Nakchu, a route Pasang knew well. We would then turn east on the main Nakchu–Chamdo highway, and branch south to Diru along a road some 120 kilometres east of Nakchu. We met no one that had been to Diru or who could tell us anything about the road conditions. Thereafter we had the single photograph of Sepu Kangri from the Chinese book Ian McNaught Davis had given us. We believed it to have been taken from the south, and there was a map of the valleys adjacent to the mountain. We decided vaguely that an approach from the north seemed most sensible, largely because we did not like the look of the vast snow face in the single photograph. As we drove out to the Lhasa–Nakchu tarmac highway, this was the sum of our knowledge of the way ahead.

We soon climbed above 4000 metres to reach the plateau, a vast empty space with thousands of yaks and sheep grazing on green grass in a land-scape punctuated by the occasional village and *bas*, the summer tents of yak-herding families. To the left on the western horizon there emerged the

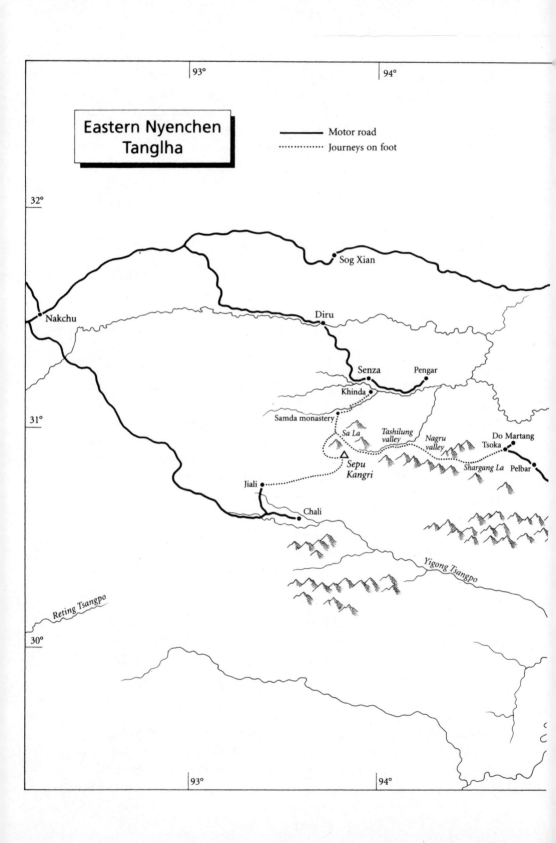

Eastern Nyenchen
Tanglha

——— Motor road
············· Journeys on foot

32°

Sog Xian

Nakchu

Diru

Senza   Pengar
Khinda

Samda monastery

Sa La   Tashilung   Nagru   Do Martang
           valley   valley   Tsoka
△
Sepu   Shargang La   Pelbar
Kangri

Jiali

Chali

Yigong Tsangpo

Reting Tsangpo

30°

93°   94°

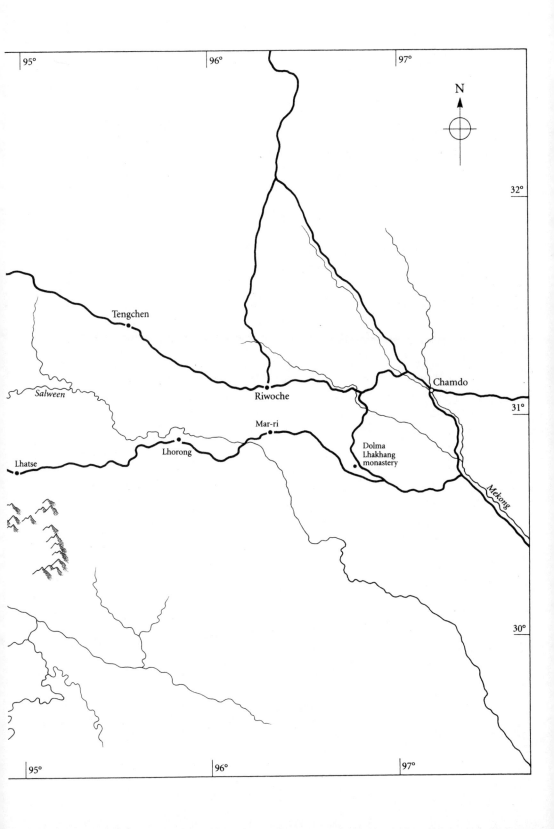

peaks of the western Nyenchen Tanglha. These were mostly rather as I had expected, somewhat dull bumps rising out of a flat landscape. An occasional giant of around 7000 metres would peep out of the clouds. One was Nyenchen Tanglha itself, at 7088 metres the highest peak of the range, which had been climbed by the Japanese. Pasang pointed out the road to its base camp winding across the plateau.

By 7.30 p.m. that evening I was sitting on a grassy 4600-metre hummock with limestone outcrops. A cluster of prayer flags fluttered in the wind beside me. Below to the west was Nakchu, an unbelievably ugly town desecrating the expanse of the plateau. It was a town of open drains and muddy streets, garish modern buildings and corrugated iron shacks. Pasang had decided we should drive straight through, avoiding as he always did the off-chance of a brush with authority. Whilst we had permits, he knew we might be questioned by the Public Security Police. We usually followed his advice closely. Smoke from our little camp beside a water source indicated that dinner was approaching. It was already near freezing and a crisp wind swept the clouds across the sunset. This would be our first night in tents: our journey had truly begun.

I walked down the hill and saw that Pasang was doing the cooking. Noodles and stir-fried vegetables was to become a common meal. Mingma was detailed to wash up. I slept badly because of the altitude. Charlie looked tired and grey. We had gained height too fast but there had been no alternative. Next morning we were crotchety. Having breakfasted we packed and drove off in the rain. The road became mud almost immediately outside Nakchu. We bumped across a dismal landscape in the drizzle and crossed three ill-defined passes before reaching the only right-hand turning, an unmarked and rutted road. 'Yes, it goes to Diru', Pasang was told by a passing truck. Traffic was sparse.

After several hours, in the mid-afternoon, the landscape changed. We descended to see our first trees since the outskirts of Lhasa. It felt as if we were dropping into Nepal. Terraced fields, growing barley and wheat, lined a steep valley. Pine forests filled the side valleys while below there was a dark brown swirling river. This was part of the Salween, or Nak-chu, the Black River of Tibet. There were several fortress-like monasteries and a massive wooden cantilever bridge. We pressed on in the rain and suddenly came to a halt. A mud slide blocked the road. A huge lorry came in the opposite direction and blasted its way through, leaving two ruts for us to follow. Tsering drove cautiously, while through the side window I looked down a near vertical slope into the gorge below.

'Always bad roads in the rainy season. It can go on like this for days,' announced Pasang with a grin.

Neither Charlie nor I had spent any time researching the weather and had been wholly unaware that the summer rains in Tibet were akin to the monsoon in Nepal. I couldn't help wondering about our chances of making an effective reconnaissance if we never had a clear view of the mountains through the clouds. Towards dusk we drove into Diru, a grubby institutional town of barracks and government buildings. The place seemed full of dogs, mangy creatures eating rubbish in the streets. A monastery stood on the left of the main street, the only vestige of a traditional building.

'I think we go on and camp,' said Pasang, anxious once again to avoid officialdom.

For several kilometres there was not a place to pitch a tent, and in the teeming rain the prospect of camping was distinctly unsavoury. We decided to turn back and seek shelter in the town. A few enquiries led to the post office guesthouse whose guardian was a friendly postmistress, Mrs Donkar. A simple room with a wood stove, beds and blankets was a welcome respite from the rain. Charlie's diary captured something of the scene:

During the night it rained again. The water drumming on the roof with an even beat lulled us to sleep and then petered out. A second symphony woke us in the small hours, a chorus of dogs. It sounded as if every dog in Diru had joined in a massive howling, yelping, barking singsong at around 3 a.m. We both giggled helplessly at the din. It rattled the windows. This wasn't a few dogs yowling at the moon. It was as if the silence which marked the end of the rain, had woken the entire canine population of the valley. We recorded it on tape as a sound effect, and fell asleep as even this vocal orchestra exhausted itself. As the cacophony started up again at six, there was no need for the alarm clock.

The resthouse was welcome, but Mrs Donkar's lavatories were unusual. On expeditions in Asia we are both used to the lack of privacy and the closeness to reality when dealing with waste matter. There were several loo issues here. The first was the problem of access to the row of stalls at the bottom of the garden past the well. The path was lined by tall orange Michaelmas daisies. It led past a Tibetan carpenter's workshop to two concrete rows of cells. We found the Chinese signs for male and female difficult to interpret at the best of times, but here the paint had faded away. The sensation was the same as thirty years ago

when, having crossed the Afghan border, we were unable to discover
on which side of the road to drive. We had waited sheepishly for a
passing truck, having drawn well off the road to avoid influencing its
passage. Here, at the loos in Diru, there was more urgency. We could
not wait for a male or female visitor.

We were to discover that both rows, of male and female stalls, were
much the same. Excrement was piled high under each concrete hole
over which we squatted; each pyramid would collapse and melt into a
foetid stream which drifted slowly down to the Salween. The stench
was indescribable. I was not acclimatised to this real travel; I gagged and
retched. In the gloom what looked like a leaf on the floor flickered,
caught in a draught. And then another, and another. It soon became
apparent that the entire concrete floor, and the lower walls were moving
in a writhing carpet of maggots. Later, when we had become accustomed
to these realities, these lavatories seemed entirely normal. It became
fun to tease the maggots, too. One shout and they would all freeze in
unison, to resume their sinuous dance a few seconds later.

I had a bad night, disturbed by a nasty cough and the howling dogs. I woke
shortly before dawn, jumped out of bed and looked out of the dirty paint-
splattered window. 'Wonderful day,' I announced to Charlie. 'Get up, it's
fabulous.' Charlie pottered outside for a pee and told me it was raining. I
don't know what he thought as he went back to sleep. After breakfast we
explained our plans to Mrs Donkar and showed her the picture of Sepu
Kangri.

'Ah, yes,' she said immediately, 'that's above my home village. I went on
a picnic there with my family several years ago.' She returned to her room
and collected her handbag. 'Here it is,' she said, producing a photograph
of herself with Sepu Kangri in the background. 'The road from here crosses
a pass and then after a couple of hours drops down into a valley. You go to
the town of Senza and from there it's a two-day walk. And don't bother to
ask anyone else in Diru, they won't know, they never go there.'

It seemed extraordinary that we had solved the problem of our route
within a few minutes. There was however one enigma: both the views we
had of Sepu Kangri from the book and Mrs Donkar's photo were, we
thought, of the *south* face. 'Azimuth for taking picture: north-east' ran the
text in *Immortal Mountains in the Snow Region.* But Mrs Donkar could not
have been photographed below the south face of Sepu unless she had
actually crossed the range. Perhaps our scant understanding of the geog-

raphy was wrong. We consulted the book again but remained perplexed. Charlie then thought about the problem laterally and looked up a mountain we both knew all too well, Chomolungma, Mount Everest. The photograph of the Tibetan side of Everest, the familiar north face, was captioned 'Azimuth for taking picture: north'. We were clearly looking at a picture of the *north* face of Sepu, not the south.

'What does azimuth really mean, anyway?' asked Charlie. 'It'd be brilliant in Scrabble,' he added. Neither of us knew. We both felt a little incompetent.

We thought we would have a quick look at the Diru monastery and drive on. We walked up alone to the *gompa* and began to film a group of twenty or so young monks, but were not allowed inside. They were a cheerful bunch, but they suddenly fell silent as two policemen arrived. We were returned to Pasang who seemed a little irritated that his two charges had escaped.

It seemed there was trouble. We could go no further, tourists were not allowed in these areas. Pasang was rarely one to argue in these situations and simply suggested they telephone Nakchu or Lhasa to check our military and civil permits. We felt glum. The police said that they would let us know the outcome of their investigations the following day. Pasang had been quite right to avoid the towns. Here, some fifty years earlier Ronald Kaulback and John Hanbury-Tracy had been stopped by the authorities when they had approached Diru on foot from the east. Were we to suffer a similar fate?

We decided to go for a walk and crossed the Salween by a fine wooden cantilever bridge, climbed the hillside above and headed for a grassy summit. This was our first exercise. I felt slow, both from the altitude and a chest cold. I fret about my chest. In 1981 I had developed lobar pneumonia on Mount Kongur in Xinjiang; Charlie had been quick to diagnose and treat it. He only told me later that the condition has a substantial death rate, even with hospital treatment. Charlie strode ahead. After an hour or so we were sitting on a pleasant summit at 4425 metres. A flock of kites soared around us and to the south we caught a glimpse of a peak dusted in snow. It could not have been more than 5000 metres; the snowline was low with the summer rain. We bounced back down to Diru. Charlie was a few minutes in front of me and spoke to Pasang in the guesthouse. 'Guess what?' he shouted like a small boy as he ran out to meet me. 'The police say it's fine, we can go tomorrow!'

We drove over the Salween the following morning crossing by a modern bridge next to the Diru hydroelectric station and headed upwards to the Shar La, the 5100-metre pass leading to the Yu-chong valley. The road was

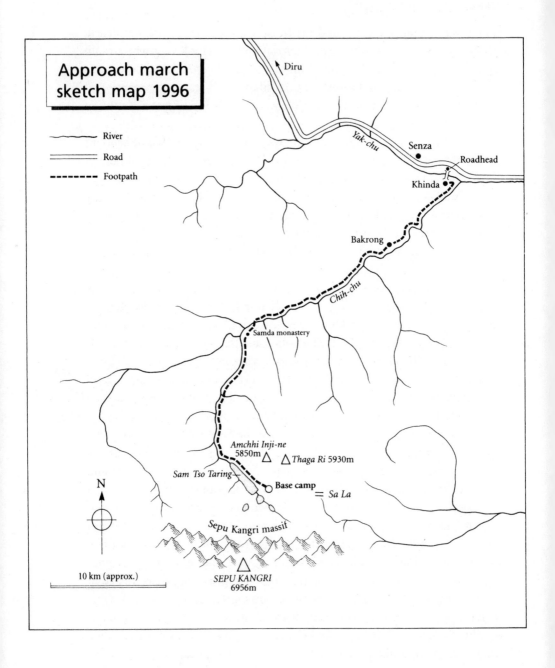

Approach march
sketch map 1996

——— River
═══ Road
▬ ▬ ▬ Footpath

Diru

Yak-chu

Senza

Roadhead

Khinda

Bakrong

Chih-chu

Samda monastery

Amchhi Inji-ne
5850m △   △ Thaga Ri 5930m

Sam Tso Taring

Base camp ○ ═ Sa La

N

Sepu Kangri massif

10 km (approx.)

△
SEPU KANGRI
6956m

good, despite the rain. Like the Diru valley, the Yu-chong was fertile. A branch of the Salween ran along the broad valley floor. We passed the small town of Senza, the district headquarters, and camped in a meadow by a suspension bridge opposite the village of Khinda, which was to be our roadhead. A small group of Chinese were fishing from the footbridge. Tsering took off his city shoes and relaxed, doubtless looking forward to a few days' rest from the road. The sun came out and we snoozed away the afternoon. Somewhere up the valley to the south lay our mountain. From now on our journey would be on foot. There was not a peak higher than 5000 metres in sight, however, which explained why Kaulback and Hanbury-Tracy had not mentioned Sepu Kangri when their caravan had passed this way.

We were both well prepared for Pasang's announcement that there would be no yaks because it was the ploughing season. In our western lives, instant gratification is the rule: the wheels turned more slowly in this traditional culture. The leader in Senza had to be consulted, the source of yaks agreed, the rate of pay and lengths of the stages. The division of work in the village had to be seen to be equitable. We would have to wait a day or two, he told us. We were not to wait for long. The following day we went for another stroll in the hills nearby. On our return Pasang told us that we would be leaving at 11 a.m. next morning with four yaks and two yak-herders. Negotiations seemed to proceed smoothly under Pasang's guidance. There were no arguments about the price.

At exactly 10.55 a.m. on 12th August four yaks walked across the empty meadow, driven by a smiling man on horseback with a long pigtail tied in a bright red ribbon. A silver dagger hung from his belt. This was Tembe.

'He has three fathers', Pasang told us. 'One here in Khinda, and two others up the valley.' Three brothers shared the same wife.

Picture two happy men walking up a glorious valley. A good path wound along the gorge gradually gaining height. We met horsemen, laden ponies and yaks, carrying wood or bags of grain. A lama from a monastery higher up the valley greeted us as he rode by. The weather had cleared with billowing white clouds in a brilliant blue sky. The grass was lush and green beneath fragrant juniper trees, willow and thorn; everywhere were wild flowers, blue, yellow, red and purple – primulas, saxifrage, gentians, miniature roses. It was so much richer and more verdant than I had imagined, yet it was also difficult to imagine that we coming so close to a huge glaciated mountain of very nearly 7000 metres. This could easily have been the English Lakes or a low valley in the Alps. We paused for a bite to eat.

'Charlie, let's have a look at the Chinese map.'

'I haven't got it,' he replied.

I thought he was joking. My first inclination was to blame him. Between us, we had carefully packed away the Chinese book that contained the map and left it in the truck. We were in no mood to return and made light of this error. The day stretched on. We had fallen behind Pasang and Tembe with our four yaks, and were now beginning to wonder when they would stop for the night. Our route had taken us past a small village of traditional Tibetan houses, single-storeyed with flat roofs and small windows, amongst fields of barley, still green but with the grain heads, tiny hairy flags, tossing in the wind. The valley had then narrowed into a dramatic gorge, with broken rocky walls of grey and red and brown, the path hugging the side of the tumbling brown river that filled the valley floor. Another bend, and it was all change, opening up into wide grassy meadows with juniper clad drumlins and gentle slopes stretching up to rounded hilltops. It was also getting late and we were relieved to see our little encampment with the cook tent already erected beside the river.

The following day took us over a fine wooden cantilever bridge to the east side of the river. We crossed a shoulder marked by *chortens* from which we had an exciting new vista of what seemed high snow peaks in the distance. Could these be the Sepu Kangri massif? Another hour's walk and we reached the Samda monastery. Charlie describes our visit in his diary:

Our visit was ill-timed and without preparation. The lamas were on their summer holidays and a skeleton staff of junior monks were the only people in residence. They were perplexed and uncertain of the motives of this strange pair of westerners armed with cameras. Their attitude was hostile and Pasang's response uncharacteristically abrupt.

'What's upsetting them so much?' I asked him.

'I told them they were monks, not the Public Security Police and that they should get on with their praying,' was his reply. No wonder they had been cross.

We beat a hasty retreat down the hillside from the group of young monks, some of whom carried long staves. Before this confrontation Chris and I had separated for a few minutes. I had been wandering around some buildings under construction, including a large prayer hall, the *dukhang*. To my surprise someone spoke to me in Chinese.

'*Neeha, neeha,*' (the usual Chinese greeting) came from behind me. I turned and saw a tall smiling skinny man carrying a large saw, a plane and a bunch of keys. He was a Chinese carpenter from near Chengdu. Proudly he unlocked the door and showed me his handiwork in the new prayer hall, the carved pillars, stairs and shrine in the making. One pillar had graffiti in Chinese scrawled across it. It read 'Long live Mao Dzedong.'

'They often use Chinese carpenters in the monasteries,' Pasang told us. 'Tibetan carpenters are hard to find.' This had come as a surprise in a land where one generally assumes that the Chinese have little interest in religion or reconstruction of things Tibetan.

We hurried away from the monastery, turning up a wide, rather barren side valley which we understood would lead us to Sepu. There was still no sign, not even a hint of our mountain, just close cropped thinly grassed hillsides that reminded me of the over grazed uplands of the English Lake District under its usual dull grey cloud.

We tired easily at this altitude. Tembe the yak-herder had said it would be a long day. It was. We walked on easy ground for several hours, past the occasional *ba*, the dark yak-hair tent used as a summer home by nomads or local people for their seasonal grazing. Distant ice summits appeared, but the geography of the head of the valley remained perplexing. We had been going for seven hours and walked slowly up the final stretch, a tedious slope that led suddenly to a lake.

The abruptness of the view was as spectacular as reaching a summit. There was immediately an extravaganza of ice peaks, glaciers and water. Before us Sam Tso Taring, the Sacred Lake, stretched into the distance for some eight kilometres, ending in a vast glacial amphitheatre. This watery scene was more fitting for the Antarctic than a mountain region so far inland. To the left rose rolling hills with the odd snow peak of nearly 6000 metres. Towering to the right was the vastness of Sepu Kangri's north face. It was several minutes before either of could assimilate the complexity of the landscape; we were overwhelmed by its breathtaking beauty and scale. Mrs Donkar's family photo and the picture in the Chinese book had done little to capture the magic of one of the finest mountain views I had ever seen.

4 Daunting Prospects

14th August – 1st September 1996

CHARLES CLARKE

Tembe knelt and pressed his forehead on the grassy shore. Pasang and Mingma did the same. This was a magic place. We both felt the glow of success, though we had had little part in its achievement. We would have been equally likely to arrive had we simply given Pasang instructions, jumped in a box and anaesthetised ourselves. It had not been an arduous journey. We sprawled on the grass, pitched camp on the shore and went to sleep very happy.

I poked my head out of my tent the following morning into a crystal clear windless dawn, the first of our journey. It was the 14th August, just over a week since our arrival in Lhasa. Ice had formed on the grass. First the distant eastern peaks caught the light and were lit with gold. As the minutes passed the face of Sepu Kangri blushed pink in the morning sun and was then reflected perfectly in the still waters of the lake. Chris shot several rolls of film before breakfast. Tembe was to leave us for a few days. 'I am going to see my other father,' he told us.

Before leaving he outlined the names of Sepu's neighbours. There was Chomo Mangyal, Sepu's Wife, a 6200-metre peak to the east; Gosham Taktso, the Son and Prime Minister of Sepu, another 6000er, and Seamo Uylmitok, the Turquoise Flower or Sepu's Daughter, a peak that looked over 6500 metres. Sepu Kangri itself he called Sepu Kunglha Karpu, the White Snow God. Sheepishly, neither Chris nor I mentioned the forgotten map, which carried heights and bearings. We sat outside and breakfasted in the sun on fresh coffee and fried eggs.

There was an abundance of places to go. We decided that first we needed to gain height, and thought the country to the east was enticing. We hadn't seen around the corner to the left of the head of the lake and we remembered from the forgotten map that there was a 5600-metre pass there, the Sa La.

Also there might be an easy summit rising from the pass. During the afternoon Pasang and Mingma helped us carry a tent and food to the far end of the lake.

Bonington was not a happy man next morning, and it was partly my fault. Breakfast was almost inedible. As cook that morning I shall never know quite why I had tried to make a mixture of porridge oats and some indifferent muesli into a hot gruel. It tasted and felt like cardboard, and was hard to swallow. We retched. Chris gallantly washed the pan with some difficulty. We thought of Mingma's eggs and coffee. Chris's neck ached, too, his personal signal of altitude. We were a crotchety pair on the patch of grass on the shore.

There had been a storm in the night and much noise. It hadn't worried us. Had it been thunder or distant avalanches, or crunching icebergs? A ship of ice about fifteen metres high now sat sedately in the lake beside us, like some giant swan, having split off from the glacier during the night. We left about 7 a.m., relieved at last to be walking into the unknown with light loads. We were heading for the Sa La, the 5600-metre pass through the cirque of peaks which enclosed Sepu Kangri to the east. The yak-herders had told Pasang that they sometimes took animals across to graze in the high pastures and sometimes to sell them. From the Sa La, we would have a fine view of the north face of Sepu Kangri.

We surprised two ruddy shelducks from a little moraine pool before we met the real wildlife – the dogs. I usually love dogs. I stroke dogs in India, and often on expeditions befriend the yak dogs. If they bark, I shout back and pretend to throw stones and they run away. I have never had a moment's anxiety with the dogs of Asia. A wild growl and two pairs of ferocious fangs soon changed all these preconceptions. The Tibetan guard dog is either a mastiff, with jaws strong enough to crunch a yak leg, or a mongrel of doubtful provenance. A pair were racing towards me, having disregarded Bonington. Did I smell? I whirled ski poles and picked up imaginary stones, but still they barked and bared their teeth, stopping only at poles' length. I was very frightened. Chris walked on. I tried to follow but my legs were shaking. I suppose the episode did not last more than a minute or two, but it was with real relief that I climbed slowly above the dogs while they stayed near two small tents, the home of a family on the high pastures. The shepherds simply grinned and waved. I remembered a confident telephone conversation to Chris dismissing the need for rabies vaccine – 'Just commercial medicine from the travel clinics,' I had said. 'Forget about rabies.'

We walked on. There were no further signs of habitation, and no more dogs above.

The pass was a grey smudge in a grey wall of rocky peaks. Tracks through steep loose rocks marked the way: curiously the route to the apparent pass was higher than an easy snow col a few hundred metres east. We headed for the col. It looked four hours away. An easy snow peak rose above it. We had already sunk into this measurement by time, predicting duration accurately at a glance. In the Alps they still sometimes measure distance by a *pipée*, how long it takes to smoke a pipe. It was four and a half hours, of tramping over shale and odd half tracks, with an occasional cairn. A barren, cloudy scene. A tiny snow slope led to the col itself, our first taste of snow and the crunch of boots. We had ice axes and it felt like climbing.

We were tired as we reached the top and peered over the edge: a steep and rotten gully dropped to the east, which explained why the tracks had not led here, but to the higher pass in the rocks. Sepu Kangri appeared across the valley, emerging bit by bit through the clouds. We filmed and recorded our thoughts about the slopes of Sepu which we could only see head on about eight kilometres away. I thought the mountain looked difficult, too hard for me. We could see the whole north face. Chris gazed at it with a hardened eye, picking out lines, sérac falls and avalanche tracks. I gazed over to the east, down a barren valley as far as the eye could see, and over towards Maya, Mawo Kangri and Kok-po, massifs of 6000-metre peaks that seemed to join up with Sepu Kangri. A circumnavigation of the range would be a long way and we would have to cross the massif itself. But that was a dream for another year.

Bonington was fired up and sped off upwards into the snow towards the small summit south of the col. I felt a little hesitant. We had no rope and I began to see crevasses and other dangers which were not there. I thought of the cheese and chocolate in my sack and especially a packet of People's Liberation Army biscuits. In half an hour Chris was back; the only summit of the expedition climbed, trivial and unnamed. I lied to him about the amount of chocolate we had had but had left him enough to keep him happy. We filmed 'trudging in the snow', and 'boots in footsteps', 'puffing with exhaustion', and a 'stout Cortez gazing on Sepu Kangri' sketch. It was just as well we did it then. We were learning never to miss the opportunity to film. We would barely touch snow again.

There was a lightness in our steps as we turned to leave the col. It was not just that we were descending. It was our first achievement, and we were beginning, after a little more than a week, to forget about the altitude. We bounced down, and had another nasty brush with the dogs, which I had taken a huge detour to avoid. But we were back at the tent in a couple of hours. We were happy; we ate and slept deeply.

It was a chilly dawn. We were off back to base camp. We had thought of crossing the river to the south to walk round the entire lake, but wisdom and heavy loads soon put paid to the idea. Blocks of ice were sweeping down an unpleasantly deep stream. Two figures appeared on the horizon, in the unmistakable colours of friends. They were Pasang and Mingma. We greeted them like old comrades, gave them half our loads and were soon back at base for lunch. We began to count days to the end of August, and realised we would really have to leave immediately. Tembe, with pigtail, dagger and yaks, was due next day. But we were bursting with energy and there were still eight hours of daylight. We bolted some food, grabbed the cameras and set off south, to climb the peak on the south-western, Sepu Kangri side of the lake.

We gained height rapidly over grass and rock. Within an hour of steady plodding upwards we were looking directly at the north face of Sepu Kangri across a moraine valley with a high glacial lake. Below, we could see the specks of our base camp and figures moving. We had climbed a thousand metres in a little over three hours to a diminutive summit, a shoulder on a ridge at 5700 metres. Once again a snow slope led upwards. It wasn't steep but there was an unpleasantly long drop if it avalanched. The snow was waist-high. First it was me, as ever, who thought of home, and then Chris. We descended separately, drying out wet boots as we walked, wrapped in our thoughts and the wonder of the place. Just as dusk fell we were home at base camp, happy, relaxed and still wondrous at the beauty of the spot. Nothing disturbed the night.

The bed tea arrived at seven. We had maintained this vestige of imperialism. While Mingma fried eggs, Pasang was already packing, confident that Tembe would arrive on time. In the almost automatic way with which events took place on this journey, around nine o'clock there was a distant jingling of a horse and a figure with a red headband zigzagging behind his yaks. Tembe was on time. Within an hour they were loaded and gone.

We had not been alone at base camp. Norge, a grandmother of sixty-two with a wry smile and toothless grin, lived with her granddaughter in a little stone house a hundred metres away. Ringma, a nun of about sixteen, was staying with them. We had exchanged smiles and they had become friends with Pasang and Mingma, sometimes fetching water, or even washing up, perhaps as a novelty. They agreed to be photographed before we left, after various protestations of modesty, and a lengthy spell in the house, while they changed, did their hair and put on jewellery. A Polaroid picture of Tembe had swayed them. Pasang mentioned that the locals were concerned that with our ice axes we were prospectors for minerals and this pastoral scene might be ruined by mining. He also exchanged our ages, pointing out to everybody that Chris was exactly the same age as the 'very old lady'. As for me, Grandma Norge had little time for the medical profession, having been told she was about to die the year before.

'And here I am', she cackled. 'What do you doctors know?'

But she beckoned Chris and me into the hut. We sat beside the fire and feasted on fresh yoghurt and innumerable cups of Tibetan tea, with the inevitable scoop of butter applied to the rim of the bowl with the edge of a dirty thumbnail. We had now forgotten about personal hygiene and supped tea and yoghurt for nearly an hour, emerging hunched and replete. We smelt of smoke and were blinded by the bright sun. As we said goodbye, the yak train was a distant bundle of colour below. We were alone. We realised that we had not arranged a rendezvous for nightfall, but the tracks after all led down the centre of the valley, so meet we must. We thought little of it.

Chris and I gave the Samda monastery a wide berth and wandered down by ourselves. I thought of home and the pace of late twentieth-century travel. Less than two weeks previously we had been trippers in the Lhasa Holiday Inn. Now we were acclimatised, grubby travellers and had achieved, if all else failed, a partial reconnaissance of an unknown range. As ever, we had scarcely done it ourselves, for without Pasang or a man of his sagacity, we would probably still be in Nakchu, or holed up in Mrs Donkar's guesthouse in Diru.

The afternoon drew on and the shadows lengthened. We passed the halfway camp of the upward journey, the rope bridge and the site where I had seen an arctic tern, familiar places of the week before. Chris caught up with me. We were both weary and as the march went on, progressively more irritable. Where the hell were they all? We had been walking for eight hours. Surely they hadn't legged it down to the roadhead in one? It was a thought we tried to avoid. We had no food, no sleeping bags and no torches. And I had a very sore bottom, a recurrent problem on this trip. Night was approaching, fast. We cursed them. We planned an unholy row, various disciplinary measures (we could not think exactly what) and complained about everything. Pasang had borrowed 50 *yuan* (less than £5) from me a few days previously. Why hadn't he given it back? God, we were grumpy. We were about to start blaming each other, but just as darkness began to fall we spotted the TIST on the big green tent. Within a minute we were drinking cups of tea and it was all forgotten. We felt ashamed we had been so annoyed. When before had a yak train travelled further than we had wanted? Usually we were moaning about a two-hour working day. We slept to the sound of the roar of the gorge and the throbbing of the little water mill beside us.

I felt a distinct trend of increasing appetite, bordering upon gluttony. I ate a monster breakfast of four eggs, bread, now showing its age, honey by the spoonful, and a cup of fresh coffee – Lavazza Espresso from Mr Ferrari, my local deli in Islington. The day became punctuated by food. By elevenses we were at the bridge beside the roadhead. Tsering, with his jacket and black shoes, still looking the man from Lhasa, was pleased to see us. With an eye for glamour, he was being photographed with Tembe's three sisters, whose attractiveness was the very obvious feature of the group photo. We soaked up the sun in the field beside the Jinbei truck.

A man crossed the bridge carrying a basket. Two brown bottles protruded from it and he held one up to us. Within minutes we were very content indeed. We were lying in the sun, drinking the second litre of cool beer, eating an early lunch of bread, matured cheddar, and speck, the delicious smoked ham from Mr Ferrari's. I dozed off. A cloud crossed the sun, and the chill woke me. Pasang and Mingma were loading the Jinbei. We waved goodbye to Tembe. His sisters hid their faces and smiled with their eyes. It was time to return to Diru.

Within three hours we were showering by the well in Mrs Donkar's courtyard. The water was icy, so cold we whimpered with pain as we washed our hair. The lavatories now seemed to us normal. Soon batteries were charging, clothes were drying, diaries and postcards were written. Tsering was covered in oil as he delved into the Jinbei, extracting every filter he could find. Bits of engine and bearings covered the concrete veranda surrounding the courtyard. We didn't ask why this service had to take place now, because the truck sounded fine; I thought Tsering just wanted to tinker, and to show off. What, after all, had he been doing alone for the last five days? Soon the Tibetans were all playing cards. Mingma seemed to be winning and he let it be known that he might be fed up with cooking. We feigned reluctance, and prepared for a night on the town.

The restaurant was Chinese, a shack in the main street. The Sechuan family had come from Chengdu, and settled in this remote spot three years before. There was the same sense of incongruity one has on entering a Chinese take-away in a small Welsh town. A tall, sad and careworn restaurateur greeted us, the only diners, while his wife, a small, helpful and efficient soul, realised wisely that trade might be a little more than usual that Friday evening. The floor was mud, and there were three metal tables. Four large posters were on the walls: the inevitable Chinese pin-up girl; a beach scene with palm trees, looking suspiciously like the Caribbean; a mountain scene with lake that would have been appropriate as an ad in a Mid-West diner for a family holiday in the Rockies; and a four-masted square-rigger. There was nothing remotely local. The feasting began. Chicken? Yes, please. Yak? Yes, please. Cabbage and chillies? Yes, please. Rice? Noodles? Eggs? Mixed vegetables? Yes, yes, yes. And far far more. I remember being finished by a dish which was almost entirely large pungent cloves of garlic and chillies. The meal became spicier course by course. There was beer from more brown bottles. The night for five of us cost under £20. We walked slowly back along the deserted main street. An occasional bicycle loomed out of the darkness. We stumbled into bed. The dogs of Diru did not wake us that night.

After our sobering view of the north face of Sepu Kangri, which we had supposed was the south face, we were now even more eager to see what the real south face had to offer. We planned to go to the south of our range by driving back through Nakchu and taking a small road we had seen signed to the town of Chali. We reloaded the entire expedition next morning from the upper balcony into the courtyard below. Lugging boxes and kitbags down the stairs was tedious so I rigged up a hoist to lower them directly into the truck. Quite why this very obvious manoeuvre gave me such personal pride is hard to imagine, but such are the little triumphs of technology. We were soon ready to leave. Chris was nowhere to be seen. He had been out filming or, I thought unkindly, avoiding loading. We drove into the main street before Pasang was told by a passing monk that Chris was at the police station. It became clear that whilst we now regarded ourselves as locals, the authorities were not happy for the foreigners to be loose, and not keen on the camera. Pasang sighed and looked resigned, with the air of a teacher whose charge had misbehaved on school journey. Everyone apologised and we were on our way.

We had a long day's bumping over the passes, with views of spectacular monasteries in the Diru valley. There was no time to stop, and perhaps we would not be welcome. By evening we were back in our campsite on the outskirts of Nakchu, the industrial hellhole of central Tibet. I half hoped for another guzzle in a restaurant, but Pasang politely made it clear that we were not going into town. Early next morning we drove through Nakchu to the filling station on the Lhasa road. Again, Pasang's expedition security was strict. We were to wait outside on the roadside, and not to take photos, while Tsering joined the queue and filled up.

The turning to the left some thirty kilometres down the metalled Nakchu–Lhasa road was not difficult to find. It was after all almost the only turning in the area. We were soon trundling and bouncing along a dirt road, high over the plateau. Distant peaks sometimes appeared through the cloud, but it was hard to position them on the map. We were heading for Chali, the only major town around, which looked a long day's drive. We stopped for the night in hills, barren but for acres of blue poppies. Occasional nomads' tents smoked in the distance. Still energetic, we climbed a hill for an hour. There was no view. My legs felt heavier than they should, I thought. We were just over 5000 metres. Pitch tents, food, sleep, wake, food, pack, and drive.

Next morning we passed a small range of strange grey limestone mountains, looking like the Dolomites, a useful training ground for some future trip. Chali was a few hours on, we thought. We had little idea of where we were in relation to a route leading to Sepu Kangri, the tourist map being even vaguer than in the north. This was a barren, treeless land. By late morning we passed a row of new Tibetan houses on the outskirts of a town. 'Retirement homes for government officials,' announced Pasang, with authority born of knowing how to answer our questions before we had asked them and, when he didn't know the answer, immediately using his imagination. We had arrived at Chali, birthplace of the two rivals for the post of Panchen Lama. A dusty main street ran between corrugated iron roofs, and unpleasant military-style buildings. There were few people about. It looked a seedy place. There was not a mountain in sight, simply the rolling hills of the Tibetan plateau.

Pasang ushered us into a small restaurant and we had a plate of noodles. A policeman and a town official joined us to tell us gloomily that the high mountains were over week's journey away, and there were neither yaks nor horses.

'But tell him we have already been to Sepu from the north,' I said. I nudged Pasang and asked him to say this again. Pasang clearly did not do so. He later said that if he had told them that we had already been to the place named on the permit, we wouldn't have been allowed to proceed. It wasn't that they were unhelpful, it seemed, they were simply bemused by our presence and that we were unannounced. Lengthy discussions followed and it soon transpired that to proceed further east was out of the question.

We would run out of time before we reached the range. It was around 150 kilometres away. There was, however, a possibility of doubling back, taking the first turning on the right, crossing a pass by this road into the Jiali valley. From there we could try to hire horses, cross a further pass and drop down into the valley which bordered Sepu Kangri to the south. The road was difficult, there was a broken bridge ... and so on. Like those directions given to a passing motorist about turning right at the pub, left at the church and then third left down a small alleyway, ending with 'you can't miss it', the possibility of success seemed an illusion. Still, we turned about and retraced the road for a few hours until the right turn.

The road, never good, became appalling. Broken rocks half a metre high formed a jumbled highway, more suitable for a tank, but just passable with a full size truck. This was no place for a small vehicle like the Jinbei. We could just about make progress in first gear, stopping frequently to shift stones. Tsering's face hardened, with a combination of determination and pain at the punishment his new pick-up was taking. Equally, it seemed he aimed to prove the vehicle's worth. For several hours we climbed higher, heading for the pass, the road becoming increasingly steep and rough. A thunderstorm threatened. With a shout Tsering reached the pass. We all jumped out, pee-ed and looked ahead. A barren valley stretched away below us. We dropped down. Gradually the road became a little easier. We reached the Jiali river and camped. I noted that I was a little off my food.

We set off next morning for the broken bridge. The river was thirty metres wide, and it looked over knee-deep or, more to the point, deeper than the floor of the cab. The central span of the bridge had been swept away. Two struts projected from either bank into nowhere, as if they had been hoping to meet in the middle. We walked into Chali-chu, the village-of-the-river, crossing by a footbridge which was still standing. Within a few minutes, the headman confirmed that there were no big trucks, no horses, and no yaks. The place was nearly empty, as the villagers were away, moving herds down from the high pastures. It seemed as though we might have reached the end of our journey. Chris calculated with his Global Positioning System (GPS) that we were still around 150 kilometres from the summit of Sepu Kangri. We had three days, possibly four, to reach the massif and be back where we were. Below us, the entrance to the village-by-the-river was guarded by two large gates that were firmly shut. Above, the golden roof of a monastery glinted in the sunlight.

Suddenly there was a shout from Pasang and the silhouette of the Jinbei appeared behind the high gates, the cab door opened and Tsering leapt out, waving, several hundred metres away. We could hear the engine throbbing. He had driven through the river. We ran down, jumped in and drove off towards Jiali, some fifty kilometres away. By 4 p.m. we were in a grassy valley over a kilometre wide. Jiali was a small settlement, a concrete and corrugated iron building and a few houses. There were yaks grazing on the hills around, men with horses, tents and nomads on the move, and of course, dogs. This was barren country in comparison with the wooded valleys of the north.

We camped beside a little stream, uphill from the evil effluent of the village, distrusting our source of drinking water. Children played and sang, peered into tents, and fiddled with everything they could find, a contrast to the friendly reserve of the people of the north. Dogs sniffed around. They were a pack of mangy, scraggy mongrels, docile, starving and lifeless. Occasionally they attempted a tilt at sexual foreplay, but they seemed too frail even for this. A thin miserable black creature came and sat beside me and wagged his tail. He nibbled a crust I threw him, relishing each bite. He growled when another dog came near. I seemed to have a little friend. I called him Mangy.

Pasang within minutes had ascertained the state of play. The pass to Sepu was at the head of the valley, some three days' march away. There were no horses, and no yaks available. The GPS said we were now seventy kilometres from Sepu Kangri. We would simply have to walk as far as we could. Pasang would come with us, we would travel as light as possible and take one tent and three nights' food. It would be a hard few days, and a squash in the tent. Maybe we would see something, but from where we sat there was nothing remotely resembling a high mountain in sight. Tsering looked relieved that his Jinbei was to go no further.

Next morning Chris announced that he had lost the Global Positioning System. 'Aren't you glad I brought the compass then?' I chirped. He was livid and in no mood for banter. He turned out his sack, emptied his tent, and was appropriately agitated by the question that wives, mothers and VISA card telephone receptionists always ask in these situations, 'Well, when did you last have it?' He didn't know. The kids, we thought, must have been those kids, they were all over the place.

I seemed to remember the night before that he had been sitting away from the tents, recording his diary and taking a GPS fix. I wandered off for a crap in that direction. The mangy black dog followed. At first I thought it was a simply a fresh yak turd on the ground, but there in the pasture was the shiny black plastic case of the GPS, glistening in the dew. The kids hadn't picked it up. I shouted, we laughed, and I brought it back. I hurried back to have my crap. I squatted and saw the mangy black dog a few yards away. You are a faithful friend, Mangy, I thought. I finished and moved away slightly, as one does, to sort myself out. Like lightning, Mangy was there, licking his chops as if he had just bolted the Sunday chicken. I suddenly felt very sick.

Pasang, Chris and I, with unpleasantly heavy sacks, walked up the valley, negotiating another violent dog scene; again they made a beeline for me. Mangy had by now deserted me. We had been walking for a couple of hours when a shout and a cloud of dust from behind announced the approach of a yak caravan, some fifty strong with a dozen or so horses. The yak were saddled but unloaded, and there were several free horses, riderless but saddled. Could we believe it? A tall aristocratic man drew up beside us, beckoning with a smile that we mount horses. He took my ski stick as a staff to direct his men. Others took our loads.

'Could I possibly get some trousers?' I whimpered to Pasang. My legs were already becoming burnt in shorts.

'Just jump on, quickly,' he replied.

The caravan barely stopped. We were on our way.

I last rode a horse for any distance in 1974, a fine tall gentle beast, in the Harki Doon valley in India, beating a retreat from a peak named Swagarohini with frostbitten feet. Chris muttered something about South America and 1963. The Tibetan ponies were small, no-nonsense-with-riders creatures with tiny wooden saddles and stirrups designed for someone the size of a Newmarket jockey. We bumped along. I was addressed by Temba, our leader.

'He says sit up straight and hold the reins like this, in one hand,' shouted Pasang with a smile, looking a natural horseman himself.

Temba trotted back and forth, hailing his men with my ski stick and pointing to each wandering yak to be brought back to the tracks. I learnt gradually how to steer, nervously, like coaxing a large yacht that belongs to someone else. The accelerator was easy, the brakes less certain. Trotting became a nightmare. My knees ached, my thighs burned. I tried desperately to hold a cine-camera in one hand. Whenever I aimed at Chris he sat bolt upright like a cavalry officer. Occasionally, and I suspect as part of the morning's entertainment, Temba would call and point at me, indicating that it was my turn to recover a yak. I learnt to trot after them and chivvy the animals back into line. We were making ground at high speed. Turn followed turn in the valley and we gradually climbed, along treeless pas-

Our first aerial view of Sepu Kangri (the dominant peak on the right central skyline) from the plane from Chengdu to Lhasa.

RIGHT Mingma the cook, Tsering the driver and Pasang the guide on our recce.

CENTRE Crossing the cantilever bridge on the way to the Sacred Lake – swept away in the floods of '98.

BELOW Charlie enjoying some yoghurt with our neighbours at the head of the Sacred Lake.

Reaching the Sacred Lake, with Sepu Kangri in the background.

Tembe, our yak-herder, and three of our neighbours at the northern end of the Sacred Lake.

RIGHT Chris on the reconnaissance above the Thong Wuk Glacier, with the Sa La in the left background and Chomo Mangyal (the Wife of Sepu) the dominant peak to the right.

BELOW Charlie at the first camp of our reconnaissance with Chomo Mangyal on the left and the Gosham Taktso (Son and Prime Minister) on the right, above the glacier flowing into the lake.

OPPOSITE RIGHT Hill country to the south of Sepu Kangri on the second stage of our reconnaissance.

OPPOSITE BELOW Chris with yak train on the south side of Sepu Kangri.

ABOVE Lhallum Tamcho in the left foreground, Lhazo Bumla (Thousand Buddhas) centre, Sepu Kangri on the right, from the south. The route eventually taken was up the ridge from the col between Lhazo Bumla and Sepu Kangri.

RIGHT Our Jinbei truck stuck in the river on the return from the southern reconnaissance.

OPPOSITE TOP A typical *ba* – summer home of nomads or villagers.

OPPOSITE BELOW Interior of a *ba* – the hearth in the middle is left in place when the family moves. They usually return to the same site.

1997 Expedition   TOP   The expedition just before its banquet in Lhasa.
From left to right, Jim Curran, Jim Lowther, Duncan Sperry,
Jim Fotheringham, Chris, Charlie, Tibetan PLA Officer, John Porter.

ABOVE   The banquet for the CTMA in Lhasa, with various exotic
dishes – in the middle is the tortoise.

Base camp in the spring. Note, the Lake is frozen in the background. At the puja (blessing) at our Base camp, Laphraoig whisky was an important part of the blessing. Dorbeh, one of our neighbours is carrying out the puja – he knew the prayers better than our sherpas.

The communications tent at Base camp. Fotheringham on left is writing love e-mails to his future partner, who at the time was in Boston, U.S.A., while Jim Lowther, on the right, was trying to manage his estate by e-mail.

RIGHT
Sam Ten Tsokpu, the
hermit who lives below
Sepu Kangri.

OPPOSITE
Jim Fotheringham leading
the steep and very difficult
ice and rock pitch to the
crest of the ridge leading
to the Frendo Spur.

BELOW
Charlie with Karte, whose
wife Charlie has just
treated – she had an
ectopic pregnancy.

John Porter, Jim Fotheringham and Jim Lowther at camp II, at the foot of the Frendo Spur, Gosham Taktso in the background.

Fotheringham and Porter pushing the route up the Frendo Spur, fixing ropes.

OPPOSITE
Fotheringham on the Frendo Spur.

Jim Lowther leading through séracs on the Frendo Spur.

The weather deteriorated and never improved. Fotheringham digging out a tent at camp I.

Lowther left, Porter right in the snow hole at camp II, discussing Porter's health – he suspected pulmonary oedema. We decided to retreat.

LEFT
Jim Lowther leading in a blizzard as he and Chris pushed the route up the Frendo Spur.

'The Retreat from Moscow' – we cleared Base camp in a blizzard.

High tech communications at camp 1 – Chris using the BT Mobiq, not only to call UK, but also to transmit digital images and stories through the Apple Newton.

tures, open and windswept, so different from the northern gorges and forests. Everyone was moving. Nomad families stood by their half-packed tents and chattels waiting for the removal men to take them down from their summer grazing. A few hours passed. We arrived at a great *maidan*. Temba dismounted and held the bridle, motioning that he was off up a side valley. I climbed down and could not stand. My knees ached and were locked. I was scorched like a crispbread. Chris looked, I thought, a little better. I longed to walk again, gently up the valley. We had already come about twenty kilometres, we guessed. There was still not a snow peak in sight.

Pasang smiled and shouted, pointing to another yak caravan. Our journey was becoming like a game of pass-the-parcel. Within minutes we were all on horseback again, the bruises on our bottoms being tortured by new saddles. Our new masters were less jolly than the first, and less aristocratic, but this Second Eleven caravan was equally fast. Within two hours we could see a pass at the head of the valley and nomads camped beneath it. We dismounted an hour below it, as the Second Eleven had reached their destination. We walked slowly up to the nomads' camp. The family were all packed, waiting to leave with a lone horseman. There was a tea kettle brewing on a yak dung fire. We stopped. Thank God, I thought, we're here for the night. I'm buggered. Why was I going so slowly?

Chris had arrived a good twenty minutes earlier. Before I had taken off my sack, the Bonington boom began. Chris drops all punctuation when he's excited:

'Hi Charlie we thought we'd go over the pass tonight and this horse is taking our loads to the pass he's leaving now so give him your sack I am going now.'

He is of course joking, I thought, it's after six.

I sipped a bowl of tea the nomad passed me. I smiled and thanked him. Chris wasn't joking; he wasn't at all. I gazed wanly up at the pass. It was over an hour away. There were two hours before nightfall. It was obvious that this was the correct decision. It had to be done. I could manage an hour. You can always manage an hour. In the space of thirty-six hours we had crossed an impassable river, and almost by chance travelled fifty kilometres on foot and horseback. We had gained about a thousand metres. Sepu Kangri and the Yapu Gully of the *Immortal Mountains* map lay, if we were correct, just over the rocky pass. Never before have I felt that we had been in more right places at the right times. The horse was laden with our sacks. It was time to go.

The others were soon far ahead. I plodded slowly on. It was an easy well-frequented trail. A few bright yellow anemones were growing in the stream bed beside the path. There was little other vegetation and we were soon looking back down on the yak pastures from a steep rocky track. Behind us the family was leaving. Samu, our horseman, would join them later. I was twenty minutes behind Pasang and Chris and I could hear them talking above me on the last stretch. They could see nothing of the mountains. I caught up on the pass. Looking into the next valley, the rocky path dropped down easily, and seemed to lead into another broad valley, presumably the Yapu Valley, perhaps an hour away. It was nearly dark.

Samu had unloaded the horse. Pasang was trying to persuade him to come and pick us up in two days' time. He argued that he would be far away, back down the valley. Money in increasingly large sums did not seem to be talking. Then he spied my binoculars.

'You can have them as a present, if you come to meet us,' I said.

A gleam of pleasure shone through his eyes. I remembered receiving my first catapult as a child. I had been given the binoculars free with a mail-order fax machine. Such is the strength of the right currency. Samu trotted off quickly into the dusk and was almost out of sight as we shouldered heavy packs. It was at least all downhill until we had to return.

Half an hour later there was a white glint in the twilight. A stream gurgled past a perfect campsite. Within minutes there was a brew on in the two-man tent. We were too tired to be hungry. Chris slept outside in my bivouac bag but came in as soon as it started to rain, cursing that my bag, brand new, was porous. The snoring started. Pasang, who had never had the experience of sharing a tent with Chris before, giggled. He soon moved outside. I slept fitfully, awoke in the small hours with a blinding headache and took some dexamethasone. I slept again.

Chris and I are both early risers.

'It's still dark,' I mumbled. 'What the hell are you doing?'

'No it isn't, it's six, and just light. Get up, I've got the stove on.'

I fumbled about and found I was in a tangle, hot, sweaty and frightened like a child. I couldn't see. For a few seconds I didn't know where I was, until I realised it was dark only because I was halfway down my sleeping bag trying unsuccessfully to burrow out.

'Y'allrightmate?' Chris asked, handing me a mug when I surfaced. I thought I was. We dressed and set off.

We were soon bouncing down the little valley, carrying lunch, film and the GPS. As the dawn really broke we found ourselves in another wide valley, heading down to the north. This was the Yapu. Along this trail which was part of the Gya Lam, Abbé Huc had ridden in years gone by, and later George Pereira. As the sun hit the peaks there were the unmistakable silhouettes of Sepu Kangri and its satellites, the other side of the jigsaw we had seen from the north. The peaks arose out of a deserted valley, recently the scene of summer grazing that the nomads had just left.

There was a wide stream to cross, ankle deep. We thought of the rest of the day in wet boots and took them off to ford it barefoot. Quite what persuaded me to try to throw each boot over the torrent to the opposite bank is beyond me. We were carrying nothing and the pair of boots would have easily dangled around my neck. Perhaps it was simply the elation of being there. Chris watched, incredulous, as I began to hurl my first boot and missed my footing. The boot landed in the frothing water and was soon heading off downstream, bouncing down the rocks. Chris screamed at me and I shot after it, just rescuing it before it disappeared down the valley. Where would we have been, with one boot and possibly a broken ankle? It is easy to do these unbelievably stupid things.

A lone horseman rode by half a mile away. It may be that he did not see us, for he did not pause or wave. We felt like trespassers in a secret land. As the morning passed we dropped down further to 4500 metres and walked for some ten kilometres along the Yapu valley floor. Compared to the northern approach, this side of Sepu Kangri looked steep, complex and very forbidding. There was no obvious way to approach it without a longer and detailed reconnaissance of the side valleys that fell from its glaciers. Still, we had seen the massif. This was a privilege enough. After lunch in the azaleas and a minor snooze, it was time to head back to camp.

We were in by 7.30 p.m., just before dark. It had been another twelve-hour day. Pasang said that he had been lonely. He would have done better to come with us. We thought about the next five days and what we had to achieve.

We needed a full day in Lhasa to sort out 1997 with the CTMA. The plane left on the morning of Saturday, 31st August, day 5. We were due home the following day. I had patients booked on Monday, 2nd September. There was no room for anything to go wrong. Put it another way, everything had to go just right, and rather a lot had gone right already. Somehow, we both felt rather carefree at the prospect of being delayed. Chris slept soundly, and snored away. I had another bad night, unusual for me at this now, for us, modest altitude of 5400 metres. I took some more dexamethasone and I coughed a lot. Pasang curled up outside. It did not rain.

I am rarely unwell on expeditions apart from the misery of arrival at high altitude. Next morning we woke, brewed and packed as usual. It was the first stage of the long journey home to England. I seemed painfully slow; I did not know why. Chris and Pasang started up the easy path through the rocks to the col, a distance of less more than forty minutes. Quickly they drew away. My engine simply wouldn't go. I was breathless, coughing and I could barely put one foot in front of another. 'If I go slower I can keep going, if I go slower I can keep going, if I go slower ...' I was already going very slowly indeed. It took me two full hours to reach the 5600-metre col.

This bloke doesn't seem very well, I thought, in a vague way. He doesn't seem very well at all. Not much to be done about it. Wonder if he's got pulmonary oedema. He's coughing a bit. He's never had it before. Anyway, he's left most of the drugs back in Jiali, so he'd better get on with it, and then get down. I was talking to myself. There was a 'him' and I seemed to know 'he' was ill. 'He' couldn't walk fast. I plodded slowly on.

'Are you all right? You look awful,' Chris asked, as I eventually sat on the rocks by the col.

'Not really, sorry, but I'll be OK.' He took some of my load and we walked down the other side. Chris looked rather worried.

The descent took on a spirit of its own. After several hours we had all but given up on Samu the horseman and I thought I might retain my binoculars. Then he suddenly rode up, took our loads and claimed his prize. We pushed on, free and faster, but there seemed no chance of reaching Jiali by nightfall. I just wondered whether we'd reach there the next day, in a bemused, slightly muddled way. I could not go faster. The afternoon drew on.

We saw an unusual sight on the plain below us, where we had been scooped up by the Second Eleven yak train. There was no road up this valley, but there in the *maidan*, the broad alluvial meadow, was a large green truck. Its engine was running and it was being loaded. Samu broke into a gallop and dropped the loads, Pasang ran after him, Chris pushed on and I followed, slowly, but as fast as I could. The three reached the truck and a discussion took place. Samu galloped back, ordered me on to his horse and rode us both down, urging all speed.

In the truck were a curious group, the strangeness of which we complemented. There were two goats, which nibbled a leather bag bearing the Red Cross of a barefoot doctor. There was the Tibetan doctor himself, and his patient, an exhausted young nomad mother who had had a baby three days before, and two other little children, one about eighteen months and the other five years old. The children grinned whenever the baby's head peeped out of its swaddling. The father had sent word down the valley asking for the truck because he really did not feel his wife could manage the long ride home on horseback. What a gent, I thought. We left within a minute of arriving on the *maidan*, bumped down the valley to Jiali by evening, pausing only for every encampment to glimpse at the new arrival in the nomad's family. We may have seen the next Dalai Lama, I thought. There was something miraculous about it all. Mingma and Tsering greeted us in astonishment. We opened a bottle of whisky. Mangy was waiting by my tent, hungry.

It should have been an easy drive back to Lhasa. We knew the way, we could cross the river and it hadn't been raining.

'We're not staying in the Holiday Inn,' we told Pasang.

'No, I've just the place, the Khada Hotel,' he replied with a twinkle.

I dozed and felt awful. We bumped down to Chali-chu, the village-by-the-river and the broken bridge. We were making good time. Tsering drove straight into the middle of the river. As we started up the gradient to the opposite bank, the Jinbei groaned and spluttered. Black smoke poured out of the exhaust. Water washed a little over the cab floor. Tsering slammed into reverse and the engine growled even more. He tried another place on the bank, failed and swore. The engine stalled. We were in mid-stream. There was an eerie silence, with only the sound of running water and a revolting smell of burnt oil, which swirled away from us downstream. We waded ashore. Pasang walked back to the village. A small crowd gathered. Tsering looked dejected. There was neither yak nor truck to be seen. A child in policeman's cap and jacket came to say hello. It soon dawned on us that he was neither a child, nor in fancy dress. He was a member of the Tibetan Police Force. We felt we were getting old. We were very civil to him thereafter.

We sat having a snack when a cloud of dust arose from the village half a mile away, followed by the purring deep throb of a diesel. Pasang arrived waving with a truck. Within half an hour, after an anxious few moments gazing at a fraying wire tow rope drawn as tight as a bowstring, the Jinbei was on the bank, dripping black oil from every orifice. Tsering stripped the filters and drained the sump, gearbox and differential into the washing-up bowl. He poured the oil back in as it separated on the surface of the water. The big truck then towed the Jinbei round the field. Within seconds there was a cough, a bang, black smoke and a roar. We were off again.

I still felt dreadful, and I seemed to become worse as each day drew on. I remember dimly the awful road over the pass towards Nakchu. Then I began to see things on the roadside. I saw my grown-up daughters, Rebecca and Naomi, come to see me as little children, in frocks. They had come to say goodbye. I spoke to my grandmother, Granny Hart, who died when I was eight, in 1954. She asked me to untie knots in the string from parcels and wind it into neat little hanks, just as I remembered as a child. Sixpence a hank. She had made her lovely chocolate cake. I then saw a stone by the road. It looked like a dog. Then the stone became a dog, a real dog. And then I saw religious people: a priest, Christ, the Madonna and an old monk were each sitting by the road in turn. These were half dreams and half real. He's really not very well, I thought, but I expect he'll be OK. To this day I recall little of that road journey, when I usually have an eye for detail. When we drove into Lhasa two days later, I decided I was recovering, though with a distinct lack of objective evidence. Must have been a touch of pulmonary oedema, I thought, and lacking any critical insight into the matter, I found I was still breathless, and my chest was painful low down on the right whenever I took a deep breath, a frequent occurrence. Pulmonary oedema would almost invariably have settled by Lhasa and it rarely causes pain.

We drove into Lhasa at darkness on Thursday, 29th August, night 3. Pasang greeted the receptionist at the Khada Hotel with undue familiarity, I thought. We were shown a pretty room, decorated in traditional colours, in this attractive family hotel. Soon we were sound asleep in clean sheets. Pasang was back with Yishi, his wife and Tenzing, his son. Mingma was with his mum, next door to Pasang's flat, having added 'chef' to his CV. Tsering was home with his family outside Lhasa.

I remained unwell. In Lhasa the night sweats began. I was wet through, even in the cool nights. My Indian cotton pyjamas were drenched by three in the morning, so much so that I would have to change clothes, often twice a night. Two days later we were on the plane back to England.

'I have good news for you about your upgrade,' the British Airways man said at New Delhi, as we waited for a connection in the middle of the night. 'There is *one* seat in Business Class!'

Chris suggested, without much enthusiasm, 'I suppose we should toss up for it.'

Well, we wouldn't have had it at all without Bonington, I thought and suggested that he took it. He accepted with alacrity. I dozed in the Tourist Class while Chris drank champagne. At Heathrow we hugged each other as we said goodbye. We had had a memorable month; we had enjoyed each other's company and the warmth of a happy team. At 6.30 a.m. in the soft summer morning of 1st September, day 6, I bought the Sunday papers, some milk and crept into our garden in Islington, making sure the back gate didn't squeak and wake the dog. I threw some earth up at Ruth's window. The curtains parted.

'What the fuck are you doing?' she shouted with a smile.

'Sorry. I haven't got the back door key. Can you let me in?'

It was all over, but not quite. I left for work as usual early on Monday morning. I was very tired, but thought little of it. Two days later, I was dragging myself about. I found I could not walk without stopping even to the end of the road, both because of my chest and an utter sense of fatigue. The distance was 200 metres.

'You're going to see a doctor tomorrow,' announced Ann Tilley, my secretary with a steely glint. 'You're off work, and I've cancelled all the patients.'

Dr John Moore-Gillon, a chest physician colleague at St Bartholomew's, at first couldn't say what was wrong. I felt in good company. But after blood tests, X-rays and a lung scan, he decided it had been a viral infection, like glandular fever, with presumably some pleurisy, and a mild inflammation of the brain. Maybe I had had a touch of pulmonary oedema too. I was off for a month, and gradually recovered. I could not stop thinking about the year ahead.

5   Behind the Turquoise Flower

7th April – 9th May 1997

CHRIS BONINGTON

Lhasa again, after views of Gaurishankar, Menlungtse, Everest, Lhotse and Makalu appearing between clouds, and then as we turned north over the Arun valley, Kangchenjunga coming into view on the right. The border between Nepal and Tibet was marked by an abrupt change from dusty green to arid brown as we commenced the long descent into Lhasa airport some fifty miles to the south of the capital at Gongkar on the Yarlung Tsangpo river. It was April 1997.

The six months since Charlie and I had returned had been challenging. The reconnaissance had been one of the best trips I have ever undertaken. We had done practically no climbing, we had attained no major summits and yet I had enjoyed a quality of exploratory adventure that I had not experienced since the first trip I made to the Himalayas, to Annapurna II, in 1960. It really had been a venture into the unknown. Everything about it had been fresh and full of surprises. Being just the two of us had enhanced the quality of the experience, both from the point of view of decision-making and the way we were able to get to know both our Tibetan staff and the few people we had met on the way. Organising the trip had been wonderfully easy and there had been none of the problems of fund-raising. We had simply paid for it ourselves.

Setting up a full-scale expedition was a different matter. First there was the question of the team. The original group had been Graham Little, Jim Lowther, Jim Fotheringham and myself as the climbing team. Graham's partner, Christine, was about to have a baby and he therefore decided that he couldn't possibly be away for so long. So I invited John Porter, a very experienced mountaineer with an interesting background. He was an American from New Hampshire who, like so many at the time of the Vietnam war, decided he could not become involved in an enterprise to which he was totally opposed. With some difficulty he had therefore fled to Britain where he continued his studies at Leeds University. He was already a talented climber and with Alex MacIntyre, joined some of the top Polish climbers first in an expedition to the Hindu Kush, travelling with neither visas nor permission through the Soviet Union. John then went on to Changabang in the Garhwal in India to make the first ascent of the south face. He has been involved in many other expeditions and I came to know him when he served as vice-president while I was president of the British Mountaineering Council. He was now living in Caldbeck, the village just below my home. His acceptance meant that our expedition was very much a Cumbrian team. Charlie, of course, was coming as our doctor and Jim Curran as film-maker. Tragically, Paul Nunn who was going to help Jim with the film had been killed in an avalanche while Charlie and I were in Tibet.

This was going to be an expensive expedition. We had learnt in Lhasa that, as a mountaineering expedition, we would have to work through the China Tibet Mountaineering Association and pay a peak fee of $15,000. The CTMA also placed a premium on all other costs we would have to meet in Tibet. This meant that we were going to have to find sponsors. It was no longer a bill we could meet out of our own pockets. Attracting a sponsor meant we needed to have a high media profile and I therefore decided not only to make a film but also run a website from base camp. This meant setting up satellite communications and would involve much work during the course of the expedition, so because I wanted to concentrate on the climbing I decided I needed a web wizard. It was at Paul Nunn's memorial gathering at Sheffield Hallam University, where he had been a lecturer in history, that I met up with Duncan Sperry, a friend of Jim Curran. I invited him on impulse. He was running a high-tech data transfer company and seemed just the man for the job.

We had a superb objective and a good team, but no money. Christmas 1996 came and went, and there was still no sponsorship. Everyone was becoming edgy. I tried to maintain an outward optimism, assuring the team and trying to convince myself that I had never failed to find sponsors before, but it was getting uncomfortably close to departure. We had to pay the peak fee in early January. I did so out of my own account. And then, as so often happens, it all came together at the last minute, mostly on a local Cumbrian basis. John Porter, who was manager of the Carlisle Training and Enterprise Council, found us two sponsors, his own TEC and Sealey's, a local manufacturer of beds. As a result of a fortunate meeting at a fund-

raising dinner for the local mountain rescue I also gained the support of
the International Powered Access Federation. But our major funding came
from an individual who wishes to remain anonymous. He had wanted to
join us on our trek to the mountain and had offered a substantial sum
towards the cost of the expedition. Sadly, he was forced to pull out at the
last moment, but very generously left his contribution in the pot.

Another vital sponsor was the computer software company, Logica. Their
PR manager, Tarquin Henderson, had worked for Apple in 1985, when I
had taken an Apple computer with me to Everest. They could give us no
money, but designed a software program to enable me to download images
from my digital camera on to the Apple Newton, a very small hand-held
computer which was light enough to take up onto the mountain. I could
then download these and send them via the British Telecom Mobiq, a very
compact satellite phone, back to their computer in the UK. My son Rupert
could then pick up the images and stories to include in the website which
he was managing. Tarquin also obtained media exposure for us on radio,
television and the computer press which helped not only Logica but the
rest of our sponsors. We had just enough money to cover the cost of the
expedition.

My own planning had been made much easier than on previous expeditions by the development of trekking agencies in Nepal which are happy
to handle every aspect of local organisation. I had made the arrangement
through Himalaya Kingdoms, a British-based company, who quoted a
single price for the hire of camping equipment, provision of food and of a
high-altitude porter, cook and cook boy, organising the import of our
equipment into Nepal and its transfer overland to Lhasa. A smiling,
immensly energetic Nepalese, Bikrum Pandey, who runs his own trekking
company in Kathmandu, Himalaya Expeditions Inc., had made it all
happen. I had asked Charlie and Duncan to go out a week early to supervise
the purchase of food but they had found they were almost superfluous.

And so, here we were, trailing into the smart new Lhasa airport building,
slightly apprehensive about all the communications equipment we had,
even though we had the necessary permits. But the customs official barely
glanced at the satellite phones and just waved us through. On the other
side of the barrier was a welcome and familiar figure, Pasang, his face
slightly puffier than when we said goodbye to him eight months earlier. He
had a fresh scar on his cheek; he was quick to tell us that he had been
involved in a fight. He was to be our interpreter. My letters to the CTMA,
asking them to employ him had been successful. He introduced us to Dorje,

our liaison officer. My first impression of Dorje was that he was very young but he was twenty-eight. He had quite long hair, in an almost Beatle cut, and was casually but smartly dressed. Pasang assured me that he was a good friend and would look after us well.

In the hour or so we had spent clearing customs the clouds had rolled in and by the time we had boarded our minibus the wind was gusting a few scattered snow flakes that mingled with the air-borne dust. The fields at the edge of the road and the hills on either side of the valley were a drab brown, their tops dusted in snow. It was all so very different from the previous August when all had been lush and green, but for the rest of the team it was new and exciting. Only Jim Fotheringham had been to Tibet before, when in 1987 he and I had travelled overland from Nepal to Menlungtse, some 300 miles to the west.

We pulled into the compound of the Khada Hotel with its classic Tibetan architecture and the smiling girls in traditional dress whom we had met the previous August. There was a lot to do. Nawang our Sherpa cook had already arrived, having travelled overland from Nepal with all our baggage. This was stored at the offices of the CTMA, just around the corner from the hotel. We had to sort all this, meet up with the officials of the CTMA to finalise our arrangements, and set our satellite communications into action. The latter was Duncan Sperry's sphere. All of this had to be done before we could visit the Potala Palace, the temples and monasteries. We had a lot to do in three days.

Duncan was struggling. He has an allergy to wheat and it is very difficult to avoid eating wheat-based foods, particularly when travelling. He was feeling ill, he was affected by the altitude, yet he still battled on to establish contact with the world. We had the three communication devices – the Saturn B data terminal, weighing thirty kilos with its large dish and chunky control unit, and two British Telecom Mobiqs, which were so small and compact it was difficult to believe they could function. The Mobiq was no larger than a laptop computer, its lid acting as a dish to gain contact with the satellite located far above the Indian Ocean. Inside was a handset that resembled my own office phone.

Duncan pointed the dish to the south, keyed in a number and we were in contact with someone. I was impressed, particularly by the ease and confidence with which he slipped into cyberspeak. Apparently he was talking to an engineer at a telephone exchange in New York. The line was as clear as if he had been just down the road, but the engineer wanted nothing to do with us. We weren't in his computer. Eventually Duncan and he worked out that we had inadvertently got aboard the wrong satellite. Shortly afterwards Duncan was able to call the correct one, linked to British Telecom, who had kindly given us free air time. We were now able to speak to the world. Standing on the roof of the hotel with the Potala towering over the rooftops, I was able to call Wendy at home and wake her in bed at seven o'clock in the morning. It felt so close and so immediate.

But we were less successful in sending out e-mails and digital pictures, either through the little Apple Newton or the laptop. The computer at Logica that was to receive the pictures and messages from the Newton did not acknowledge us. Duncan was having problems with the e-mail address he had set up with his service company in England. He was to spend our entire time in Lhasa struggling with the satcomms equipment which had been delivered to him only a few days before our departure. In the meantime there was much else to do, loads to be checked and repacked, so that we had everything we needed to hand for the road journey and beyond.

Charlie worked with our three Sherpas who had travelled from Nepal, our sirdar Dawa, the cook Nawang and Pemba his assistant. Together they shopped for more fresh food and other items we still needed. We were surprised at just how much there was available in the Lhasa markets. It was so different from 1982 when there had been hardly any shops, very few vegetables and a feeling of bleak austerity. Now the market just opposite our hotel was crammed with stalls brimming with vegetables, many of which had probably been brought from Chengdu or even further afield. Some bananas carried a sticker to show that they had come from Ecuador. There were stalls piled with bowls of spices, others with yak and sheep meat, hanging red and gory from hooks.

I was anxious to start the road journey as soon as possible. The others wanted more time. In particular, Jim Fotheringham, a practising Buddhist, had a very special assignment. He had been entrusted with a pair of shoes for the fourteen-year-old Karmapa, a reincarnate lama who, after the Dalai Lama, was the holiest man in the Tibetan religious hierarchy. His monastery was two hours' drive from Lhasa and he only held audience on certain days, so we resolved to deliver the shoes on our way back.

That first night Dorje took us to eat at a local restaurant. It was smart and airy with pictures of European cuisine round the walls. The menu was extensive and Chinese. The following morning Jim Lowther and I called at the CTMA to settle the final arrangements for the expedition. We were shown into the office of Gao Mouxing, the Secretary General. He was Chinese but had lived in Tibet for over thirty years. I guessed that he was an old Communist Party member who had worked his way up the bureaucratic ladder. He spoke no English and looked Tibetan even though he was born in China. He seemed to leave much of the day-to-day work and liaison with foreigners to Dou Chang Shen, a young Chinese who seemed much more than an interpreter. We learnt later that he and his wife were also part-owners of the restaurant we had visited the previous evening.

The meeting started well with Gao Mouxing saying that we were now becoming friends because we had met the previous August. This became even more evident during the course of our negotiations. We were planning to make a film of our expedition but were required to pay a fee of $4,000 to the CTMA for permission to do so. However, we had not managed to pre-sell the film to a television channel and were therefore working speculatively. I explained this to Dou Chang Shen and suggested that they waived the filming fee but that if we managed to sell the film on our return home, we would then pay them the $4,000. I was impressed by his trust and readiness to accept this line of argument. We were also invited to a banquet that evening. We responded by suggesting that they joined us the following night.

The next two days passed in the usual turmoil. Charlie, with whom I shared a room, not only co-ordinated the shopping and packing, but somehow at the same time managed to write an article, complete a chapter of a medical textbook and a book review for a medical journal in the UK.

The banquet hosted by the CTMA was memorable for the number of toasts and the quantity of alcohol consumed. The newcomers to Tibet were introduced to the bottoms-up custom of the *moutai* toast, a lethal short, swigged between glasses of beer. Back at the hotel we rounded off the evening with a bottle of malt whisky. The next day, everyone felt the worse for wear.

The following night we hosted our own banquet. The Khada Hotel rose to the occasion with turtle blood-flavoured *moutai*, an entire tortoise, huge king prawns and black chicken – a prized poultry dish with a blackened skin, garnished with a swan carved from Chinese cabbage. The dishes just kept on coming. My neighbour, one of the officials from the CTMA, could not take his eyes off the tortoise and it soon became evident that the head was a particularly succulent morsel. He could not disguise his look of delight as he plucked it from the dish with his chopsticks and popped it into his mouth. There were more speeches, more toasts and we were presented with a box of phials containing a pink elixir named 'Rhodiola – the Strong and Healthy Preparation' by one guest, a middle-aged somewhat

rotund officer in the People's Liberation Army who ran a factory manu-
facturing herbal medicines.

I had decided we would follow the route of our northern reconnaissance
and head for Diru and the Sacred Lake. We would attempt Sepu Kangri
from the north. Next morning we piled ourselves and our gear into three
Land Cruisers and a ubiquitous Dong Feng Chinese truck designed to
survive rough tracks and do-it-yourself maintenance. It was still wintry
with snow on hills that had been completely clear in August. We stopped
at a transport café for lunch. Big blow torches, a popular heat source for
cooking in Tibet, roared under huge woks, pretty plump young women in
traditional dress bustled from table to table serving groups of Tibetans, their
long hair braided with red thread. The atmosphere was smoky, bustling and
friendly. Up to that moment I had been preoccupied with problems with
satellite communications and organisational responsibility, but I now felt
relaxed, able to enjoy being in Tibet and part of the expedition.

We reached Nakchu in the late afternoon. On the recce we had driven
straight through because Pasang was worried that we might be delayed by
the police, but this time we were more relaxed, stopping in the main street
to go shopping in the large covered market. The stalls sold everything that
a visiting nomad could want from kitchen utensils, harnesses and music
cassettes to clothing, knives, shoes and a wide variety of headgear. I chose
one of the latter, buying a fine felt hat with a leather chin strap. The Tibetans
tend to wear these as they come, but I squashed the top to resemble a
dashing broad-brimmed trilby. Duncan, who had been unable to do any
shopping in Lhasa because of his communication duties, was looking at
traditional Tibetan sheepskin coats, but was discouraged when he discovered that they cost about $1,500.

Nakchu might be an eyesore with its brash new buildings and broad
muddy streets but it has all the vitality of a frontier town. There was a real
feeling of the Wild West with swaggering Tibetans and their womenfolk
arrayed in turquoise and jewellery on their annual visit to town. Pasang
had commented the previous August that the people of Nakchu got on well
with the Chinese and distrusted Lhasa. Before the Chinese had built the
motor road from Amdo in the north, the town had been little more than a
large village, but even then it was a trading centre for the nomads who had
scant respect either for central government or the law. Banditry had been
a popular profession.

We camped outside the town at the same place as we had the previous
summer. It was snowing by the time we put up the tents. As we crowded

into the mess tent there was that first night atmosphere when the Sherpas are getting the feel of the cooking arrangements. Nonetheless Dawa and Nawang produced an excellent meal. It was Duncan's birthday and Charlie, ever thoughtful, had bought a cake in Kathmandu and had kept aside a bottle of champagne. It was a good start to the expedition. It was bitterly cold that night. Nakchu is the one of the coldest and highest cities in Tibet and we were experiencing the end of the Tibetan winter. I shivered in my high-altitude sleeping bag and wondered how I was going to fare on the mountain.

Next morning dawned clear and fine with a brilliant light blue sky. There was also a cutting wind on which the early morning sun made no impression. We all trekked our separate ways to the top of the little hill above the camp to take pictures of the prayer flags that were piled in chaotic profusion around some cairns. The brown of the wind-blasted hills was just beginning to break through the light covering of fresh snow. A line of pylons snaked across the plateau towards Nakchu whose corrugated iron roofs glittered in the early morning sun.

After breakfast the others drove off while Duncan and I kept back one of the Land Cruisers to concentrate on solving the problems with our satellite communications. We could telephone anywhere in the world but we were unable to download pictures to Rupert at home in Cumbria, either through the Newton-Logica connection or by e-mail. Duncan's e-mail server was still out of action and the main Logica computer didn't recognise us. It was bitterly cold even in the sun with a driving wind gusting over the plateau. The eight-hour time difference between Tibet and Britain meant that we couldn't call anyone at Logica without waking them up in the early hours of the morning. Eventually we gave up, piled into the Land Cruiser and set out to catch up the team.

The main highway to Chamdo was a corrugated dirt road. It felt far further than it had done the previous August and I became convinced we had overshot the turning to Diru. We hadn't and soon, 120 kilometres from Nakchu, we saw both the turning and the other Land Cruisers. The rest of the team were photographing yaks as they grazed on the scanty brown wind blasted grass. There was no hay or fodder for them. The yaks eat what grass they can find throughout the year. If there is a prolonged heavy winter or spring snowfall thousands die from starvation, a disaster for the nomads.

We drove throughout the day, counting off the passes as we crossed them. There was enough snow on the high ones to make driving alarming as we followed the deep ruts left by the big trucks. It was late in the evening by the time we reached Diru. I decided we would stay in the guesthouse we had used on the recce. It hadn't changed at all: neither had the little Chinese restaurant on the main street. The improbable picture of the island in the sun was still on the wall and the tiny kitchen produced a vast array of good Chinese food.

Dorje, our liaison officer, had gone to see the local police chief as a courtesy and to verify not only our permit to proceed further, but also to confirm that we could visit the monasteries in the valley. Jim Lowther, ever curious and willing to help, had gone with him. We were halfway through our meal when they arrived back. Dorje reported that the police had agreed that our climbing permission was in order but they were less happy about our visiting monasteries. They would have to refer to Nakchu and would let us know in the morning.

A policeman arrived about nine o'clock next day. He told us we could visit just one monastery, the one opposite our guesthouse, but we must not take any pictures. Outside, the place was a building site. This was where we had been turned away the previous August, but now we were shown through a side door into the cavernous main chamber. It was little more than a shell on which they were obviously still working and there was just one huge unpainted Buddha. The abandoned dark red robes of the monks, worn to keep them warm in this cold dank place, lay scattered on the low couches. There was a solitary monk in a side chapel, chanting a mantra, keeping time with drum and bells. The wall here was lined with gold-painted Buddhas and a rack full of Tibetan prayer books in their oblong boxes. They had obviously finished this chapel first before working on the main room of the *gompa*. Jim Fotheringham made three full prostrations before the Buddha while we looked on. It was only in this room that I began to feel the sanctity of the building. There was however a sense of anticlimax exemplified by the presence of a bored policeman, the empty ugliness of the main chamber and the absence of most of the monks.

We all trailed out and piled into the Land Cruisers to set out on the final stage of our journey. This took us down the valley beside the Salween river that now, at the end of winter, was little more than a stream and past the hydroelectric plant which provided the entire valley with electricity. Above the road stood another *gompa*, like a fortress, perched on a hill. The place had caught my imagination on my last visit, more so than any of the other monasteries we had glimpsed. We stopped to take pictures.

Dorje turned and asked me suddenly, 'Do you want to have a look at it?'
'But we were only allowed to look at that one monastery in the town.'

'That's OK. There are no policemen here.'

Dorje recruited a passer-by to guide us up a side track and over a rickety bridge to zigzag up the hill on a faint path through a juniper-scattered meadow towards the buildings. It was all so unspoilt, so refreshingly beautiful, with a tall white *stupa* on a small col just below the hill on which the *gompa* stood, like the keep of a citadel. The living quarters of the monastery were sprawled across the hillside opposite. There was no sign of anyone, but Dorje found a gong by the side door and gave it a good bang. A few minutes later three monks appeared. Even though we must have been the first Europeans they had ever seen there, they seemed to take us for granted and, after asking us to refrain from taking pictures inside, agreed to show us round. Apparently most of the monks and the reincarnate lama in charge of the monastery were visiting another shrine.

The three young monks told us that this *gompa* was only twenty years old, which was difficult to believe for it seemed rooted to the hill as if had been there for a thousand years. It was only on closer inspection it was apparent that the wooden beams were of new timber. The interior was fully finished with effigies of the Buddha, reincarnate lamas and the fierce guardians of the *gompa* freshly painted in gleaming gold and clad in brightly coloured silk. The young monks pointed out the site of the old *gompa* nestling on the col. You could just see where the foundations had been before the place had been razed to the ground during the Cultural Revolution, like all the monasteries in the valley.

We were invited to tea in the house of one monk and were introduced to an older monk who had been at the original monastery when it was destroyed.

'They came in trucks,' he told us through Dorje.

'There were Tibetans as well as Chinese. They didn't kill anyone here but they beat us and destroyed everything. They took away anything precious. Nothing has ever been returned.'

The monks waved as we descended the track to resume our journey up the long deep valley and hairpinned ascent to cross the final 5000-metre pass, the Shar La. On the other side we dropped into the Yu-chong valley. Charlie had gone ahead with Pasang to start negotiating for our yaks and as we lost height we could see the blue cook tent already pitched beside the footbridge over the river to Khinda. The expedition really was under way.

That afternoon we learnt it would take three full days to assemble the yaks we would need for the approach march. In many ways I welcomed the extra time. It gave us the opportunity to sort out all our gear, to get our communications working effectively, and also to start building up some fitness by climbing the hills nearby. Our first day in Yuchong was spent yet again struggling with satellite communications. I was the only one who understood how to transfer the digital images from our cameras though e-mail to our web site. This entailed downloading the images as enclosures on e-mail. The concentration brought on a bout of the severe neck pain I experience from time to time. This legacy of an old injury can be triggered by stress, altitude, exhaustion, cold, or mixing my drinks! This time it was definitely the former. It was a nagging ache that made any kind of thought or work difficult, but I just had to fight my way through and try to ignore it.

The others also had a lot to do. Jim Lowther and John Porter had volunteered to organise the loads and Charlie was assembling a bright red inflatable survival bag used for treating altitude sickness. The patient is placed inside and the pressure increased with a pump to simulate descent. This is both more effective than using bottled oxygen and saves weight.

I escaped towards the end of the day. The pain in my neck had vanished and I set out to climb a hill on the other side of the river. I had been there the previous August, so I was on familiar ground. This time I had my new Avocet altimeter watch that not only recorded the altitude but also the rate of ascent and a host of other information. That afternoon I climbed 535 metres to a height of 4435 metres at 405 metres per hour. It is perhaps childish to record these statistics but I have always loved gadgets and this one provided some measure of my fitness.

Next day was much better. Our satellite communications were working and I spent the morning helping Charlie and Jim Fotheringham write reports on my Apple PowerBook for the website. After lunch I set out up the hill behind the camp, passing a row of houses set high on the hillside, then on up close-cropped grass and narrow yak paths flanked by stands of juniper. I slowed as I gained height but was making steady progress. I felt at peace with myself, partly because I was on fresh ground and had the excitement of wondering what view there would be at the top. I also felt relieved that not only was our technology working but that it was accepted, and even welcomed by the team. There was the added interest and obvious enjoyment of contributing articles for the website and the pleasure of being able to contact home on the satellite phone.

On reaching the crest there were yet more rolling ridges and deep cut valleys stretching to the north but no glimpse of Sepu Kangri to the south. It was hidden by the intervening mountains, some of them snow-capped and around 5800 metres in height. I walked along the broad ridge for a distance, looking up at the yaks which were grazing high above. As I started back I noticed a young girl, probably no more than ten or so, bounding up the hill, no doubt to bring the yaks down to the little hamlet for the night. She was carrying out what to her was a commonplace daily chore: for me this had been a major physical effort. Nevertheless I had a deep sense of contentment and that night wrote in my diary: 'I felt for the first time a sense of joy and wonderment. Such freedom being alone and moving well in this glorious environment, the valley far below. OK, it's drab and brown under a dull grey sky, with the sun struggling to penetrate it, but it has an entrancing beauty'.

After another day at the roadhead we were ready to set out with forty-seven yaks and half a dozen yak-herders, all of them mounted on stocky Tibetan ponies. I started off with John Porter and Jim Lowther, but they were setting a faster pace than I found comfortable so I allowed myself to drop back, relishing the solitude in the long valley. That night we again used a campsite we had passed on our previous approach, a rolling alp clad with clumps of juniper. Apparently this was the first good pasture, essential this early in the season when the yaks were still weak from the winter. The herders quickly lit a fire and ate *tsampa* and made tea, passing round a haunch of dried yak. We sat with them under a clear starlit sky, sipped their salted tea and chewed on the amazingly tasty dried yak. It had a fibrous texture and a pungent gamy taste.

Next morning we set out for the Samda monastery, crossing the fine cantilever bridge on the way. We had had an unfriendly reception when we had last visited Samda. This time it was very different. Perhaps it was our extra numbers and Dorje's status as liaison officer, but the monks gathered round, pleased to be photographed and happy for us to be there. We were invited for tea in the monastery kitchen. Stoves glowed with yak-dung fires and in a side room, rows of yak carcasses hung from beams. We forced down the Tibetan tea, closely watched by our hosts, and then went for a tour of inspection. Although of the Bon or animist sect, it resembled many other *gompas* with the Buddha in central position flanked by the effigies of reincarnate lamas. This remote shrine had also been destroyed during the Cultural Revolution but reconstruction had started some twenty years ago. A large prayer hall was being built for the expanding monastery. Once outside, we lined up for a group photograph with the monks. With their eye shades and gold wrist watches, the monks were a trendy looking bunch.

We dawdled on to our next campsite about an hour's walk up the Sepu

Kangri valley. It had been a short day and the following one would be even shorter. This was just as well for we would be reaching 4700 metres where we planned to make our base, and it was essential to have enough time to find a good position. I envisaged one at the end of the lake near where Charlie and I had taken a camp on our recce towards the Sa La.

Next morning John Porter, Charlie, Jim Curran and I set out early, well ahead of the yak train. The ground was frozen hard with little banks of old winter snow in the gullies and the sides of the streams frozen after a cold night. Our mountain objective slowly came into view and, as we reached the elbow at the head of the valley, we could finally see the huge north face of Sepu Kangri itself. John Porter gazed through my binoculars, picking out potential lines. It was that heady moment at the start of an expedition when almost anything seems possible. Through binoculars distances seem shorter and memories of the cruel effects of moving at altitude are forgotten.

We continued walking up the valley past the two little flat-roofed huts of our neighbours from the previous summer. Norge, 'the old lady' from 1996, recognised me, clasped my hands and smiled. I tried by sign language to show her that I had given the photographs I had taken previously to Tembe, our yak-herder from the previous year. The lake was a sheet of gleaming white, frozen hard in the cold of winter. John and Jim looked in wonder at the place. We had not exaggerated its beauty. It seemed strange and a little daunting to walk on the ice for the full three miles to the head of the lake where we searched for a good campsite, one that would get plenty of sun, offer a little shelter from the wind, and give us a view of the face. Also, we needed a clear sighting to the satellite over the Indian Ocean. We finally settled for the lake shore immediately below a couple of houses which we discovered were occupied throughout the year. The yaks and the rest of the team arrived an hour later and we spent the remainder of the day organising our home for the next few weeks. The communications tent had three tables so that several people could work at the same time. It was dark enough inside for the VDU screens to be visible. Colour screens are hard to use in natural light. The mess tent was to be our communal home, next to Dawa, Nawang and Pemba's kitchen. Our sleeping tents were scattered around and soon we had established a small village on the frozen turf of the shore.

The other team members, and I too at first, had had reservations about our satellite link with the world, feeling that one of the charms of expeditioning was getting away from worries of home and work. But –

because it was there – I noticed my companions were not slow to use the benefits of instant communication. John Porter was able to talk to his two children before they went off to school, Jim Lowther checked up on his estate, and Duncan was conducting by e-mail the final tortuous stages of selling a house. Everyone also became involved in contributing to our website – it was an instant magazine or diary over which we had complete control and in which we could tell our own story from day to day. Were we losing some of the romance of mountaineering in our use of modern technology? I don't think so. There was room for the Shiptonesque as well as the satellite. It was simply a matter of using the tools of communication we have today.

Two days later, we had settled into base camp. This was to be the morning of the *puja*, but first we had a reminder of the world beyond Sepu Kangri. It was the morning after the UK General Election on 1st May and I was able to listen to the news of the Labour landslide on my short-wave radio. It all seemed very distant. Power in China also changes abruptly but by different mechanisms. I was brought back to the present by the Sherpas who produced a long string of prayer flags which they stretched from the top of the bank immediately above the camp to a pole on the lake shore. We then sat above on the bank, in a half circle around the flagstaff, facing Sepu Kangri. Dawa quickly handed the ceremony over to Dorbe, one of our neighbours, whom we came to know well in the following weeks. He had a Tibetan drum and cymbals and read from the oblong sheets of a Tibetan prayer book. I found the *puja* ceremony particularly moving, both because of Dorbe's rhythmic chant and the beauty of the White Snow God, Sepu Kangri, gleaming in the early morning sun above Sam Tso Taring, the Sacred Lake.

After the ceremony we were impatient for action. John Porter, Jim Lowther and Charlie set out to climb one of the hills behind base camp to get a good view of Sepu Kangri and possibly determine which was its highest point – the sharp pointed summit on its left, Taktse Dunlhu, eldest son of Sepu, or the big rounded dome on its right, the White Snow God. The Chinese map in the back of our book indicated that the former was the higher, whilst the Soviet map, a copy of which Graham Little had obtained for us, hinted that the rounded top on the right was the true summit.

Jim Fotheringham decided that he would visit a hermit who, we had been told, lived at the foot of Sepu Kangri and then continue up the valley to see if there was a feasible way round the back of the mountain, to the south-west. The previous year I had identified a possible route to the west of Seamo Uylmitok, the Turquoise Flower, the Daughter of Sepu. I decided to go with Jim, partly to keep him company and partly because he was to be my climbing partner. Pasang joined us as interpreter. We walked over the frozen lake and up an icefall formed by a frozen stream from the valley above. The home of the hermit was on a small shoulder protruding from the end of the long ridge of the Turquoise Flower. Clusters of willow, still bare of leaves, surrounded the two single-storeyed, flat-roofed huts where the hermit lived. He must have seen us approaching for he was waiting for us. Long dark ringlets framed a moustached face; he looked the archetypal holy man. He beckoned us into a little courtyard with a fine view down to the lake. Jim made an obeisance and offered him our gifts of butter, sugar and *tsampa*. There was a canopy providing shade on one side of the door, with some cushions to sit on. He gestured us to sit down, and went inside to bring out the ubiquitous Chinese vacuum flask of hot water.

Conversing through Pasang, we learnt that his name was Sam Ten Tsokpu, that he originally came from Chali, to the south of Sepu Kangri and had lived alone here for the last four years. He had studied at the Samda monastery. He ate no meat and took no stimulants, not even tea. He depended entirely upon the generosity of the local people for his supply of food and never went far from his hermitage. It was certainly an idyllic spot. Plump little blue-tits perched on the wall, obviously fed regularly by the hermit. There was a gap in the wall overlooking the valley. This seemed to be the place where Sam Ten sat meditating and contemplating the hills opposite, the glacier calving its icebergs into the lake below and the holy peaks, the family and court of Sepu Kangri.

Jim asked him for a blessing. We were beckoned into the single room which was cosy and welcoming, with his bed against one wall, a small stove, some prayer books and clutter on a small table. The hermit sat cross-legged on the bed, murmured some prayers and gave Jim a handful of the ceremonial silk *kataks* tied in special knots for all of us.

As Jim and I continued on up the snow-floored valley, we both felt a sense of peace. But we were also excited with the anticipation of what we might see later that day. Above, another frozen cascade led to a second icebound lake into which the Thong Wuk Glacier flowed. We decided to cross this lake to gain a further view to see if there was a way round the back of Sepu Kangri to the west. There seemed to be a feasible route up snow slopes that rose all the way to the crest of the ridge. I was moving from a sceptical stance about Jim's proposal to a much more open-minded one. It seemed to be making sense.

We set out on a formal reconnaissance two days later. This was certainly no lightweight affair. Charlie and Jim Curran came to the head of the glacier, while Dawa and Pasang carried loads as far as our proposed camp. We skirted the lake on its right, west bank stumbling over snow-covered boulders along the edge of the glacier to reach a spot where we camped immediately below the side valley whose left-hand retaining wall led up to the crest of the ridge. This seemed to give access to the western slopes of Sepu Kangri.

The following morning we started at 3 a.m., hoping to camp on the crest of the ridge and push on into the basin behind the Turquoise Flower. My load seemed ridiculously heavy as I struggled up the initial moraine, wallowing in deep snow between the piled boulders. It was pitch dark: I had left first and was isolated in a little pool of light from my headtorch. When I looked back I could see the lights of the others – Fothers, Jim Lowther, John – each picking a line up the fifty-metre-high slope. In the dim half light we could see that beyond the crest of the moraine there was a flattening and then the main slope stretched away, still in darkness. To begin with the snow was firm and held my weight but every now and then the fragile crust would break and I would sink in thigh deep. The slope seemed endless. Jim Fotheringham had pulled ahead out to the right. We were each trying to pick a better line, none of us with much success. At last we reached the crest and dropped down to a flattening that could have been a frozen lake. On the far side rose a steepish wall and here the snow was even worse. Fothers was out in front and the three of us were content to follow his laboriously ploughed track. We topped another crest just as a cloudy threatening dawn arrived. A blast of wind and flurries of snow disheartened us further.

'We could always stop here,' I suggested.

'Great place for digging a snow hole,' commented Fothers.

I didn't feel enthusiastic about that. I was too tired. I just welcomed the thought of stopping. But then the cloud cleared. We dithered about whether or not to stay, but it was still early in the morning so we decided to press on. Fothers remained in the lead, Jim Lowther just behind him. John and I were in the rear, glad to take advantage of well trodden steps. Fothers headed up towards a rocky notch in the ridge. It seemed steep enough to justify roping up, and there was a risk of avalanche. We moved one at a time. Progress was slow, both because of the altitude and the weight of our sacks. The cloud had rolled in once again bringing flurries of snow. Looking towards the end of the ridge we caught ominous glimpses of sérac walls and huge crevasses between the ridge and the west face of the Turquoise Flower. The north ridge which we could see in profile was beginning to look more attractive.

I was last to reach the notch, to find Fothers slumped exhausted against the rock wall. John was resting as well. We were all discouraged by what we had seen of this possible route round the back. The ridge itself was narrow and rocky, piled with snow. On the other side the slope dropped steeply to a glacier far below. I dumped my sack and scrambled along for about a hundred metres, while Jim Lowther went in the opposite direction to gain a different perspective. I reached the top of a small gendarme but a rounded snow hummock barred my view of the route beyond. I could just see complex sérac walls and even bigger crevasses than before. I returned discouraged. Jim Lowther and John Porter were equally sceptical. We decided to retreat and returned to the snow-clad moraine to dig out a campsite for the night. The north ridge of the Turquoise Flower was a better bet and, as it had a passing resemblance to an Alpine classic, the Frendo Spur, on the side of the north face of the Aiguille du Midi, that is what we christened it and decided to go for. And yet, even as we took that decision, I couldn't help feeling that we hadn't really pushed our recce far enough. We hadn't seen enough to rule out 'the way round the back', behind the Turquoise Flower.

But we had made up our minds. The next morning we retreated to the glacier. We were sandwiched between two layers of cloud, a uniform grey ceiling and a grey carpet covering the valley, the lower peaks and foothills to the north. The scene had an eerie beauty, but heralded disturbing omens for the future.

6 Our Frendo Spur

10th – 28th May 1997

CHRIS BONINGTON

Jim Fotheringham was muttering feverishly, letting out little groans interspersed with calls of, 'Watch the rope.' He always does this when the climbing becomes hard, but he also keeps going. He was out in front on the first real difficulty of the climb. We had left our camp on the glacier at 7.30 on the morning of 10th May and had cramponed up a huge avalanche fan of firm frozen snow leading to the gully and snow ramp we had picked out from below. This appeared to give the easiest access to the foot of the Frendo Spur. It was a lovely cloudless morning but moving on a west face, we were in deep shade, the frozen slopes guarded from the softening rays of the sun.

It felt good to be climbing and even better to be doing so lightly laden. I had arrived first and secured a belay while Jim volunteered to lead the first pitch, an icy scoop leading up to broken snow-covered rocks. It was very similar to a Scottish gully in winter. As Jim started he quickly discovered that the slope was steeper than it looked, that the ice soon changed to powder-snow and the rock strata were all downward sloping, giving poor hand and footholds.

Jim was now twenty metres above us and, although he had managed to hammer in a couple of rock pegs, neither seemed firm placements. He was panting with the exertion at an altitude of around 5400 metres. He let out little whimpers as he bridged across the gully, trying to gain some purchase with his ice tools. He was obviously very insecure and, had he fallen, would undoubtedly have injured himself. 'Christ, I'm coming off,' he shouted. I braced into the belay, clutched the rope and waited.

With some more scratching of crampons on rock, he pulled over a bulge, completed a precarious mantelshelf movement, inching cramponed boots level with his hands, and somehow straightened up. He was at last able to secure a good anchor. Thereafter it looked as if the angle eased. He tied off the rope, abseiled back down to me, said something about having had it for the day, and started to descend.

I jumared up the rope to his high point and as I did so I could see just how hard the pitch had been. Jim had done well to climb it at all. I led on up the gully on much easier ground with better placements for my ice tools. An awkward pull out to the top led to snow. A few metres higher I was able to place a good anchor at the full stretch of the rope. I brought Jim Lowther and John Porter up to join me but by this time we could see the sun had struck the upper part of a ramp above us. Already a few icicles and lumps of ice were rattling down. We decided it was time to retreat.

We set the alarm for 2.30 a.m. next morning but when I woke I could feel the wind hammering against the tent. I could hear the patter of driven snow. I snuggled down into my sleeping bag and dozed off again. When I next woke, it was still blowing a gale. I peered out to see snow streaming in the wind and an overcast sky. There was a gleam of light in the other tent. John and Jim Lowther must have been brewing up, so I steeled myself to light the gas stove and make our first brew of the day.

John Porter and Jim Lowther were soon away, setting out at 3.30 a.m. We were an hour behind them but it was their turn to be in the lead, so our delay didn't really matter. We plodded up through the dark, with glimpses of their tracks ahead in the freshly fallen snow. By the time we reached the foot of the gully John and Jim Lowther had already jumared up the rope. John was starting a fresh pitch. A wild cloudy dawn was just breaking. A powder-snow avalanche tumbled down the gully, buffeting me, the fine snow dust penetrating my clothing and stinging my face as I jumared higher. I just clung to the jumar cords and, when the avalanche had passed, continued climbing until I had reached Jim Lowther.

Above, John Porter was shouting about coming back down.

Jim Fotheringham caught up with me and said breathlessly, 'Do you think we should go on in this? It looks a bit bloody dangerous.'

'It's only spindrift, but it's up to you,' I replied. Jim and John discussed things, too, in a shouted exchange. John decided to press on. I felt relieved. I wanted to keep things moving. There were a few breaks in the cloud, then a few more and the cloud and wind suddenly dissipated. The morning became fine, clear and windless, with the sun beginning to creep round to us. Within a few minutes it all felt so different, and doubts that had been so serious before vanished. John Porter stayed out in front kicking into deep but reasonably firm snow, placing anchors in rock cracks for the line he was fixing. The rest of us followed, passing fresh ropes up as John ran out more pitches.

We were on the crest of the ridge by midday. There was a little snow saddle where we could pitch tents in safety and from where we had a ringside view of the Frendo Spur and anyone climbing on it. The angle appeared to lay back and didn't look too formidable. In the bright sunshine we felt optimistic. We had already decided to run a line of fixed rope up the side of the Frendo to the high saddle between the Turquoise Flower, Seamo Uylmitok, and the main summit to give ourselves a high jumping off point for a summit attempt. To provide this line of retreat seemed sensible in view of the unsettled weather and the length and potential complexity of the route to the top. We descended the fixed ropes feeling well satisfied with our day's work. We really were making inroads on the climb.

We planned to establish camp II at the foot of the spur the following morning, but once again the wind was blowing and the snow had returned. I felt tired from the previous day's effort, as I suspect did every one else. We shouted to the others and decided to wait to see if the weather would clear. It didn't. We discussed what to do. In this unsettled weather it seemed silly to have more people than necessary sitting at the top camp eating supplies, so I suggested that just one pair should move up, supported by the other pair and our Sherpas from camp I. It made sense to have the strongest pair out in front and I proposed that Jim Fotheringham and John Porter should go ahead the next day, on the grounds that I was the slowest, being the oldest, and Jim Lowther was the least experienced.

Next morning the weather was as bad as ever, but we set out anyway, Jim Lowther and I laden with ropes, food and tents, while Jim Fotheringham and John Porter were travelling light, carrying only their personal gear. The going was slow. I still felt tired and lethargic, but made it to the top of the fixed ropes in three hours. There is no doubt that as you get older your ability to hump heavy loads declines and the time needed to recover increases. By the time I reached the top of the ropes, the lead pair had already set out to push the route up the Frendo. Jim Lowther and I spent most of the morning digging a snow cave for camp II on the col before returning to camp I. It had been a good day. That evening John Porter radioed down that they had run out five rope-lengths.

We set out late the following morning. The weather pattern seemed to have settled into snow and wind during the morning and evening, with a clear patch in the middle of the day if we were lucky. We decided to pitch a

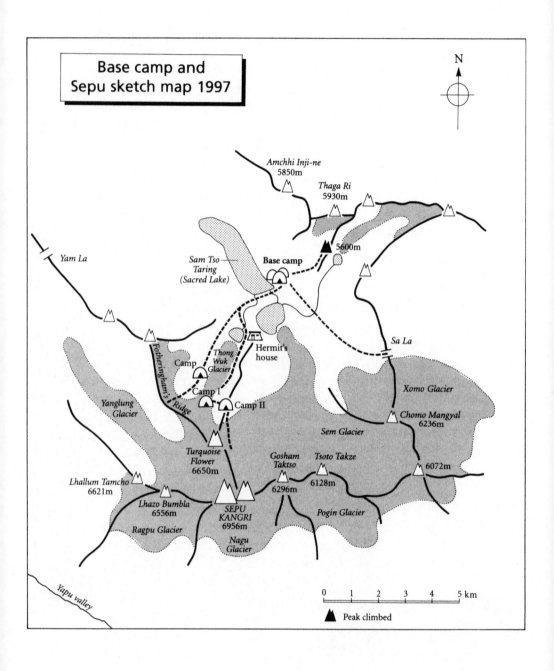

Base camp and
Sepu sketch map 1997

N

Amchhi Inji-ne
5850m

Thaga Ri
5930m

5600m

Yam La

Sam Tso
Taring
(Sacred Lake)

Base camp

Sa La

Hermit's
house

Xomo Glacier

Fotheringham's Ridge

Camp

Thong
Wuk
Glacier

Camp I

Camp II

Chomo Mangyal
6236m

Yanglung
Glacier

Sem Glacier

Turquoise
Flower
6650m

Gosham
Taktso
6296m

Tsoto Takze

6072m

Lhallum Tamcho
6621m

Lhazo Bumbla
6556m

SEPU
KANGRI
6956m

6128m

Ragpu Glacier

Nagu
Glacier

Pogin Glacier

Yapu valley

0   1   2   3   4   5 km

▲ Peak climbed

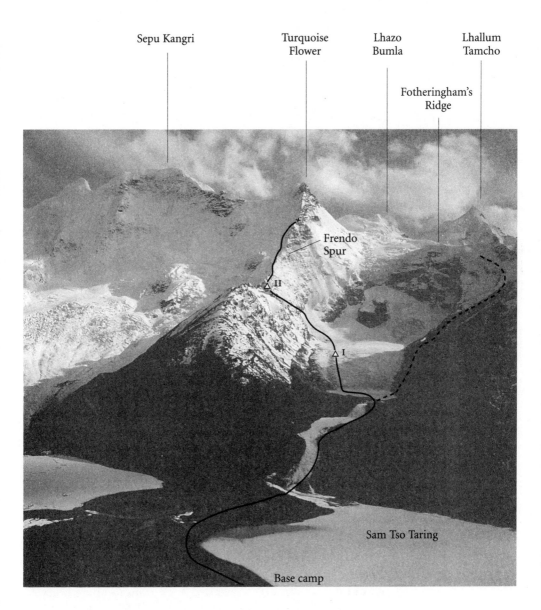

Sepu Kangri

Turquoise
Flower

Lhazo
Bumla

Lhallum
Tamcho

Fotheringham's
Ridge

Frendo
Spur

II

I

Sam Tso Taring

Base camp

Recce to Fotheringham's Ridge – – – – – – –

1997 ATTEMPT: SEPU KANGRI FROM THE NORTH

tent on the col beside the camp II snow hole, since I had brought up the Mobiq satellite phone and was hoping to transmit reports and pictures of our progress using my Apple Newton, the small hand-held computer.

That day the weather cleared around ten in the morning and stayed fine. We were able to watch John and Jim Lowther as they made their way slowly but steadily up the face to the left of the Frendo Spur, weaving through sérac walls and crevasses. When they returned in the late afternoon they had reached a height of 5850 metres but warned us there was a very real avalanche risk and there were some places very exposed to collapsing sérac from above. Nonetheless, as we sat out in the late afternoon sun in a cloudless evening, our spirits surged. Jim Lowther and I seemed to have settled into a partnership and were going out in front the following day. Given a bit of luck in the next few days, I thought, we'll be poised for a summit bid.

It is amazing how once out in front you gain renewed energy. I also enjoyed climbing with 'The Lowther'. He was always full of enthusiasm and very steady. Once again it was cloudy with gusting snow showers as we climbed up the fixed ropes above camp II. A snow ridge led to an icy corridor through the séracs, with some gaping black holes. We even climbed a small vertical ice wall. It took us a couple of hours to reach the previous day's high point beside a small sérac that gave a secure ice screw anchor. We now took turns to lead, running out a full length of rope each time. It wasn't technically difficult, just nerve-racking, for the snow was very deep and had it started to avalanche we would have had little chance of survival. We couldn't find any ice for anchors but were using snow stakes, which would just be carried away in any sizable slide of snow. The séracs above were also beginning to look more threatening.

There was an occasional break in the clouds with tantalising glimpses of distant mountains. There were magnificent unknown peaks some miles to the north-east. I even wondered if one could be Amne Machen, but this great mountain must have been further away. Then the cloud would roll in again bringing flurries of snow in noisy gusts. We ran out about six rope-lengths. We were gaining height and had reached a point where a broad glacial shelf swung out and up to the left towards the crest of the ridge. It was three o'clock in the afternoon, too late to progress further. We had reached a height of 6050 metres. By traversing back from the high point towards the Frendo Spur we could find some protection from the séracs above, avoiding their fall line, and could place a secure belay in an ice wall that would also provide shelter for a camp.

We retreated, well satisfied with our day's work. The cloud had cleared and the peaks across the valley were bathed in sunlight. But Jim Fotheringham and John Porter failed to share our enthusiasm. They didn't like the route we had chosen, feeling we had verged too far into the centre of the snow face. They were downbeat and we were defensive. We discussed plans for the next few days. I suggested that we should make the present end of the fixed ropes our attack point and try to push through to the crest of the ridge in a single day. We would have one higher camp, and then go for the summit. All we needed were three more fine days. We decided to spend the following day sorting out gear and food for the summit push. Then we'd go for it. As I dropped off to sleep I felt excited. At last the summit seemed attainable.

I woke to the familiar sound of snow pattering on the tent and I could hear the wind roaring across the spur. The weather was back to its previous depressing routine but with a bit of luck it would clear up by midday. I heard someone outside the tent. It was John, who had emerged from the snow hole.

'I'm not feeling too good,' he told us. 'I'm thinking of going down.'

'Let's all get together in the snow hole and talk it through,' I suggested.

Jim Fothers had a pan of water boiling by the time we joined them. But John was buried in his sleeping bag at the back of the cave, from where he stated his position.

'I've been coughing up a lot gunge and my lungs feel full of fluid. It feels like pulmonary oedema to me. I've had this kind of thing before. If I go down I should be able to throw it off and I can then come back up and join you if you haven't already gone for the top. I'll be fine getting myself down.'

We talked the problem over. There were no crevasses to worry about and the fixed ropes were in place below if John were to descend on his own. The two Jims wanted to stay on and grab the first opportunity for a summit bid. This was the obvious solution but I felt unhappy at the prospect of anyone wandering down the mountain by themselves. Even stronger was a feeling that we were climbing together, as a team, a group of friends who should stick together, come what may. I therefore suggested that we should all go down with John, have a rest at base camp and return in a few days. It was an emotional reaction that had little to do with logic. I put it to the others. They agreed, with some reservation.

And so, leaving almost everything in place, we descended, arriving at base camp just after lunch. That night as we slept, there was a soft patter on the tent. I became dimly aware of it and thought it was a brief snow shower. But the snow continued for many hours. By daybreak the entire base camp had almost vanished under a heavy white mantle. The two-man tents were mounds of snow buried under a fifty-centimetre fall. In the event our retreat had been providential. Camp II itself would have been safe enough, but ascent or descent would have been desperately dangerous. On the other hand, if it had dawned a perfect day, we would have been cursing ourselves for missing an opportunity of completing the climb. Such is life. It was pure luck rather than clever judgement that had turned our decision to descend into the right one.

At base camp, life appeared normal and everyone seemed settled. Duncan worked hard at the communications, Jim Curran filmed and the Sherpas cooked, and when there was no work to do they played cards endlessly with Pasang and Dorje. We had few visitors, as this valley lay on no trading route. Our neighbours in the small stone cottage above the camp, Karte, a thirty-five-year-old yak-herder and Tsini his wife were pleasant people. We had seen them briefly in 1996 when Charlie had been terrified by their dogs when the family were camped on a high pasture below the Sa La. But in their home a drama was unfolding that was to alter our relationships. Tsini was seriously ill. Charlie takes up the story:

On all expeditions local people ask for help. We noticed it little in 1996. Matters changed in May 1997. I thought Tsini was going to die. This was to draw me closer to life in the small villages and Tibetan tents. As with illness within our team there are several generalities which separate this medicine-in-the-field from practice at home. The first is language. Pasang was a long-suffering, kind and accurate interpreter who helped me through many a difficult consultation. To complicate matters, the patient in Tibet, especially if young or female, is often overshadowed by the senior family member, usually male, who recounts how they perceive the problem, rather than allowing the patient to tell the story. Secondly, physical examination is difficult. Crowded smoky surroundings, poorly lit and with privacy unknown, make it hard to carry out one's business. Our neighbours' home, stone-walled and single-storey with a roof of peat blocks and branches, was a single L-shaped room, some four metres in each longest dimension. Smoke from an open range against the main wall either found its way through the roof between the open beams above or filled this living quarter. In winter, or when the nights were chilly, a free-standing yak-dung stove of beaten iron heated the room; we would find its chimney scalding hot if we touched it by mistake. I invariably did so. In the corner was a small Bon shrine. Around the walls were wooden and stone couches, draped with yak skins, rugs and a carpet. A hand-turned grindstone for *tsampa* was by the door. Several old leather chests and, incongruously, a stereo tape recorder completed the room. Five adults lived here with the children. There were two adjacent outhouses containing slaughtered meat hanging on hooks, saddles, sacks of grain and rice, and tents for the summer – the impedimenta of a wealthy family in these parts. They owned some forty yaks, goats, and four horses. Outside, in a muddy yard, twelve kid goats scampered about.

Tsini was thirty-four, but curiously, in this land of regular festivals she did not know her birthday. It was so with many Tibetans. Tsini and Karte were now childless; some eight years earlier, Tsini had had a baby. 'He caught a cold and died when a year old,' Pasang told me later. One morning, Karte walked into camp to ask Pasang to bring me to the house because Tsini was ill. We walked slowly up on a gloomy day. Snow was blowing in the wind; the mountains were invisible. Somewhere in the clouds were the climbing team. Some three months earlier Tsini had become pregnant. Ten days before we had arrived she had had severe pain in the abdomen and since then she had been unwell. I sat with Karte and drank tea, still unaccustomed to the rancid taste, while he went over the story. After a few minutes, as the smoke cleared, I saw Tsini, a silent woman with fear in her eyes, huddled in yak skins on the couch opposite. She was pale, sweating and in terrible pain. A mass the size of an orange bulged from the abdomen low on the left. The lump was intensely tender. During each wave of pain lasting several minutes she would wince and turn away. This was the cheerful woman who a year earlier we had seen milking yaks, and who had shown her prowess with a slingshot of plaited yak rope. Tsini could fire a stone with deadly accuracy at a yak's bottom fifty metres away. She was gravely ill, whatever was wrong.

I am not a gynaecologist, but gynaecological it must be, I thought. A tubal ectopic pregnancy seemed the only answer. The foetus had not implanted in the womb, but in the Fallopian tube leading from the ovary. If this were correct this was a possible surgical emergency, and potentially lethal. Another possibility was an ovarian cyst, I thought, or an abscess. An abscess would be full of pus – but there had been no obvious fever, so this seemed unlikely. I gave her some codeine, a simple painkiller, and told everyone what I thought the problem was. Orsa her mother-in-law agreed, having seen it before; she knew how dangerous it was. I said I needed to think about the problem and turned to leave. Orsa came outside, solemn but composed. 'Just do your best,' she said to Pasang softly. 'We understand.'

I walked back down the hill and lay in my tent. What on earth should I do? I wondered. There was no possibility of getting a helicopter. A journey to hospital would commence with a two-day horse ride down the valley: this was out of the question. Whatever was to be done, or whatever was going to happen, was to evolve where we were. To telephone a colleague back in the UK may now seem obvious, but I felt at the time that it was a stroke of genius. I waited until the afternoon and rang Marcus Setchell, a consultant gynaecologist, tracking him down early in the morning to his office at Homerton Hospital. As always, Marcus listened attentively, and said he too thought Tsini's problem was an ectopic pregnancy. I felt like a successful candidate in Medical Finals.

'Don't worry too much,' he said, with a grim tone. 'If she has survived as long as this, she might recover. The dead foetus will be absorbed . . . and Charles, don't *you* do an operation. Treat her pain, and give her antibiotics if you think she's infected, and hang on.'

I thanked him profusely and hung up. The Mobiq satellite telephone had been invaluable. I talked the issues over with Pasang before we saw Tsini again. I asked him what would happen if she were to die, which seemed rather likely.

'Chop, I think so, here,' he replied. He meant the traditional means of offering the dismembered remains of the dead to birds and animals.

When we returned to the house, codeine had had little effect. I don't mess about with minor painkilling drugs on expeditions. People in severe pain require strong medicine. The next step up was diamorphine, the other name for heroin. I gave Tsini an injection. Within minutes the pain eased and she relaxed into a sleepy state. We discussed the issues again. Frankness in these situations is hard. Often there is implicit faith that everything can be cured and terrible anxiety when the news is doubtful. I told everyone what Marcus Setchell had said, and set about organising regular painkilling injections and tablets. The heroin had its usual dramatic effect in reducing pain, but above all reducing fear.

Over the next three weeks Pasang and I visited Tsini several times a day. There were various crises of increasing pain. Once I took a needle and plunged it into the orange-sized lump, to see if it contained pus. I withdrew nothing except a little dried blood. Very gradually, Tsini began to improve. A party went to see Sam Ten Tsokpu the hermit to consult him. A young Bon monk from Samda came to her bedside to chant and beat his drum. The mass in the abdomen began to melt away.

While Charlie was handling this emergency, I was concerned that each day the weather seemed to become worse, with more snowfall. At the same time the lake was beginning to thaw with water oozing round the shore. We had retreated to base on 17th May. Our flight from Lhasa was booked on 1st June and all my fellow climbers were committed to returning home on time. As the days slipped by, the tension increased. I wanted to delay our return to Lhasa as long as possible, to give us the best opportunity of snatching an improvement in the weather. The others, understandably, were concerned about their families and work back home. Charlie, who had worked throughout the expedition as organiser and load-carrier, as well as doctor, wanted to explore a different way back to Lhasa from base camp. Everyone was perhaps more realistic than me about the dangers of the route on the mountain with the ever-increasing accumulation of snow.

I calculated, in some desperation, that 25th May was the last date on which we could possibly set out for a summit bid. We could push through to camp II in a single day and this would enable us to reach the high point, gained by Jim Lowther and myself on the 26th. We should make the crest of the ridge on the 27th, somewhere close to the top on the 28th, the summit on the 29th, return to base for the 30th and rush back to Lhasa. It was a tight schedule but it could just be done; but we also needed safe snow conditions and some settled weather. Neither materialised.

We played bridge. I also played Warcraft, a computer strategy game to which I am addicted. We sat and sent and read our e-mails. Each day it snowed for a few hours; then the sun would shine and it would begin to thaw. Cloud clung to the summit of Sepu Kangri. Our chances of making a bid for the summit became slimmer. Indeed we were beginning to wonder if we would be able to evacuate all the gear that included cameras, video tapes and satellite phones from camp II at the foot of the Frendo Spur.

On the 22nd a team waded through thigh deep snow to evacuate camp I. I clung to the knowledge that we could do this and still make a summit bid by going straight to camp II from base. Two days later there was no sign of the weather improving. Even I gave up hope and agreed to ordering the yaks for the evening of 27th May to clear base camp. It looked increasingly as if we were going to have to abandon everything on the mountain, even the precious video tapes. Then, on the afternoon of the 25th, the weather cleared at last. For the first time in days we could see the summit of Sepu Kangri. It was too late to contemplate a summit bid but at least we had the chance of clearing camp II.

Huge heaps of avalanche debris lay piled at the foot of the slope above camp I below the fixed ropes, a sign of just how dangerous the face must have been. Assuming that everything that was likely to avalanche had already come down, we picked our way gingerly up the long incline. It was amazing just how much gear and spare food we had accumulated. We each had a bulging sack of around thirty kilos. Fothers was first away and when he reached the end of the fixed ropes below, he decided to let his sack slide down the slope since it was a clear run all the way to the bottom. I thought this was a great idea and did the same. But as my cargo began to cartwheel down the slope the top burst open and the BT Mobiq, the Apple Newton, a solar panel, clothing and socks distributed themselves over the lower slopes. I had failed to fasten the flap of my sack securely. I was disgusted more at my own laziness and incompetence than at the potential damage and loss of gear. Weaving back and forth through the avalanche debris I eventually recovered all the scattered equipment. Thankfully both the Mobiq and the Newton had survived their tumble.

A large party from base camp came up to meet us by the shore of the upper lake and I was immensely grateful when Karte took my sack with a smile. It began to snow, yet again. This came as a relief in one way, since it underlined our decision to bail out. I stumbled into base, tired and in several moods. At once I felt dejected at failure but happy to be safe. Above all I knew we had all given our utmost in our attempt to climb Sepu Kangri.

We left base camp two days later in a blizzard. The prayer flags were rustling in the wind. I was behind Jim Curran and Charlie as we walked away. Orsa and Tsini stood on the hillside above the camp, their hair and clothing fluttering in the wind.

Jim turned to Charlie. 'God, she's so beautiful,' he said, 'and anyway, well done, you old bugger.'

'Oh, it was only nature and a few painkillers,' he replied. I saw Charlie was crying. We were both already planning to return.

7   A Brief Visit Home

June 1997 – June 1998

CHARLES CLARKE

As we walked down the Sa Valley and drove back across the Tibetan plateau to Lhasa at the end of May 1997, we were as a team far from sombre, despite failure on Sepu Kangri itself. Ours had been a happy trip. There was much talk of returning. For Chris and myself, it was apparent that we had been the most captivated by the region, both by the mountain itself and by its people. We were both smitten. It became almost unthinkable that we would not return and sometimes on our journey back to Britain there was the strange feeling that we were simply popping home to reorganise ourselves. There were several components to these emotive thoughts.

Perhaps the first was that another team might climb the mountain, the massif which both Chris and I felt was 'ours' by right of first sight and first footing – an assumption which was as arrogant as it was unrealistic. However, it would be invidious to read, as a short paragraph in a national newspaper, 'Team from somewhere climb Tibetan peak'. Secondly, by any measure, our exploration of the laboriously named Eastern Section of the Nyenchen Tanglha, a range in extent greater than the entire Swiss Alps, was incomplete. In the reconnaissance of 1996 we had but scratched its surface. In reality we had trekked for only a week into the valleys leading to Sepu Kangri from the north and south. We both wanted, and myself especially, to continue the exploration of the region. Finally, we had developed an unusual affection for the people we had met and their families. Tsini's illness had drawn me particularly close. We had seen the poverty and hardship of their lives, enjoyed their humour and marvelled at their honesty. Had our campsites been anywhere in Europe, and especially in Britain, they could never have been as open.

For four days in late May and early June 1997 Chris and I were plotting and dreaming in the Khada Hotel in Lhasa. Our first thought was to return in the autumn of 1997, in a mere three months. A cooler examination of this ludicrous idea made it worthy of no further consideration. Our wives and families, such realities as work, income tax, and financial sponsorship loomed larger as we came nearer home. Also, expeditions do not simply end when the key turns in the back door; or when, I remind myself, having forgotten the key, I'd thrown earth at Ruth's window. There is work to do, thanking sponsors, lecturing, writing, and closing accounts. There is also a period of readjustment to family life. However, such was our determination that we began work in earnest immediately on our return to the Tibetan capital: there seemed not a minute to lose.

One of our first visits was to the Tibet Meteorological Office, somewhat shamefaced that we had not contacted them previously, to ascertain rainfall and temperatures. We were welcomed by the director, Mr Ni Ma Dan Zeng and his staff, and shown round a dazzling assortment of computers, satellite weather maps, and international on-line information. It came as something of a surprise (an unwarranted western preconception) that rainfall and temperature had been collected methodically since the mid-1950s and the information was readily available. Whilst no data had been collected from the Sepu Kangri massif itself, nor for its surrounding valleys and pastures, there were figures for the towns of Sog Xian, on the Nakchu–Chamdo road to the north, and for Chali, which we had already visited, to the south. Each is around 4000 metres, some 700 metres below base camp. We confirmed that June, July and August were indeed the months of the rainy season, with rainfalls between 120 and 135 centimetres. Either side of this period, average temperatures were around zero, whilst in December and January, they fell to about minus 10°C, with extreme temperatures between minus 30° and minus 40°C; the rain or snowfall during these winter months was negligible. Security, Mr Dan Zeng explained apologetically, restricted our access to *seeing* the figures (I think the photocopier was broken) but we soon had a hastily scribbled table for the year. A glance showed that March–April was a possibility, but with the certain disadvantage of increasing precipitation as the spring progressed. Also, at that time we would have, as we knew already, an icebound base camp and approach. It had been quite cold enough in May! The alternative was towards the end of the summer rains and into the autumn.

In our makeshift office in a room in the Khada Hotel I drew a graph of the figures and tried to picture our expedition approaching during the summer, or even grappling with the mountain in the depths of the Tibetan winter. We had had a glimpse of extreme cold on the way to Everest in early

March 1982, and did not wish to repeat the experience. I scribbled across the page, 'Chris, I think you should aim for the summit on 1st October 1998.' In the event we chose an approach in early September.

The second issue was permission. Would the China Tibet Mountaineering Association (CTMA) grant exclusive access over a year in advance? We had kept fairly silent about Sepu Kangri, but it was quite clear in the mountaineering world that this major summit was for the picking. Equally, how could we combine an expedition to climb the mountain with an exploratory journey? The two have different objectives, style and organisation. The computers and printers in our 'office' soon generated headed paper, and plans bearing a formality and gravity which far outweighed the reality of our organisation. Chris applied for a permit through the CTMA to attempt Sepu Kangri in the autumn of 1998, whilst I went to Tibet International Sports Travel (TIST), the trekking and travel organisation, to talk about my proposed journey through the Nyenchen Tanglha during the latter part of the rainy season, in August 1998. Somewhat to our surprise, outline permission for both projects was granted. No money changed hands. There remained the issue, possibly more difficult, to break the news of these schemes at home, and for myself, at work.

Already, whilst we were in Lhasa, it became clear that there would be changes to the climbing team. Jim Lowther was ready and able to come, but neither Jim Fotheringham, nor John Porter could commit themselves, and Duncan Sperry felt unable to repeat his role in communications. On our return to Britain, Chris chose his team with his usual deliberation:

In addition to Charlie and myself, I wanted to keep the team small, to allow, if at all possible an alpine-style ascent of Sepu Kangri, either using our 1997 route, if this seemed safe and feasible, or approaching the mountain from its western flank, using the route which Jim Fotheringham had favoured – but which we had rejected. Graham Little could get away for eight weeks, now that Ryan his son was nearly two. My other choice was Victor Saunders with whom I had climbed on our expedition to Panch Chuli in 1992. An architect by training, he had been a member of a select group of London climbers who would regularly drive up to the far north of Scotland on a Friday night to snatch prized unclimbed winter lines from the local Scots hot shots. They would then drive all the way back to London during Sunday night to be at work first thing on the Monday. He also had an impressive list of alpine routes to his credit and had made some fine Himalayan ascents, of which the Golden Pillar of Spantik with Mick Fowler in 1987 was undoubtedly his finest. In his mid-forties Victor had abandoned the security of the architect's office in Hackney Borough Council to become a mountain guide. He was also a distinguished mountaineeering author. He was fun to be with, had a quick, mercurial intelligence and a wide range of interests, including a willingness to play bridge with me, a game I had discovered, thanks to Graham Little, on Panch Chuli in 1992. It was a wonderful way of filling in time. Victor is a great games player; he would even play computer war games with me. Adding his name to those of Jim Lowther and Graham Little, I felt I had a combination which would provide a powerful four-strong climbing team.

Chris's plans for the main expedition crystallised towards the autumn of 1997, at least in terms of timing, equipment and logistics. There were however several holes, which became more evident and embarrassing as the months passed into early 1998. We had no sponsorship, and no media support. Chris was keen that the expedition should have a strong communications background, ideally with the ability to transmit TV film direct from base camp, partly to give a technological flavour, and partly to attract sponsorship. Also, I surmised, the Bonington love of electronic gadgetry would remain unfulfilled without it. Such financial and media support did not materialise until the eleventh hour, but in the event Chris and I agreed to underwrite the expedition ourselves, at an overall cost of between £50,000 and £100,000. Neither of us consulted our wives about this import-ant issue; this was nothing new. As this reality approached, each of us became a little evasive. 'The Money' became a subject which neither of us discussed much.

Meanwhile I continued to plan a journey of mountain exploration through the Nyenchen Tanglha, approaching the Sepu Kangri massif from the east. The information I had was sketchy in the extreme. The first objective was to reach Chamdo, the market town which was the capital of Kham, eastern Tibet, about a thousand kilometres by road from Lhasa. There were two routes to Chamdo, a northern circuit via Nakchu, Sog Xian and Riwoche, or a southern route, passing the approach to Namcha Barwa (7782m). This latter route seemed the more interesting, and I barely con-sidered the northern route. We'd done most of it, I thought. It would only be a couple of days' drive from Nakchu.

From Chamdo, the Tibet tourist map, which had proved itself as reliable as any during the reconnaissance, showed a minor road heading west for some 300 kilometres to the town of Pelbar and high mountains. Thereafter we would walk through the Nyenchen Tanglha and try to approach Sepu base camp by crossing the Sa La, the difficult 5600-metre pass. Chris and I had reached a col beside the Sa La in 1996; Jim Fotheringham and I had tackled the steep pass itself just to the west in 1997. An attractive possibility after this would be to leave some of the equipment with Karte and Tsini and cross passes to the south of the range, before meeting Chris, with the climbing team and supporting the expedition during September and October.

In 1997 I had had the opportunity to question local people about the terrain to the east. Whilst they had not completed the proposed route themselves, they had not scorned the idea of travelling to Pelbar from base camp, and thus the reverse seemed reasonable. The journey would involve linking between valleys over a distance of some 200 kilometres and crossing, I thought, about six 5000-metre passes between them. To achieve this objective I felt that the trip needed to be lightweight in every aspect, some of which would be unpalatable – the smallest tents, a minimum of food and clothing, with the barest essentials of climbing equipment. We would try as best we could to live off the land and befriend nomad families on the way. In addition, to comply with and maintain the expedition's commitment to communication, we needed to develop and adapt lightweight equipment to enable us to have voice, e-mail and picture transmission. This would need to be solar-powered. Inevitably such a decision made our baggage more cumbersome than originally planned, but it did add another dimension to travel through a remote region. Also, if difficult to put into any useful practice, communication could be valuable in case of accident or illness – *if*, as someone pointed out, the sun was shining.

Our party was to be small, and no more than three persons. One was to be Pasang, our resourceful Tibetan friend who had been with us both in 1996 and 1997. The other was less certain. Ruth, my wife, suggested that he should be male. Chris insisted that I needed a cameraman and photgrapher, recognising the failings of my own skills. I also required someone with whom I could share the technical communications issues, and, particularly, an equable companion who was adaptable to a journey which might have to abandoned, because of illness, bad weather or difficult terrain – for there might simply be no feasible route from Pelbar to base camp. Lastly, and it may seem trivial, the third person needed to be able to survive, and if possible enjoy, a basic Tibetan diet of *tsampa*, Tibetan black salt tea and dried yak meat. A degree of physical and gastronomic hardship was guaranteed.

In the event Elliot Robertson, a somewhat laconic twenty-six-year-old university friend of my daughter Rebecca expressed interest, if with some amazement at my own lack of order and the dearth of information I had. A keen mountaineer and geographer, he confirmed his ability to convince the outside world of his attributes by being appointed Communications Officer at the Royal Geographical Society on the eve of our departure.

May 1998 passed. Orders went out for clothing to Berghaus, and to Terra Nova for tents. Both generously supplied equipment free. Food and climbing equipment were also donated from many sources. I bought solar panels and a Toshiba Libretto, a miniature laptop PC, while Chris remained with Apple who provided the latest G3 PowerBooks. British Telecom supplied Mobiqs, the satellite telephones. Gradually the paraphernalia of a forthcoming expedition accumulated, except for one vital component, 'The Money'. Chris seemed intermittently calm, then agitated. We spoke on the telephone most days, usually in an attempt to wake each other increasingly early, as if to demonstrate endeavour. Could it be, we discussed in bleaker moments, that the Bonington formula was fallible? Could a factor be that most of the chairmen and managing directors, film producers and bankers we approached for major sponsorship were a decade younger than either of us? Was there a tacit message saying STOP? Chris stayed remarkably sanguine, recalling at the time:

> I just felt we had a magic story, of exploration, of a fabulous mountain and a chance for a remarkable film, but convincing either the media or potential sponsors was not easy. Letters, phone calls, meetings were all unsuccessful and I was getting increasingly worried, though I tried not to show it to Charlie or the others. In the event it once again all came together with a rush – but nail bitingly later than the previous year. I had been speaking to the senior managers of National Express at a conference in Harrogate, and sitting next to Phil White, the chairman at dinner that night, I enthused about our expedition to Sepu Kangri. At the end of the evening I asked if he was interested.
>
> He said, 'Yes, fax me some more details and I'll let you know by the end of the week.' His secretary phoned two days later to say that Phil would be delighted for National Express to be our main sponsor. We were now very nearly covered. Then Barclaycard and Burton McCall, agents for Victorinox, Maglite and other leading brands, came in with

further financial support, and one of Charlie's employers, the National Hospital for Neurology and Neurosurgery, even combined one of its medical appeals with the expedition.

By mid-June Chris seemed to have solved our problems. We had sponsorship, a committed climbing team, a film team, live coverage from ITN and permission for both expeditions. And then another crisis occurred. Jim Lowther was forced to drop out in mid-July because his mother was seriously ill. It was not going to be easy to find a replacement at a few weeks' notice. Chris remembered that Graham and Jim Lowther had invited a young Scottish climber named Scott Muir to join them on their expedition to the north face of the Kulu Eiger in 1995. Jim had spoken highly of him and Chris had climbed with him and Graham that winter. He had just finished a teachers' training course in physical education and would therefore probably be free. Graham liked the idea and Scott accepted Chris's invitation with alacrity.

The main expedition – Chris, Graham Little, Scott Muir and Victor Saunders – would leave London early in September, with a media/film team, whilst Elliot and I would slip away a month earlier. We planned to meet around 10th September, at or near base camp, 6000 miles away.

8   A Journey to Chamdo

5th – 15th August 1988

CHARLES CLARKE

In late July 1998, the week before Elliot and I were due to leave London, word came from Kathmandu, our final port of call en route to Lhasa, that there were problems with the entry visas due to be issued by the Chinese Embassy in Nepal. For several days it seemed that our journey through eastern Tibet was in real jeopardy. The crux of the matter was that travel must be arranged within Tibet on a group basis. Individuals or small groups are either discouraged or banned; but these regulations, and their practical application, vary. In August 1998 the minimum group was five persons. There also seemed to be a distinct air of finality about the matter.

Bikrum Pandey, our Nepalese agent in Kathmandu who runs Himalayan Expeditions Inc., is a staunch ally in these times of bureaucratic crisis. He had several suggestions, which he faxed, e-mailed or telephoned through to London and Cumbria. His boldest ruse was to apply to the Kathmandu Chinese embassy as an approved party of five, the group to comprise Elliot and myself, plus three named Sherpas; the latter three would vanish, mysteriously, before boarding the Kathmandu–Lhasa flight. Neither Chris nor I felt happy with this subterfuge, certainly at this early stage of the expedition. Chris therefore presented the conflict to the China Tibet Mountaineering Association (CTMA) in Lhasa, who forwarded it to the head office of the Chinese Mountaineering Association in Beijing, indicating firmly that Elliot and I were simply the advance party of the main Sepu Kangri expedition, and expected to collect our Chinese visas in Kathmandu on the date agreed in Lhasa more than a year previously.

However, the matter remained ambiguous. We left Heathrow for Kathmandu on Wednesday, 5th August with a degree of uncertainty. If Elliot sensed that this was to be an unusual journey, he kept quiet about it. His last contact with regular travel was to be the pleasant and sometimes luxurious flight with Qatar Airways from Heathrow to Kathmandu, which included an upgrade to First Class on the Doha–Kathmandu sector. It was his first visit to the capital of Nepal. Far from the eastern promise he anticipated, within an hour of arrival he was installed on the roof of the Marshyangdi Hotel above the Thamel bazaar, an apparent prisoner, battling with a computer crash which seemed insoluble. He also discovered he had lost his bag of climbing equipment – it had never been loaded at Heathrow. He was not to leave the Marshyangdi for thirty-six hours.

Our months of preparatory work seemed useless. We could neither send e-mail, nor download photographs via the Toshiba Libretto PC. We seemed to be having a frustrating re-run of Duncan's problems in 1997. Some aspects of the computer/e-mail server/helpline industry have defences as powerful as that mythical paramedical dragon, the doctor's receptionist. Eight international satellite calls to the helpline of UUNET, the e-mail server, were made. Each call, lasting about half an hour, was fielded by a different voice. Despite introducing themselves as personal friends by their first names, each knew nothing about any previous discussion. Each time we began again from the beginning; each time the proposed solution failed.

I saw Elliot gazing hopelessly and longingly over the parapet down to the bazaar streets of Thamel below. I tried to soothe him with a vodka and tonic.

He then hit upon a potential solution: 'I'll phone Apple.'

'You'll phone Apple? What on earth do you mean? The Tosh is a PC.'

Twit, I thought, but then, I didn't know him well. Throughout our preparations there had been an amicable but running Apple versus PC battle. Bonington, a long-term Apple user, staunch devotee and beneficiary of Apple Computer, Inc., had failed to convert me from a PC, the system I use at work. For our lightweight journey, I had bought a Toshiba Libretto, a miniature PC barely larger than a video cassette. Elliot had been involved in co-ordinating both these systems.

So he telephoned Ian Summerfield, Chris's Apple support man, based in London, not the Apple HQ in Cupertino. Ian, whilst himself unable to help, said he 'knew a man who could'. From another south London building, the friendly voice of Tony Dixon, unknown to either of us, guided Elliot through a maze of modems, baud rates, networking and passwords. At 10 p.m. on the day following our arrival in Kathmandu, we were back on line, if none the wiser why we had had the problem.

The tide had turned. Elliot's missing bag of equipment had been found at Heathrow after a determined telephone chase by Ann Tilley, my secretary.

An hour later Bikrum left a message that he had our visas and that we should be ready at 6 a.m. to leave for the airport to catch the twice-weekly Lhasa flight, on Saturday, 8th August. Somewhat surprisingly it seemed we were really off to Tibet.

The China South-West Airlines Boeing 737 Kathmandu–Lhasa service is a symbol of a changing China, clean, and efficient, if distant from either the magic of the Himalayan scenery during the sixty-five-minute flight, or the fact that we were travelling to Tibet. The glossy airline magazine, the equivalent of British Airways' *High Life*, advertised China and matters distinctly Chinese; a delightful recipe explained the skills needed to choose and cook puppy. 'Choose a nice young dog; one with a yellow coat is tastiest ...' it began. The stewardesses were Han Chinese, not Tibetan, and so were the cabin signs and announcements. It was some minutes after we had passed the Everest massif and its satellites that anyone bothered to tell the passengers about the 8000-metre peaks visible below them through the left-hand windows; most photographers were however already on a second reel of film by the time the cabin loudspeakers crackled into life.

I looked down at the south-west face of Everest, in Nepal, and then as we turned north into Tibet, we passed above the Kangshung, the east face. Both held memories of friends lost on expeditions I had been on – Mick Burke in 1975, Peter Boardman and Joe Tasker in 1982. I had long lost that urge to climb to high summits, and had never distinguished myself when I had the ambition. It seemed an anomaly, nearly twenty-five years on, that I was still taking part in major expeditions. My passport is primarily as a doctor, but on this trip I was also fulfilling an ambition – a journey of exploration through the Nyenchen Tanglha.

The immigration authorities at Lhasa airport could not have been less interested in the pair of us. I almost felt tempted to write 'smuggler' as Elliot's occupation on his immigration form, but thought better of it. The customs officer waved through our pile of electronic gadgetry without a murmur. By early evening we were installed among old friends at the Khada Hotel, the Tibetan family venture in old Lhasa. As Elliot was soon to discover, this was luxury, Tibetan-style. Within minutes, and it was difficult to avoid working furtively, we assembled the communications equipment like spies; unlike the Kathmandu disaster, everything worked well. We transmitted our first digital photograph, of a thirteenth-century Buddha, from the hotel roof, with the Potala Palace as our horizon, but soon found we could do so as easily via the bedroom window.

Pasang Choephel, our friend, interpreter and guide from 1996 and 1997, was soon at the Khada Hotel. He and Yishi, with their 'two small Tenzings', aged three and two, still lived in the rooftop flat ten minutes' walk away, in a sidestreet off the Barkhor market. His friend, Mingma, who had been our cook with L-plates in 1996, had been to prison in the intervening period: a fire had broken out in the Barkhor when he had been on security duty, and he had taken the blame. But he was now a policeman. We went through our plans with Pasang.

'No problem, I think, but I must see about the southern road to Chamdo. Very bad rains this summer. Many landslides. I think Nakchu maybe better.'

The two days in Lhasa passed rapidly by. We were soon used to the bustle and the traffic and said good morning on a daily basis to the cheerful prostitutes whose stalls surrounded the hotel. We ate simply, in tiny family restaurants. One evening an army jeep drew up outside the hotel. Several PLA soldiers jumped out; they were simply returning their videos next door. We had brief meetings with the CTMA to finalise details for the main Sepu Kangri expedition and the arrival of Chris and the team in September, and had a similar half hour with Tibet International Sports and Tourism, who were dealing with our journey. We shopped in the Barkhor market, mulling from time to time over the conflicting messages about our possible routes to Chamdo. I had decided that we would import no food supplies, there being an ample selection readily available in Tibet. Elliot was able to spend a day sightseeing. As on previous visits, the bureaucracy seemed minimal, provided one had agreed details previously. One Land Cruiser, and one Dong Feng truck, largely to carry fuel, would be available the following morning. Any suggestion of the southern route to Chamdo was eventually vetoed on the grounds of landslides, though I sensed there was also a degree of ignorance about actual road conditions in the north-east. We met no one in Lhasa who had ever driven to Chamdo.

At the agreed time of 8.30 a.m. on Tuesday, 11th August, almost to the minute, with a punctuality which was characteristic, we drove out of the Khada Hotel courtyard towards the Nakchu road. We were in no hurry. An hour or so from Lhasa we visited Pasang's village, Chupsang, a few kilometres off the road. Dhekey, his mother, is used to impromptu visits from her son, the village boy who, still in relative youth, had led such a life of adventure. In her simple farmhouse, she gave us wild mushroom noodles and yak-butter tea. Pasang showed us the shrine to his father, and one of his four sisters who had died in childhood.

Some seven hours later we arrived at the Nakchu Hotel, a stark grotesquely ugly, cold modern building, redolent of an age of central government. Pasang decreed that we had to stay there; unfortunately they had only a single room free for the five of us, ourselves and Pasang, Lobsang the Land Cruiser, and Tenzing the Truck. The day had been cold and rainy, and the spectacular peaks to the east of the Lhasa–Nakchu metalled highway had been hidden in cloud. Elliot seemed unimpressed by his first taste of the Tibetan plateau in these dismal conditions, and the altitude of 4600 metres was oppressive. Nakchu, whose streets I had never found attractive, was like a war zone, with ditches dividing doorsteps from the road in preparation for the long awaited main drains. Our communal hotel room was spartan, and the lavatories too near the reality of mass defecation at this early stage of journey. We climbed over the ditches to a grubby restaurant and had an unhappy meal – cold pig's ears and trotters are an acquired taste for *hors d'oeuvres* – but soon left for an evening at the Nakchu racecourse.

The annual Nakchu horse-races in August have been famous for over a century. Behind the main street were 300 embroidered tents which housed horses, shops, bars, families and restaurants for this week-long celebration. Around 10,000 people attend, from the town and from surrounding nomad encampments far afield. By dusk, the time we arrived, the races were over but the party mood and dancing were in full swing. So were the riot police. These young men, exclusively Han Chinese, looked threatening in riot gear, crash helmets, visors, cloaks and batons. They patrolled the crowd in groups, but behaved pleasantly, both to the dancers, to the surrounding crowd and ourselves. Their commander, a jovial man in more conventional police uniform, megaphone in hand, stood by on the dais reserved during the races for the stewards. A line of a hundred or more Tibetans danced a simple forward and backward step, the women as usual in traditional dress, the men in more varied attire. The mood was jolly, sober, relaxed and informal. We filmed and photographed at leisure in the failing light. As darkness fell bonfires were lit; we were tired, headachy with the altitude, and turned to leave. As we wandered back to bed we saw an unusual sight – the riot police, their batons and helmets put aside, had joined the line of dancers.

Twelve hours later at ten in the morning both Land Cruiser and the Dong Feng truck were off the dirt road, up to their axles in mud. We were an hour out of Nakchu on the way to Chamdo. Pasang, Lobsang and Tenzing dug, swore, and broke the tow-rope, twice. Fifteen other trucks were also stuck in mud on the road while we had made an unsuccessful and foolhardy detour. Elliot and I were irritated and blamed Lobsang for leaving the convoy. Three hours later, all of us covered in mud, we were free. The convoy remained in the bog. Lobsang was exonerated. We crossed the rolling plateau of Nyenrong county, over barren windswept moors, past nomads' tents, and the occasional settlement. There were two unexciting passes, the Langlu La (4300m) and the Janghku La (4700m) before the right turn to Diru at the stone marking 1871 kilometres, presumably from Beijing. We were 120 kilometres east of Nakchu. This turning had been the road to base camp. We continued straight on through this landscape into Sok county, over the Gang La (4800m) and the Shara La (4700m), and by late afternoon dropped down to the Sok valley.

The land became fertile, with cornfields in the valley floor. On the hillsides barley was growing in fields chiselled out in steep terraces, looking sometimes as if they had been sculpted into Tibetan letters. The rain continued. It had scarcely stopped all day, and poured on us as we entered our first town, Sog Xian, or Sok Tsanden Zhol, on the Sok-chu, a tributary of the Salween. A spectacular hilltop monastery, Sok Tsanden *gompa*, dominates the old town, but we drove on past looking for the 'Yigzam resthouse and adjacent restaurant' mentioned in our guidebook. No one seemed to recognise the name, and we were directed to a government compound.

A tall and intellectual-looking Han Chinese man greeted us, his smartness accentuating our scruffy and travel-worn appearance. Pasang told us he was a visiting senior civil servant from Lhasa. 'Welcome to China. But may I see your passports?' he said in perfect English, with a commanding smile, then, 'Have a nice stay here; maybe see you later,' as he handed them back. A Tibetan woman, dressed traditionally, if soberly, largely in grey, stood by him and fell into apparently casual conversation with Pasang about the local monastery.

'What did she say?' I asked him later, as we sat down in the Chinese restaurant, the only one in town, to trotters and pig's ears, followed by Sechuan chicken, cabbage and rice.

'She said if you visit the *gompa*, they will go home to England and you will stay in the police station.'

This conversation typified the response on the sensitive subject of monasteries for the rest of the our journey. I knew from previous experience that there was a general reluctance to grant permission to visit monasteries to parties who had other agendas. Our stated purpose was mountain exploration, not Buddhism. Also, I was well aware that it was entirely likely we would have plenty of opportunity to visit shrines far more remote and more intimate than those of Sok Tsanden, impressive though it was.

Next morning we stood below the *gompa*, again in the rain, and gazed upwards. Before the Lhasa–Shigatse civil war (1639–41), the Sok area, like much of the surrounding country, had been a stronghold of Bon, the animistic religion which preceded Buddhism in Tibet. Sok Tsanden *gompa* is said to have been founded by the Mongol chieftain Gushi (or Gushri) Qan Tendzin Chogyel during the seventeenth century, becoming one of the major Buddhist monasteries of the region, and in its heyday supporting 600 monks. A renowned sandalwood image of Avalokiteshvara, a patron deity of Tibet, is housed within its upper storey.

The monastery towers above the old town. A simpler and older building lies below it, the Kabgye *lhakhang*, fronted by a modest traditional court-yard. We felt that it would tempting providence to do more than peer through the entrance gates. Its own history has been chequered. The Nying-mapa shrine, a Buddhist school following very traditional teachings, was founded there in 1169 by a *terton* or treasure-finder named Nyangrel Nyima Ozer. *Tertons* were the discoverers of sacred texts or objects (*terma*) con-cealed at places of spiritual power in Tibet during the seventh to ninth centuries, thus fulfilling the ancient prophesies which indicated that the *termas* would be discovered in subsequent centuries. The place flourished for some five centuries until Gushi Qan's Mongol army destroyed it, as it was alien to the prevailing Buddhist school at the time. The monastery was refounded a century later, and again destroyed in the Cultural Revolution. Today, we gathered, it is a thriving Buddhist shrine with thirty married couples, *mantrins*, religious folk who cannot sustain the abstinence of nuns and lamas. Distant drums sounded from within. We pressed on to the Chamdo road towards Tengchen.

We were told later that there had been unrest in Sog Xian several years previously. The Tibetan population, apparently *en masse*, had decided that they wished to be rid of the Han Chinese immigrants. In these small towns, the shops, eating houses, and much of the trade is run by Han families, many of whom have settled within the last five years. Tilling the fields, tending yaks and goats remain the province of Tibetans. With some blood-shed, Tibetan Sog Xian folk had ejected its Han population. Because there were no evident ringleaders, there had been no prosecutions and, after some arbitration, the Han families returned. Perhaps this was the reason for the pointed 'China' greeting from the Lhasa civil servant.

The Sog Xian–Tengchen road was running in mud, and as we drove along the valley floor, through the cornfields beside the river, it became clear that our journey to Chamdo might well be halted completely by landslides. Ten kilometres out of town one truck lay overturned by the roadside and an entire convoy had been halted by mud. We dug in the rain, pushed stones under wheels, levered with crowbars, until the leading truck was free, then motored slowly on, rarely touching 20 kph.

Elliot wrote in his diary:

Another day in the Land Cruiser, shaken around like dice. We've had twenty-four hours of rain and the dirt road is bad; the route back to Nakchu is now blocked. Wrecked vehicles, crashed into the river, are a vivid reminder of the consequences should Lobsang make an error. On more than one occasion today Charlie and I clawed for door handles as we slithered towards the edge.

We have crossed four major passes today, each time having to climb roughly a thousand metres. The landscape has changed dramatically from high plateau to a complex network of interconnecting gorges. The water that lay as sullen marsh on the high ground has taken fright and scattered into rivers in all directions. Each deep gorge we've descended is filled with raging water, although there is seemingly no pattern to the overall direction of flow. Charlie, from his assortment of British, Soviet, Chinese and Indian Survey maps – some dating from 1920 – assures us that, despite their contrary directions, all the rivers flow into the Salween, and down to Burma. Pasang and I meet his air of authority with caution. The road was slow throughout, the weather abysmal and there were no views of anything except nearby rolling hills, and rain; it teemed continuously. Finally, towards late afternoon, having crossed the Chak La (4500m), we looked for an advertised resthouse in a small town called Rongpo Gyarubtang. No one there knew of anything resembling accommodation and waved us on to the Shel La, a 4800-metre pass, and the Sertsa monastery. We climbed to the rocky pass, thinking that a remote monastery might offer us a room, or at least a campsite. The pass was desolate. We searched its south-western side for a monastery. There was no track, no road, and no people. And as far as we could see, no monastery – it simply must have been tucked out of sight. There seemed little alternative but to press on in the dusk to Tengchen.

Darkness fell around 8.30 p.m. Elliot and I were exhausted. There was no sign of Tengchen. The milestones had disappeared long ago, on our first day out of Nakchu, and we relied on the various maps, all of which gave different distances, and on the word of mouth of passing drivers, or the occasional person on the road, who were equally vague. As darkness fell some lights appeared in the distance. There seemed to be a sharp right turning on the brow of a hill. We stopped. The apparent right fork led over a precipice. Lobsang drove cautiously into Tengchen at 10 p.m.

The town was muddy and dismal in the rain. It had also closed up for the night. We disturbed the keeper of the local government compound, a grey concrete single-storey block, and begged a room, which was cold, grubby but adequate. Pasang left in search of food. Cooking for ourselves seemed an unacceptable alternative. By banging on several street doors he roused the occupants of a Chinese family restaurant and within an hour we were eating chicken, beef, noodles, rice and cabbage, all in chillied Sechuan-style. There were two tables and home-made benches, with a tarpaulin stretched across the room behind which the family lived. The chef's wife remained fast asleep, while we drank beer and smoked, with the relief of weary travellers who had found succour. We were a jolly party; we had come to trust the drivers implicitly, and felt they were getting to like us. It was after midnight before we were asleep.

We were woken, not by the rain, which had continued through the night, nor by barking dogs, which had punctuated our sleep, but by music. The rousing tones of a loudspeaker in the courtyard brought first 'a cheerful morning wake-up tune', and then a blast of Han Chinese 'verbal encouragement'. The majority of the inhabitants of the compound were Tibetan, whom we gathered understood little of the screeching message which, we learnt, was about how much better off the Tibetans had become in the last ten years. We were glad to leave and to return to the Chinese restaurant for breakfast of dumplings, rice porridge and jasmine tea, but there were loudspeakers throughout town, blasting the same message. I thought this sort of thing had died with the old regime; it seemed a relic of a different era. Any thought of looking for the two important Bon monasteries in Tengchen was out of the question and, anyway, we were keen to move on towards and possibly into Chamdo, around 250 kilometres away.

By noon it was obvious that Chamdo was a distant dream. We had grumbled forty kilometres in four hours. Our report e-mailed that night to the website in Cumbria – we had used the Land Cruiser's cigarette lighter for power – tells how we felt:

Friday, 14th August 1998. Camping on the banks of the Mekong. It is still raining. Near Riwoche, 3695m, on the Chamdo road. 96.50E, 31.20N.

It soon became clear this morning that the way forward to Chamdo was fraught with difficulty. Mud, rain and landslides made progress slow. Some trucks turned back, others stuck fast, and we heard one had rolled off the road. There were conflicting opinions about the state of the road ahead. By 4 p.m. we crossed over the Dzeki La at 4400 metres and the scenery changed dramatically into an Alpine landscape. We rounded a corner to see a beautiful monastery surrounded by *chortens*, pine trees and meadows of gentians, edelweiss, and primulas. Kham, this region of eastern Tibet, is densely forested, a contrast to the stark plateau of the west. At times, this gentle landscape is like chocolate-box Switzerland, with wooden chalets, babbling streams and distant snows.

By seven in the evening we had descended to Riwoche, a clean pleasant town with paved streets, and feasted on pig's trotters, pork and chillies, potatoes and noodles in a Sechuan eating house. The trotters still make Elliot go green, but I love the food. The place was *en fête*, awaiting the arrival of officials and a team of ophthalmologists from Italy, for whom we were continually mistaken. Banners, largely in Chinese, and incomprehensible to all our Tibetan team, and presumably the majority of the inhabitants, festooned the streets. There was not an empty room in the place.

The rain abated for long enough to pitch camp on a grassy meadow on the banks of the Dzi-chu, one of the feeding rivers of the Mekong, a few kilometres out of town. 140 kilometres today. The road ahead was clear, they said in Riwoche. 'So it's lunch in Chamdo tomorrow?' said Elliot, as he went to sleep.

Late in the sunny afternoon of Saturday, 15th August we did reach Chamdo, but not without a final struggle. 'No problems with the road now,' said a passing truck driver to Lobsang, who showed some disbelief. We had packed up tents after yet another night of torrential rain, and left camp without breakfast. The Dzi-chu was already flooding into the meadow.

Within ten kilometres a substantial mud slide, whose centrepiece was a metre-high boulder, blocked the road. Rocks continued to fall down the chute, if fairly innocently, and grey mud to ooze from the hillside, to emphasise activity in the slope above. Compared to previous slides this seemed a daunting prospect to clear. There had been a turning to the south a few kilometres behind us, and we toyed with the idea of investigating it. Little did we know that help was nearby. Within ten minutes a band of smiling Tibetan roadbuilders, soon joined by a bulldozer, set to work. They were a team of ten, with an *esprit de corps* which ran to make-up, lipstick and some jaunty smiles – for they were all young women. Their housekeeper ushered us into their lodgings nearby, made us tea and we shared out the last of the flat Lhasa loaves surrounded by children. Within two hours the road was clear.

Just another hundred kilometres, we thought, only to hit another slide forty kilometres further on. This time there was no road gang, so we spent an hour shovelling slime and prising rocks into the gorge, while some wild raspberrries by the roadside provided a simple lunch. A bus of women students heading for Chamdo to take their exams drew up behind us, singing and laughing, and had soon stripped the precipitous hillside of fruit. We were interrupted, from nowhere, by a police jeep's siren, wholly unnecessary, as usual. Typically, too, the vehicle skidded to a halt on the clear road ahead, as if arriving at the scene of a crime. The policeman and driver simply watched us work, while a Tibetan arrived and drew from his bag ten sticks of explosive and unreeled a distinctive line of fuse. 'That'll bring the whole cliff down, for sure,' said Elliot. Between us we dissuaded him from playing Red Adair. Elliot gingerly picked up the dynamite and placed it out of harm's way. The other truck drivers stuck with us still lacked enthusiasm to try to drive through. To their relief, Tenzing the Truck took a run at our road-clearing handiwork in the Dong Feng, its massive wheeels pushing the remaining boulders down the cliff, as he reached the clear road beyond. Lobsang followed in the Land Cruiser. Lacking their bravado, Elliot and I walked across the slide.

By 4 p.m., leaving the spectacular densely forested gorges, we drove into Chamdo, the pleasant capital of Kham, feeling like survivors of a motor rally. The metalled roads, crowds, hooting taxis, rickshaws and bicycles made us feel as if we had been above the snowline or at sea for a month. Pasang stopped immediately outside the smartest hotel, an extraordinary chrome and glass creation of the late 1990s. It seemed incongruous in this pleasant market town, with its Tibetan market and monasteries, perched on a promontory between two branches of the Mekong. As we stood in the hotel foyer, we felt the residual throb of the engine and movement as if we had just stepped off a ship. Five very dirty men showered dried mud across the hall and up the stairs into spotlessly clean rooms. We were surprised at

Pasang's choice, but he was insistent that we should have the best avai
a style we liked, especially when TIST were paying the bill. It turned
that it was only around £16 a night for a room for two, and well within hi
budget.

ɔcks, Mountains and a
ery

…ugust 1998

…RKE

Twenty-four hours after arriving in Chamdo the five of us were sitting on a tarmac road, halted some twenty kilometres south of the city, eating a miserable supper of bread, cold and revolting tinned fish and water. We were all rather grumpy. Elliot had an unsightly patch of tar stuck to one buttock of his red cotton trousers, spoiling his otherwise immaculate appearance. The roadblock this time was man-made.

We had enjoyed the previous day. We had prowled around the Chamdo Chinese and Tibetan bazaars, buying a profusion of vegetables, and had enjoyed delicious chillied kebabs roasted in the street; we found a jovial Chinese baker and his wife and bought their entire morning stock of *ba-lip*, the round flat bread. Then we moved on to buying string, hats, tarpaulin, a Khamba knife, a silver engraved snuff horn, a wok, matches, rubber bands, fresh garlic, ginger and chillies, smoked pork, a new tow-rope, bricks of black Tibetan tea, yak butter and blocks of salt – some of the things we hadn't picked up in Lhasa. I bullied Pasang to find two metres of black cloth: the computer VDU was almost invisible when we worked outside. We could have done all our shopping in Chamdo. Finally, Elliot had spotted two bright blue packets of Nabisco Chocolate Chip Cookies, a mark of the penetration of the multinationals. Oddly, we failed to buy a single polythene bag, despite our baptism in the Tibetan rainy season. But at 3200 metres Chamdo, compared to the highland towns on the road from Nakchu, was not only a land of plenty but a pleasant warm and apparently relaxed place, perched between two rivers which formed the Mekong. We did not venture towards the monasteries on the hill above the bazaars and Pasang asked us not to take photographs, simply to avoid any possible trouble. He had had a minor brush with the Chamdo Public Security Police, the PSP, at whose office he had had to explain our presence and plans and get our passports and travel permits checked. Pasang always preferred to handle these potential bureaucratic hurdles unencumbered by us. The travel permits still bore the southern circle road route rather than our actual northern road, via Nakchu.

'I see you have come from the south,' the Tibetan PSP officer had said to him.

'Yes,' Pasang said he'd answered a little vaguely, 'we have come from Lhasa.'

'But there is no road, you must have come from the north illegally. It is not on the permit.'

Pasang told us later: 'I just behaved like a stupid country boy, and said I could not read properly and did not know south from north. I think it will be all right but they say they have to phone Lhasa. Anyway, Nakchu is on the permit, though on the way home.'

The PSP man had not retained our passports, a sign we interpreted as hopeful. They had been told where we were going; this seemed to present no problem. We thought little more about the matter. Indeed, we heard nothing more from the PSP.

By lunchtime on Sunday, 16th August we were ready to leave, with clothes washed and dried in the hotel courtyard. We loaded the vehicles and just as Elliot and I thought we were about to drive off, the drivers and Pasang pointed to a restaurant across the road. I wondered if they were more attracted by the staff, a jolly Chinese family with three pretty daughters, than the need for food. We dined in some style in a small private room. It was to be our last meal of such quality for months. We were interrupted by a pair of military policemen who burst into the dining room and rushed out again. 'They're looking for soldiers,' announced Pasang. Many restaurants and bars are out of bounds to the military, especially in uniform. This had certainly not been apparent in Lhasa.

To our surprise the metalled streets of Chamdo did not give way to dirt road as we left the outskirts less than a kilometre from the town centre. The highway followed the Mekong river valley. It was a sunny afternoon. We were even able to read a book on the move, so smooth was the surface. This was preferable to suffering the Magimix rattle over corrugated mud. The Land Cruiser windows were open. Elliot sat in his corner on the back seat and ate the second packet of Chocolate Chip Cookies. Pasang dozed in the front. We thought we had a hundred kilometres or so on this road, the main airport route, before turning west towards Dolma Lhakhang monastery and the Nyenchen Tanglha.

After less than half an hour's drive our state of relative bliss was brought to an abrupt halt. It was about 3 p.m. A wooden counterweighted barrier spanned the road with a queue of vehicles lined up behind it; there was construction and blasting ahead. The road would be closed until 9 p.m. at least. It would then be dark, and there was no moon. We enquired further of a man named Tsiring, the guardian of this barrier, at the hut from which he controlled all traffic. He told us initially that the road would be fully open next day, then that it would be closed for a week and finally that there were other roadblocks in the next thirty kilometres, the last being a military checkpoint. He thought we might not be allowed to proceed at all without, he said with a flourish, a permit from the Party Leader in Chamdo. Eventually, after we had been waiting for four hours Pasang harassed him gently and produced our papers; he was always one to treat officialdom cautiously. At this Tsiring told him that if he had known we already had these documents he would have let us through when we had first arrived. We were now some sort of minor VIPs. Typically, however, he felt he could not reverse his earlier decision because this would anger the other waiting drivers. Tsiring's comments engendered irritation, principally against him but also between ourselves. We wondered why on earth the Chamdo PSP had not told Pasang about the roadblock. As Tsiring said, 'Everyone in Chamdo knows this road is closed.'

We vacillated too. Should we return to Chamdo and sort this out on Monday morning by trying to obtain the permit, or try to travel in the night? By the following day, the Monday, if we chose to believe Tsiring, the road would already be closed for the week. As for the alternative by night, Lobsang and Tenzing were worried both about the state of the road and about being unable to drive back through the roadblocks on their return journey. Elliot and I fretted about being turned back at some later point for want of the correct papers. Predictably we decided to press on regardless and at least have a look. Eventually, when the barrier opened precisely at nine, we drove off in a clear but moonless night.

We first continued south along the Mekong in convoy with other vehicles. It felt as if we were travelling through occupied territory. The metalled road deteriorated to rockfall debris and clung to the side of the gorge. These things are less frightening in darkness. I cannot say much more about the terrain but at sixty kilometres or so from Tsiring's barrier we turned west, while the rest of the convoy turned east towards Dayak, a town across the river. We saw their headlights twinkling away below as we climbed through forests to a pass. On the crest a solitary roadmender flagged us down.

Pasang awoke and leant across the driving seat brandishing our papers. Lobsang brushed him aside, wound down the window slowly and offered the man a cigarette to pass the time of night. The roadman's attitude was straightforward: he simply did not want tyres denting a hundred metres of his fresh tarmac before 11 p.m. – in half an hour's time. Lobsang talked him round and crawled slowly over his handiwork without leaving a treadmark. Tenzing followed gingerly in the truck.

We descended little from this pass and continued on a good dirt road, at first zigzagging through forests before breaking into open ground and climbing again steadily, obviously towards another high point. Suddenly, on the pass itself at midnight at 4800 metres there were searchlights, noise and many people. We thought that this must be the military checkpoint, and almost thought kindly about Tsiring for his warning. It was the only fact about which he seemed to have been correct. But he was wrong again. There was no barrier at all, but a People's Liberation Army road gang in full swing with a steaming tar baby, a massive diesel roller, and flares. There was laughter from the team of Tibetan women workers. Both Land Cruiser and truck passed slowly through with a wave from the flagman.

We soon had some company on this lonely road. An empty gravel lorry had pulled out from the roadworks between the Land Cruiser and Tenzing's truck. He knew the road well and, had it been wider, he would have overtaken us. He drove unpleasantly close before pulling back to a reasonable distance. We drove as a trio down the pass and came easily to open country. As the road flattened out on a treeless plateau at around 4000 metres, the roadsign of the roadblock loomed up; it was all in Chinese. There was indeed a military checkpost. A solitary hut stood in darkness beside a wooden barrier. A rope dangled from one end near a window in the hut. The occupants were clearly asleep. Lobsang switched off the engine, dowsed the lights and cruised in quietly. It would be so easy to tweak the rope, I thought. Lobsang had the same idea. As we drew to a halt there were piercing lights flashing in the mirror. The gravel truck roared up behind the Land Cruiser, hooting continuously, clearly determined to wake the hut's occupants and anyone else around.

Almost at once a dim light shone through the curtains, while an arm fell limply out of the window and grasped the rope. The barrier rose before us. The convoy of three passed through without a word from the guards, who must have thought we were part of the road crew. We couldn't help giggling. 'That's all right then,' murmured Elliot. He gave a long warm smile of success and dozed off.

Less than a hundred metres further a sign pointed to the right, indicating its message once again only in Chinese. What Tibetan could want directions? It seemed to be in the right place, and there was only one right turn on the map in a hundred or so kilometres. We were in no mood to return to the checkpoint to ask the way. We paused. The gravel lorry roared straight on, hooting in farewell. We took the right turn.

'First place to camp, Pasang,' I suggested quietly. Pasang was fast asleep.

'Camp, now, yes,' replied Lobsang in English but drove straight on. A substantial ditch that I had not seen prevented us leaving the road to reach the plateau. It seemed an age before a hard shoulder materialised. Lobsang drove on to the grass. We all felt very pleased with the way fate had treated us.

A waning moon in a clear night lit the landscape with the Milky Way outlined like a *katak*, the silk blessing scarf. We could see for several miles. Smoke from some *ba*, the nomads' tents, drifted into the still night air in the distance. An animal howled. Pasang said it was a wolf-fox. At 1 a.m., tired and hungry, we laid out sleeping bags and slept under the stars. Six hours later in a crystal dawn, clouds of steam puffed intermittently from Elliot's bivvy bag. From the foot ice crystals melted slowly and soon vanished as the sun struck us. Pasang was never one to cook when there was chance of avoiding it, usually a prudent move. We bundled up belongings and packed quickly without food or drink and left in blazing sunshine, heading west for a remote monastery named Dolma Lhakhang and, we hoped, some breakfast.

We had scarcely discussed the possibility of a visit to this monastery since we had left Lhasa. In part we had been preoccupied with the journey. But I also knew that if the moment was right, and the place distant from a large town, we might be able to visit this former seat of a reincarnate lama in exile who bore the title Akong Rinpoche. We already had an introduction. The weekend before Elliot and I had left London we had driven to Samye Ling monastery, in Eskdalemuir, near Lockerbie in southern Scotland. We had met the Akong Rinpoche himself, a deeply spiritual figure but a man with a firm grasp of world affairs. He had been dedicated to improving and raising funds for Samye Ling. I had, I confess, found a heavy gold Rolex a little incongruous, but he was, and is, one of the highest prelates of Tibetan Buddhism.

We had pored over a map, the placenames of which were all in Tibetan. He had shown us that Dolma Lhakhang monastery was up a right turn off the Chamdo–Lhorong road. We were fairly certain we were driving along this. 'My monastery is in this remote region and is a place for nomads,' the Akong Rinpoche had told us. Like many high lamas he had left many years before in troubled times. Since 1980, however, when the rebuilding of the monasteries began after the Cultural Revolution, he had been able to make visits to Tibet and had been able to return to Dolma Lhakhang on several occasions. I had felt he believed it highly unlikely that these two Englishmen would ever find his former home, but he had given us the map, several photographs of himself and postcards of Samye Ling just in case we did. The Akong Rinpoche had also talked about his relations with Tibet; he was careful not enlarge on details that might be politically sensitive.

A group of horsemen approached from the west; Pasang asked if they knew of the monastery. 'First right; you can't miss the road, then about a day on horseback north and ride across the river,' was the gist of their reply. Some thirty kilometres further there was indeed a right turn where we stopped. The roadsign was as usual in Chinese only. A passing jeep told us that it pointed north to Riwoche 161 km, and west to Lhorong 181 km. Its occupants looked official, so Pasang asked them nothing more. At least we now knew where we were and logged our position almost to the metre on the Garmin Global Positioning System, a device that would play an increasingly important role in our travels. Coincidentally there was now a loud hissing from the truck. A front tyre was punctured. We gnawed bread, and sipped cold tea from Pasang's flask by the roadside while Tenzing changed the wheel. The right wheelnuts had reversed threads. To Elliot's surprise the little rhyme he sang, 'Righty tighty, lefty loosy', didn't seem to work. I had never heard this ditty: too clever by half, that boy, I thought. Still, he's great company. A family of nomads en route to the nearby settlement of Chakdado told us that Dolma Lhakhang was some thirty kilometres north along the Riwoche road, but they doubted we could drive across the river. They looked in astonishment at the photographs of the Akong Rinpoche who remained a most important and revered figure, despite his long absence. 'To cross the river would be easy with our horses,' they had told Pasang as they rode away.

Some twenty-five kilometres up the Riwoche road we looked up a broad valley to see the outline of a monastery etched against the distant hills. We drove on and stopped on the grassy bank of the river, the Yu-chu. Two foxes trotted across the hillside opposite. 'They aren't foxes. Those are wolf-foxes,' Pasang told us, 'not proper foxes.' Their coats were greyish-rust but their gait and form looked distinctly foxlike. We would hear from Pasang on the subject of wolf-foxes again. The river was too deep to cross in the Land

Cruiser; and Tenzing had the puncture to repair on the truck. It seemed more fitting to approach this splendid site on foot. The monastery was under a kilometre away.

A monk with a broad grin descended the opposite bank on horseback. Waving to us, he rode across, dismounted and greeted us. His horse had a chronic skin disease with sores along its spine for which he immediately suggested we might have some medicine, the first of many requests. Cheerfully he grabbed a rucksack of our precious film equipment, dangled it across his saddle, and rode back across the river, beckoning us to follow on foot. We forded the icy stream with some difficulty and walked up the hillside to the monastery gates soaked to our waists. Looking at the surrounding landscape it was clear why the Akong Rinpoche had said this was a place for nomads. Not another building was in sight. In the distance a few tents were dotted about; yaks grazed and a lone horseman rode through the valley.

A group of monks awaited us, welcoming us silently with palms turned uppermost, a sign to confirm that no one carried weapons. We came in peace. This was a homely place. Dogs lay around the doorway; puppies buried themselves in food poured out in a wooden trough. One puppy stood alone eyeing us mischievously. A *chorten* stood below the courtyard; beside it a nun cast small clay Buddhas. The yard was surrounded by a kitchen, storehouses and prayer hall-in-the-making which was still a building site. Above was a small shrine where the present incumbent lama resided. Elliot was introduced in the kitchens to rancid yak-butter tea, *tsampa* and dried yak hacked off the bone. I watched anxiously to see how he was handling this food and was relieved that he seemed to enjoy his breakfast. We were all starving.

We told the leading monk, a serious man with kindly eyes, where we had come from and gave him the photographs from Scotland. He left us to arrange an audience with the Kongtoul Lama, the present religious leader of Dolma Lhakhang. Another man entered, a Tibetan in a grey jacket and trousers. The room fell silent and we were told that he was a Party official on a regular visit. During the afternoon he was to give the monks a political lecture. He was welcomed and had tea with us. Whilst there was little to see of statues, books, gold and silver, Dolma Lhakhang had the feel of learning and prayer. Above the monastery was the hermitage, a collection of tiny rooms with a wooden frontage tied in with beams carved out of a spectacular cliff. Here the sage Pemba Lama had meditated some three centuries ago for three years, three months and three days before his recognition as a reincarnation. We climbed down ladders to reach it from above and crouched in the cramped rooms looking out over the valley.

The meeting with the Kongtoul Lama followed. He was a shy young man of twenty-two. He murmured to the monk with the kindly eyes who spoke to Pasang. In turn he translated. Conversation proceeded slowly. A blessing followed and silk *kataks*. We gave a donation and asked if the Kongtoul lama would like to telephone the Akong Rinpoche. From an open first-floor window we aimed the satellite dish south and dialled the number. It seemed ludicrous to hear in reply the Eskdalemuir monastery's answer-phone playing its recorded message: 'This office opens at 9 a.m. Please try later'. I tracked down Marian Dreyfus, the Akong Rinpoche's assistant, before she had left for work and obtained his private number. 'I am speaking from Dolma Lhakhang,' I said, apologising for calling so early. It was just after 7 a.m. in Britain. In this place where wood and yak dung were the source of power and the rooms lit by butter lamp, the solar panel and digital technology allowed one reincarnate lama to speak to another. The talk was mainly secular about supplies and the progress of building work.

By this time it was mid-afternoon. We made to leave. Elliot and I felt both an urge to travel and that perhaps to stay longer would have been an imposition. '*Dro* (let's go),' said Pasang spontaneously. We left in a hail-storm, forded the icy stream to rejoin the vehicles and drove off in silence, feeling moved and privileged. Elliot was as entranced as I was by this visit; I was glad that he entered so much into the spirit of the enterprise. We were also enjoying each other's company, and had fallen into the familiar routine of criticising each other's every move, a sure sign of friendship.

We travelled for an hour over the barren plateau before pitching camp beneath the next pass which led into Pelbar county and, all being well, the roadhead. The road proved less taxing than the drive to Chamdo but, as we left Dolma Lhakhang, we saw Tenzing now had a companion beside him in the truck. Elliot's diary tells the story of the hitch-hiker:

Tuesday 18th August. 11 p.m. Camp outside Lhorong. 30.84°N, 96.67°E. 3400 metres.

We have had various hitch-hikers for much of the journey. The wandering beggar monk who dropped off in Lhorong yesterday was the most bizarre by far. On the approach to Dolma Lhakhang monastery we had been halted by a wide, fast-flowing, ice cold river. We stripped off and, while preparing to ford, a cheery and burly monk appeared on horseback. Once dismounted we could see he was five foot five tall and dressed in traditional robes; traditional that is if you ignored a very small girl's straw boater with a pink ribbon and bow. For a beggar he was exceptionally well fed, due in part to a large sack of dried cheese, which was his inseparable companion, accompanying an infectious laugh and a total inability to remain silent.

On leaving the monastery, after prolonged goodbyes with fifty monks and nuns, we realised that our hitch-hiker, Pele who was unaffiliated to any monastery, had abandoned his mangy horse in favour of a free ride. He had simply told Tenzing he was joining our party, and leapt aboard the truck as we left. Setting up camp that evening, the beggar monk strode off and completed a quick sweep of the valley nomads, replenishing his own sack of cheese and somehow acquiring another one. Over the fire that night he supplemented his meal of rice, yak and cabbage from us, adding the contents of both his nose and ears. These he picked constantly with his forefinger while giving details of his chequered past. He had taken his vows comparatively late at the age of twenty-five, already having been married three times, or was it four? He couldn't remember. Although he seemed to have lodgings at Riwoche monastery, 150 kilometres to the north, he was not allowed to pray or study there. He spent most of his time on the road. Such a lifestyle undoubtedly honed his begging skills. That night he returned to the nomads to sleep, leaving them early next morning to peer into our tents with a loud *Tashi-de-le* greeting, shaking us out before dawn at 7 a.m., solely to demand his breakfast.

No sooner had we driven off than we started the climb to the next pass. A devout mother and son flagged us down near a nomad encampment called Gyata Sa. She carried an aluminium pitcher of fresh yak milk and a wooden churn of yoghurt. Her name was Tsering Yankyi. Her father had died recently and, having heard that we had seen the Akong Rinpoche in Scotland, she asked us to relay a silk scarf and some money to him in order that a prayer might be said for the deceased. The high lama had left Tibet roughly forty years ago. It was moving to see her so desperate for the message to reach him.

No such gentle sentiments from Pele, the Begging Monk. Having spotted the milk and yoghurt, he skipped introductions and prayers and rootled around for his bowl, thrusting it out, anxious not to miss the chance of an offering. He was already on his third helping of yoghurt when we began our first. But his cheery manner and peculiar company

Tibet '98   TOP LEFT Charlie with solar panels rigged across his rucksack trying to generate enough electricity for the satellite phone.

TOP RIGHT Charlie exploring the eastern approaches to Sepu Kangri.

ABOVE The small caravan of Charlie, Elliot and Pasang in the Tashilung.

Charlie with Puh and Jayang
leaving the Yanglung Valley, after
the reconnaissance of the western
approaches of Sepu Kangri.

Charlie calling Chris's press
conference at the Royal Geographical
Society, using the BT Mobiq.

Interior of Nima's *ba*.
Sonam Doha and her family
making *chura* (yak cheese).

Charlie, Pasang and Elliot, the great explorers.

The climbing team reaches the roadhead at Khinda to join the explorers. 7th September 1998.

The bridge from the roadhead to the little village of Khinda as it was during 1996 and 1997. Yak hides moored to the bridge are being cleaned in the river.

The bridge was swept away during the heavy monsoon in the summer of '98, and the only means of crossing was a wire, which Charlie is using to cross the river.

In the background is the concrete plinth built by a Chinese company for a major road bridge, but the local district ran out of money and couldn't continue construction.

We arrived at harvest time, and could not hire any yaks or horses for several days. Here at Khinda they are building up high level haystacks. The barley is left on the stalk to dry out.

The Bon monastery at Samda.

Victor Saunders, Charlie Clarke, Greig Cubitt, Martin Belderson and Jim Curran resting on their way up to Samda.

The annual dance festival at Samda monastery.

The white clown frightening the audience.

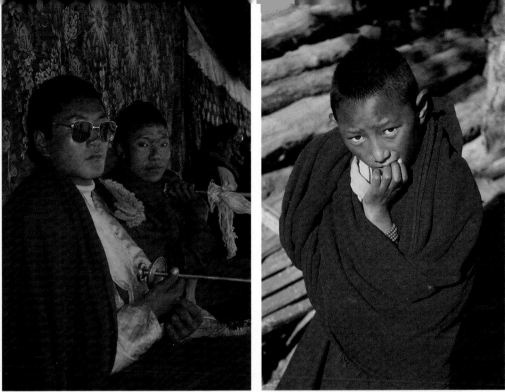

TOP LEFT Some of the monks; note the shades.

TOP RIGHT A noviciate monk.

ABOVE Wherever Charlie went, people came for treatment – some travelled up to 100 miles.

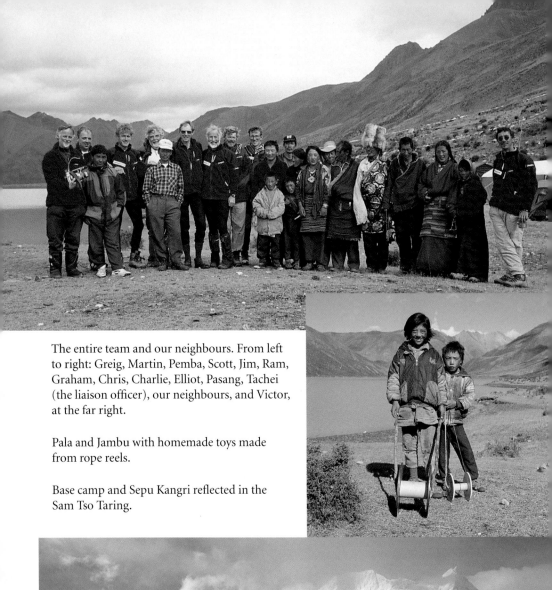

The entire team and our neighbours. From left to right: Greig, Martin, Pemba, Scott, Jim, Ram, Graham, Chris, Charlie, Elliot, Pasang, Tachei (the liaison officer), our neighbours, and Victor, at the far right.

Pala and Jambu with homemade toys made from rope reels.

Base camp and Sepu Kangri reflected in the Sam Tso Taring.

LEFT Afternoon matinée. Greig, Scott, Victor and Graham editing film they have just shot.

CENTRE Chris reporting for ITN, our two young neighbours holding the reflector.

BELOW More high tech. Scott repairing a wind generator. The high speed data terminal on the right.

ABOVE At the end of the expedition we gave our neighbours food and equipment we no longer needed.

LEFT Dorbe and his family. His wife died in 1994.

OPPOSITE TOP Orsa, Tsini, Jambu, Karte and Tsering Sonam. It was Tsini who had the ectopic pregnancy. The family lived immediately above Base camp.

OPPOSITE BELOW Puh and Kokor and their children. They lived about 20 minutes away from Base camp at a height of around 5000 metres throughout the year.

Sepu Kangri and Seamo Uylmitok (the Turquoise Flower) on the right,
reflected in Sam Tso Taring.

The north face of Sepu Kangri.

Scott on the summit of Thaga Ri.

TOP LEFT A view from the hermit's house, looking towards Base camp. Thaga Ri, climbed by Graham and Scott is the peak on the right; Amchhi Inji-ne (Victor and Charlie) is second from left.

LEFT Scott playing Atlas on the Thong Wuk Glacier.

Victor showing
Elliot the
technique of
short roping at
camp 1.

Scott and Elliot
at camp 1.

were worth the food we gave him. He departed suddenly when we
arrived at Lhorong. So did Charlie's binoculars.

This part of the drive has been fairly uneventful. The landscape is still
dramatic, switching, as we have crossed four passes, from barren and
bleak high ground to deep narrow gorges with some spectacular walls;
a future rockclimbers' paradise? We have passed the wreckage of one
or two vehicles, victims of last week's rain. We also had a near miss
head-on with a motorbike whose rider, followed by bike, left the road
in the direction of the river. He narrowly arrested his descent on a steep
bank and we hauled both to the road; he was badly shaken but seemed
none the worse for wear, and drove off. We have also managed to break
our pressure stove, so the flavour of cooking may now change – from
now on everything is to be cooked on yak dung or wood if we can get
it. Cloud and occasional rain have been the rule, killing photography
and making solar charging but an idle dream.

By the evening of 18th August we were camped in the spectacular gorge
west of the town of Lhorong. From our enquiries Lhorong seemed to be
the last major town before Pelbar. It had shops and a post office. I posted a
cheque Elliot owed me to Barclays head office in London and a postcard to
Frank Boothman who had been so helpful with the cartography. Elliot
thought he was on a safe wicket *vis-à-vis* the cheque but some two months
later over £400 had been credited to my account; Frank duly received his
postcard. We were impressed by the Chinese postal service.

Meanwhile the Land Cruiser had developed an ominous crunch as we
turned left-hand corners that sounded like a crack in the chassis. I found a
minor fissure next to a shock absorber. Lobsang was impressed at the
diagnosis. The spot weld took twenty minutes in Lhorong and cost under
£2. We toyed with the idea of staying in the town but open country seemed
more attractive. Despite the fact we were legitimate, we continued to avoid
chance meetings with authority. The countryside varied, alternating
between wooded valleys and windswept plateau. A fine bridge crossed the
Salween at a place we had been told was a ford. We descended a final pass
of 4800 metres and dropped into the wide valley of Pelbar.

The dismal weather was frustrating. Here were our first high mountains
somewhere to the south but cloud and rain obscured anything beyond a
glimpse of a grey glacier. Somewhere above were the eastern summits of
this part of the Nyenchen Tanglha – several 6000-metre peaks. We paused
briefly in Pelbar, a small village with a monastery, and were told by the

leader to go on to Tsoka where we might find horses. On Wednesday, 19th August we drove into the gloomy compound there. A friendly custodian showed us a room and made us welcome. There were however no horses. We must go to Do Martang, he told us, the district headquarters half an hour west. By late afternoon we had found the leader there, a portly, serious man called Pema Tanda Dadhul. With barely a question he smiled and announced, 'You shall have five horses at 11 a.m. in Tsoka the day after tomorrow. I shall arrange it. Have a day of rest.' He indicated a Sechuan restaurant that soon provided pig's ears, still not Elliot's favourite, and chicken, cabbage, beef and beer; then we played pool in the street. Elliot bought some eggs and spare AA batteries which didn't work. Pasang bought some wine. We drove back to Tsoka in the drizzle.

Solar power had been a distant prospect for three days but here in the compound there was electricity from a small hydroelectric plant nearby.

'You can't do that, you'll kill us,' said Elliot as I wired into the fusebox with a pair of crocodile clips.

'Piece of cake,' I replied and turned on the computer, sent an e-mail, switched on the phone and called Ruth at home.

We slept well that night. Outside it teemed with rain. Suddenly, early next morning, our road journey really did feel at an end. A cord was severed. Lobsang and Tenzing, our careful drivers who had replaced our anxiety with calm confidence in many an evil place, said goodbye. We paid them well and wished them luck as they drove off east through the mud. The three of us were alone.

10 The Sa La Is Not For Horses

20th August – 5th September 1998

CHARLES CLARKE

I can deal with most smells. I like game high and reeking. I love old-fashioned camembert, the sort one used to be able to buy in France. But Pasang's yak meat stank the place out. Our room in the Tsoka Political Cultural Centre was bare but dry and preferable to the nearly continuous rain in the yard outside. Pasang had bought the meat fresh in Chamdo. He had boiled it four days previously. Since that time the temperature had barely touched freezing; often it was 10° to 20°C. The plan was that the cooked meat would dry and with this in mind Pasang had laid it out on his bed in this simple room. It was already mouldy and on the rare occasions the sun shone the flies swarmed there. They were enormous bluebottles. They scarcely flew except to reach the rotting hunks of meat; there they crawled, buzzing with contentment and laid their eggs, spellbound at their good luck. The surface of the flesh became invisible.

Pasang insisted stubbornly that the meat was 'just fine and when it's dry you'll like it' and fried a little for lunch. It fizzed in the oil in the wok as one might expect but there then came a secondary fizzing in the mouth like over-ripe Stilton. The taste was foetid. Elliot and I commented more than once that all was not well and perhaps, we suggested, it was not how Yishi, Pasang's wife and an exquisite cook, would like it. At this he faltered and perhaps thought of her alone with the children in Lhasa. Elliot attributed his queasiness to the meat. Pasang thought his own malaise that morning was due to a surfeit of Kong Fuyan rice wine, an evil 40% proof sweet and sickly liquor in an over-decorated bottle which he had bought in Do Martang. He asked Sanchu, a pretty widow who lived next door, what she thought about the meat. 'Rotten,' she replied, 'but I'll cook it again for me and my daughter.' She took it away. Sanchu was about twenty-two. She had lost her yak-herder husband from illness the year before and had been given a room free in the compound. She was keen to earn money and welcomed the pile of filthy clothes we gave her to wash.

Besides Sanchu, her two-year-old daughter and the caretaker, whose name we never knew, there were the two other residents of the compound of the Cultural Political Centre, Dr Choephel, the general practitioner, and Li Puye, the teacher of English. Dr Choephel lived opposite our quarters, across the yard. He had learnt medicine in Chengdu, where his father had studied before the Second World War. His surgery and sole dwelling was a single room. He looked after a population of about a thousand.

'What sort of diseases do you see and treat?' I asked.

'Everything,' he replied with a smile and continued to talk to the woman who was consulting him. She had headaches and joint pains, backache, insomnia, stomach ache, dizziness and palpitations and, despite them all, looked healthy. I thought she was depressed. Dr Choephel was sympathetic, until the next wave of symptoms began. At this, he rolled his eyes to the ceiling and smiled gently and, turning to the patient and then to me, asked:

'Would you like another opinion from the English doctor?'

'You mean him?' she gestured towards me. 'I have already seen him, last night. *Amchhi Inji-ne* (the English doctor), he was no good at all, completely useless.' Pasang delighted in translating this word for word.

Li Puye, the Chinese teacher of English, also had a room nearby. The proof of his industry had been the children of Do Martang chanting, 'Hello how are you hello how are you goodbye goodbye' as they had craned their necks to have better view while Elliot and I had had to pee in the main street. He had graduated in Chengdu the previous year. I asked him how he liked Tsoka. 'Yes, I like it just a *little*,' he said with a shy smile, his head on one side, 'but the road from my home is long and shallow.' Li Puye was a man who seemed kind but rather lost in this valley far from his family. He showed us the English grammar he used; the text was almost incomprehensible. He spoke little Tibetan, Pasang told us.

These towns, like Tsoka and Do Martang, the district headquarters, were somewhat similar. Each had a government compound, with a satellite dish behind it which received and relayed central television on several channels. A small hospital, the post office and police station were adjacent to it. There were shops selling clothing, pots and pans, grain, beer, imported Chinese tinned food, batteries and radios. Several shop fronts were also restaurants. In the larger towns these would extend sometimes to a disco or a brothel. Most shops were the homes of Chinese families who lived in one small back room. A few shops which sold local produce, such as saddles, harnesses and silver jewellery, were run by Tibetans. In the main street there were several charcoal kebab stalls and battered pool tables with green cloth peeling from the surface. Pool has become a Tibetan national game.

Tsoka itself was a smaller town. A satellite dish stood behind the compound above the river. There was one Tibetan shop which bought barley and *chura*, hard dry cheese, from the locals and sold it on. I found a sealed tin of No.761 People's Liberation Army Biscuits hidden away on a dusty shelf, an emergency ration that I had searched for in vain in Lhasa and Chamdo. I carried this proudly back to Elliot. I had an absolute longing for the eight-inch cubical green tin with its jagged lip around the lid. The reason for this intense desire remains obscure: certain objects assume a strange importance on expeditions. He took one mouthful of the extra sample biscuit I had bought for him, flavour-sealed in a polythene sachet. 'Wonderful when you're hungry,' I told him. He spat it out and retched, complaining that the fawn-yellow block the size of a matchbox tasted of sweetish cardboard and faintly of sick. I quite liked this old-fashioned hard tack. Fussy chap, don't know how lucky they are, these youngsters, I thought.

We spent our first rest day since Lhasa writing, using the telephone and sending e-mails, my makeshift power supply being essential in the absence of sun. Elliot had fallen silent about how dangerous the electrical connections to the fusebox had been: I felt he was impressed, but he wouldn't admit that the old duffer had such ingenuity. I had been pleased with my handiwork. Pasang cooked an indifferent supper of noodles and cabbage and drank a little more of the Kong Fuyan wine. We went to bed early and hoped the horses would arrive next day at the promised time of 11 a.m. Our first goal would be the Shargang La, the pass which Abbé Huc had crossed some 150 years before. Everyone seemed to know where it was – 'A day or two up there.' They pointed to hills in the west.

The next morning Friday, 21st August was dull but dry. It had rained heavily in the night, snow dusted the surrounding hills that rose to around 4800 metres. They were largely barren but occasionally sustained low brushwood. There were fields of corn and barley at 3800 metres with trees beside the road in the valley floor. Pema Tanda Dadhul called in to say goodbye about ten o'clock and assured us that five horses were on their way. We were packed and a small pile of loads waited in the yard. I had removed the crocodile clips gingerly from the fusebox without incident. Eleven o'clock passed and a light shower sent us inside. Several rough-looking men with foul teeth came in with laden horses; they were not for us. They peered with undue interest at the purple bags and rucksacks and walked off.

By noon we were beginning to ask the usual questions and kept glancing between our watches and the compound gates; but Pema Tanda Dadhul had been true to his word. Five unladen horses and one foal walked in five minutes later with a horseman named Chunzi and Pema Tsomung, a woman of about twenty-five. They were cheerful but serious people. Scarcely had they greeted us than they were loaded and away. Money was not mentioned.

'How much are they charging and where are we going tonight?' I asked Pasang as I put on my sack.

'I don't know,' he replied. 'Pema Tanda Dadhul has arranged it all. It will be fine. Come on, Charlie, we're off.'

We marched back towards Pelbar along the road for several kilometres before taking a path on the right that began to gain height, reminding me that, apart from the odd stroll, we had taken no exercise for over a fortnight. We were however reasonably acclimatised, having rarely been much below 4000 metres. Just outside Tsoka we looked down from the road into a picnic garden where several families were having lunch under tile cupolas. Next to the garden was a Chinese cemetery, reminding us that Han communities in these parts were not new. Three boys were skulking about there below us, clearly up to no good. One of the two older ones who looked about twelve produced a bottle of beer from a carrier bag, opened it furtively behind a bush and, having taken a swig, gave it to a third, perhaps his younger brother of around ten. He too glanced around anxiously before putting it to his lips. Meanwhile the other twelve-year-old lit a cigarette. It was a familiar scene anywhere. I looked below. 'Goodbye road,' I mumbled to myself. 'We are really on our way now.'

Chunzi, Pema Tsomung, Pasang, Elliot, the five horses and the foal climbed up the easy path rising from the valley floor. I lagged behind, despite an indecently light rucksack. A small boy caught up with me; with a grin and a *yamo* greeting he gestured to me to give him my load. He could not have been more than eight. He carried the bright red rucksack for an hour and I gave him 2 *yuan*, about twenty pence. He clutched the *yuan* note with excitement and ran off home. We walked on for some four hours past villages and fields of barley, meeting yak caravans or horsemen from the Shargang La. This was easy country with a well-made path sometimes cutting through scrub and juniper. We would not be seeing a tree of any substance for some days. Everyone would always greet us on the way with a nod and smile. 'Ah, *Inji-ne* (from England),' they would say to Pasang and walk on, horse bells jingling. The Tibetans do not tie bells to yaks because it makes the animals nervous. The frisky yak shakes off its loads with some aplomb. Close to a village called Du Tsuka over 4400 metres we camped beside a stream. A rainbow arched over this small valley describing a complete semi-circle. I thought this auspicious. Soon however it began to rain.

Then began a ritual which was to become stereotyped throughout this journey. We would put up the lightweight Terra Nova tents – a dark green Voyager and two Solars – throw in our rucksacks and collect wood and dry dung. Often when close to habitation we would buy these precious commodities. The horsemen put up their cotton tent and within minutes had a blazing fire of twigs in the entrance. Then using hand-held goatskin bellows they lit the yak dung and a pan of water would soon be brewing for tea. I met Heinrich Harrer in London some months after we had returned home. The conversation soon turned to dung fires. He recalled a disaster with their own bellows when he had crossed western Tibet with Peter Aufschneiter, after their wartime escape from British internment in India. The goatskin bellows bag had been stolen by a wolf during the night, leaving its iron tubing. 'It was almost impossible to light a fire without our bellows,' he told me. 'We were in terrible trouble; getting yak dung to burn is such an art.'

Little has changed for centuries on these journeys. To begin with, coming with our technology we would struggle with a multi-fuel primus which was difficult to use in wind or rain. Lobsang had given us a litre of petrol to start it and we carried kerosene from Lhasa as its main fuel. In reserve we had the five gas cylinders we had carried irresponsibly on the plane from Kathmandu, breaking all the safety regulations. Perhaps it would take the horsemen fifteen minutes to brew up, invariably before us. To make tea they break off a portion of the compressed tea brick, add crystals of salt and sometimes a knob of rancid butter. The pot would boil away through the evening with more ingredients thrown in as it emptied.

After tea they would eat *tsampa*; this is ground roast barley with the consistency of flour. They pour a little tea into a small cereal-sized bowl and pummel the *tsampa* into dough with a forefinger. They also sometimes chop in *chura*, flaking the dried cheese from a block, and then rancid butter. From the same cotton or yak-leather bag as the *tsampa*, butter, salt crystal and *chura* would come meat. This would be either raw yak or sheep on the bone with hard sinewy flesh that had been air-dried over several weeks.

They would slice the meat thinly from the joint, using the large knife with a silver embossed handle that hangs on the right of every traveller's belt.

Beside this superb example of the economical camp kitchen we would struggle trying to prepare supper, usually noodles and vegetables and our own tea, a meal already requiring three cooking pots which would have to be heated in turn. Our Tibetan companions would be sitting relaxed by their fire, eating from their bag and drinking as the mood took them. As the days went by we would move gradually towards local food but it is a taste that can only be acquired slowly. At first more than a mouthful of *tsampa* is hard to swallow because it has the consistency of Weetabix with a dash of water, while the tea tastes salty or rancid. It is difficult to handle more than a morsel of dried meat. With perseverance these things changed as the weeks went by and towards the end of our journey I began to crave the heaviness of *tsampa* and felt I had not eaten properly without a bowlful. Elliot followed my example somewhat less avidly but gradually became accustomed to this simple timeless fare. It was dark by 8 p.m. and we were usually asleep by nine, after writing or dictating diaries.

Next morning we left at nine, heading towards the Shargang La in dirty but improving weather. Grasslands gave way to shale and mud with the odd patch of grubby snow. Elliot's insides were playing up and he had to stop every half hour or so. At least it slows him down, I thought mercilessly. The path climbed steadily: our altimeter watches changed every few minutes – 4800m, 4850m, 4900m, 5000m appeared on the display.

I wrote that night:

By 2 p.m. we climbed up the last rocky zigzag and reached the prayer flags, carvings, and the odd broken bottle, the trappings of a major pass. The Shargang La is 5038m on the map, and either 5135m, 5285m, or 5105m on various pieces of gadgetry and at N30°51', E94°31' from the Garmin GPS. WOW! For the first time during this journey, we saw high mountains in clear weather. Filling the south-western horizon it seemed we could see the entire range of the eastern Nyenchen Tanglha, snow and rock peaks of around 6000 to nearly 7000 metres. At its northern end, far in the distance, was a fang of ice, bearing the unmistakable profile of the Sepu Kangri massif. It was as if the mountain knew we were there and had beckoned us. Within a minute the fang was gone, eclipsed in cloud. A black thundercloud hovered over the snow-capped summit immediately south of the pass. I felt neurotic about lightning and we dropped a hundred metres, scree-running down shale. Sepu

Kangri was 67.1km away as the crow flies, so the GPS told us. Our route will be considerably more convoluted. We descended on Gya Lam, the old yak road. It seemed endless, through pastures, and reached meadows above Tsara Sondu village where we must change transport.

The meadow in the valley floor was idyllic but we had lost long before the panoramic view of the Nyenchen Tanglha. Grass and rock peaks surrounded us. There were trees in the valley below where the track of Gya Lam wound downwards. A few minutes' walk below camp a fine 6000-metre ice peak glistened to the south. Elliot had discovered it on one of his innumerable visits to the lavatory. Sheep, some looking distinctly edible, grazed close by. The three of us were weary and walked about like old men. A Tibetan with a smiling face rode into camp and drank tea. His name was Nima.

'No horses tomorrow,' said Pasang, 'but Nima says he can bring five the next day from his village up the valley on the right.'

'Great, we can have a rest,' Elliot and I replied simultaneously.

Pasang talked to Nima about the way towards the Hidden Kingdom of Nagru and to the Sa La, the final pass that we knew led into the Sepu Kangri basin. We were told that there were several routes. Nima knew them well, though he had not been over the Sa La himself.

'He says the Sa La is not for horses, I think so,' said Pasang.

We orientated ourselves with a compass, the GPS and the photocopy of a Russian 1:200,000 map, translated the Cyrillic script and asked Nima if he knew the various villages. Most of the names as far as Nima was concerned were wrong but it seemed clear that the general topography shown on this map was highly accurate. Elliot quickly reminded me of an evening in Lhasa.

'Wasn't that the map you chucked on the bed when we were sorting papers when you said, "No damn use that Russian thing, I'm sure we can leave *that* behind"?' Being an academic geographer he had then looked at the map closely and disagreed. I was ready for him. 'Didn't waste those years at Edinburgh University, did you? I thought you just spent them doing tracing and colouring, that's all you do in Geography,' I replied. Had we not brought the Russian contribution we would have abandoned the only map that bore any resemblance to reality on the ground.

Nima told us that there were plans to build a road over the Shargang La. I felt sad. I powered up the phone and spoke to my father to wish him a happy ninety-first birthday, his first alone for over sixty years since my mother had died shortly before we had left England. 'Charles? You want

Charles? He's away in Tibet,' he replied when I said my name. It was not his age: father had always been like that. I remembered returning home in November 1969 after a long Himalayan series of expeditions lasting nine months. International calls were then costly and difficult. I had phoned immediately on arrival at Heathrow:

'Hello, dad, it's Charles.'

'Charles? Charles? Charles *who*?' he had replied.

Pasang phoned Yishi in Lhasa and Elliot called home. Chunzi asked if he could speak to his brother, a monk in the Rampling monastery in Lhasa. He punched in the number, located his brother and gave the unfortunate monk a shopping list that would fill a truck. Shirts, a suit, a new saddle and halter, rice and a radio were among the requests. He could not be separated from the phone for over twenty minutes. It was clear that he felt the need for the technology of the outside world as much as we did air travel. So why not have a road? Lucky Pema Tsomung doesn't want to phone her boyfriend, I thought as Chunzi eventually hung up.

We slept soundly that night. The morning of our rest day was sunny. Chunzi and Pema Tsomung left us. We paid them off at the rate set by the leader, 12 *yuan* per person and/or per horse a day (about £1) with half rate for the return journey. Soon they became specks on the Shargang La trail. Nima returned leading two horses. Elliot and Pasang planned to ride an hour or two up the Keela Pu, the side valley where Nima lived, to buy a sheep. Elliot mounted his horse, trying to look confident. Pasang gave me a wicked grin, followed by a healthy thwack on the animal's bottom. Elliot's horse neighed and reared in a determined attempt to unseat the rider. Pasang galloped off laughing. 'Don't worry, I'll look after the baggage,' I shouted after them. 'Have a nice day.' The inane greeting of our American cousins seemed for once appropriate.

I fiddled about in the sun with the solar panels, the phone and the computer, sweating under the two metres of black cloth. The VDU screen was invisible without it, except after nightfall by which time it was too cold to work. By lunchtime the satellite phone became unusable. I had punched in the wrong passcode three times. 'Enter your unblock code or please call the BT Mobiq helpline,' its error message read. How exactly when the goddam phone doesn't work, I wondered. Next the Libretto computer crashed. A blank screen was all that remained visible as I crouched beneath my black head-dress, looking as if I was involved in some dubious rite. 'Bugger it, I've done nothing wrong,' I said aloud. It was time to do a little washing and scribble in my diary rather than battle with a keyboard. '*I hate technology . . .'* I began. It would the first of many trials, but at least the sun was shining and I could charge the batteries of these apparently useless pieces of equipment.

The riders returned around 4 p.m. A sheep carcass dripping blood dangled across Pasang's saddle. Elliott was full of stories of Nima's family and his six children, especially their wild three-year-old son. He had not been happy when they had slaughtered the sheep by suffocation. 'But I thought it only right to see how we got our meat,' he said. A rope is tied tightly round the muzzle and the animal gradually lapsed into unconsciousness; it sounds gruesome but having seen the final act done to both sheep and yak, it is less horrible than the description. He also announced with some glee that Pasang had been thrown from his horse. Then he glanced at the phone and the Libretto.

'I go away for six hours and all you can do is smash every piece of equipment we have. All you can do is make a bloody clothesline.' I explained that I had washed his underpants; they were on the line. Despite this generous act he was furious. He set to work with some resignation, like a child trying to solve that ultimate problem that no grown-up understands, how to programme a video.

Elliot cheered up with some roast lamb, some of the most succulent either of us had ever tasted. By nightfall he had solved our phone problems. We phoned Chris in Cumbria and e-mailed a report and Olympus digital photos. Chris told us to get ready for an expedition press conference he was holding at the Royal Geographical Society in a few days' time; we would need to phone in to coincide with his announcement that he was 'just going to talk to the team in Tibet'. I wrote down the direct line London number to the press conference and also the number of National Express's advertising agency. We had arranged that we could take no incoming calls on our travels. Elliot told him I had already broken everything. That was quite unnecessary, I thought. Cheeky brat.

Nima and his friend Po Thondup arrived next morning with five pack horses. Po Thondup was about fifty, a pleasant silent man with gnarled hands. He had spent eighteen years in prison commencing in the 1950s. He told us his crime had been his job: he had been a soldier in the Tibetan army of resistance. We were first to head north-east up the Keela Pu valley to Nima's house. Then we would cross three 5000-metre passes, the Gu Gyu La, the Pemo La and Tang La. This would lead us to Nagru, the Hidden Kingdom. We strolled easily up the Keela Pu for a couple of hours and were welcomed by Nima's wife, Sonam Doha, whose face was open and friendly and her gestures gentle. They lived in a large *ba* some five metres square. It was easy to stand upright inside. A central fire vented through an ingenious opening in the roof that could be closed by pulling a rope when it rained or snowed. A solar panel lit a single neon strip, the only connection with the late twentieth century. Sonam Doha gave us tea, stooping to present each bowl and pausing while we took a first mouthful. Pasang said that it was good manners to take a sip, turn slightly away and allow the bowl to be taken to be refilled. This action symbolises that the guest trusts the host. She also gave us fresh creamy yak yoghurt; Nima cut two wooden spatulas to use as spoons rather than see us attempt to quaff the yoghurt from the bowl. Two of their six children were there. The three-year-old boy was at first silent and deferential, then he began to show off by screaming with laughter and running round inside the *ba* beating the dog, which then growled at him. At this he burst into tears and ran to his mother, howling and kicking his legs as she cuddled him. He then crashed on to a couch and fell asleep. Meanwhile a baby lay blissfully asleep in a fleece bag beside us.

'How old?' I asked.

'She was born when we had snow five months ago,' Nima told us.

'And what is she called?' Pasang said the baby had no name because it was unlucky for one so young to have one.

A deterrent for the Evil Eye, I thought.

We were in no hurry and left our hosts to decide when we should leave. The family lived here during the summer and moved to a house lower down the valley from November to March to escape the worst of the cold. During the summer months they would travel to Pelbar over the Shargang La every few weeks to buy barley, flour and other essentials. Pasang grumbled that the prices were subsidised for country folk. 'The price of food in Lhasa is so expensive for us' – the usual talk of the townie. Nima said they had once been to Lhasa. It had been some seventeen years previously, shortly after he and Sonam Doha had married; they had travelled with horses for some three weeks to reach the capital.

The talk turned to wild animals. We were told there were *naar*, blue sheep, small deer which sounded like musk, marmots, and *pika*, a common rodent the size of a rat. They would also see wolves and foxes. 'And wolf-foxes,' Pasang added. There were no longer bears, nor snow leopards here, but occasionally smaller brown cats with pointed ears. These animals were very shy and rare.

'The bone is very expensive and used for medicine,' Nima said. We thought he was describing an ocelot. 'And then there are *temu*. Many *temu* in Nagru,' he added with some respect. *Temu* kill yak and sheep.

'A *temu* is not like a bear,' Pasang explained. It was as tall as a man and had long grey-brown hair that flopped about when it walked. This animal left a footprint like a human but without a heel. It had long toenails. Pasang knew well the fascination Europeans have with the *yeti* and led us on a little before admitting that there was actually a *temu* in the Norbu Lingkha zoo in Lhasa. We were left in ignorance as to what animal it really was until the day before we left Tibet.

Nima rose to go. 'Tonight we stay at Po Lo Kage beneath the Gu Gyu La.'

Four hours later we were camped by a stream eating *momos*, delicious dumplings stuffed with meat and onions and hunks of lamb roasted in the embers. A man approached carrying a hammer and pair of pincers. 'The road above is very stony,' Nima said. The newcomer was the blacksmith. He had some tea, shoed the horses and left us in the dusk. It began to rain. Next morning we walked up the rocky track to the Gu Gya La. The altimeter read 5265 metres. We had hoped for a good view of the peaks of the Nyenchen Tanglha but it was cloudy. There would be more days of disappointment. Nima pointed to the glaciers of some peaks around 6000 metres. They were called Kila Cho and Jongla Mokbu. Legend relates that these two great mountains, with the help of Sepu Kangri, had magical powers; they had stopped the Chinese from invading India through Tibet in times gone by. We had crossed into the head of the Pemo valley and, losing little height, crossed two other stony passes, the Pemo La and the Tang La, before dropping down into the Nagru valley, the scree giving way to pastures.

'Do you think there are wolf-foxes here?' I asked Pasang, keen to sort out this mongrel.

'Of course, there will be many wolf-foxes.'

'But Pasang, a fox cannot mate with a wolf.' I felt sure of my ground.

'Charlie, they definitely can. We have a story that tells how it happened. The fox sent a letter to the she-wolf asking her if she would like to have sex with him. The wolf was very angry that an animal so much smaller should suggest this and chased the fox back to its hole. What is the word? Impertinent, I think so. The fox had dived inside his hole. Then the she-wolf followed. Now the she-wolf, being larger than the fox, got stuck. Do you know what happened next?'

'Go on!'

'Quick as a flash the fox came out of the other end of its hole, went round to the entrance where the wolf was stuck, with her bottom sticking out, and fucked her. That's how the wolf-fox was born.'

I loved Pasang's fables. 'Please tell us another story Pasang,' we said as we walked along.

'You know the one about the yak and the water-buffalo?'

'No!'

'Well, you know the water-buffalo has short hair and the yak has long hair?'

'Yes.'

'Well, long long ago the yak and the water-buffalo were sisters. They lived in the plains in India. The yak had to go on a journey to the far north, to Tibet to collect salt and, knowing it was very cold, she asked her sister if she could borrow her coat. So the water-buffalo gave it to the yak, leaving herself naked. The buffalo made her sister promise to give back the coat when she returned.'

'And then?'

'When the yak reached Tibet she liked it so much she never went home to India. And that is why water-buffaloes still have thin coats, and also why they always hold their heads upwards. They are looking up to the mountains for their yak sisters. And it's also why water-buffaloes are so bad-tempered and have that sad miserable groan.'

This was easy country with a well-marked track. We had left behind the glimpses of high mountains; there were trees below in the distance. My diary tells of our introduction to the Nagru valley:

We dropped down at about 1545hrs to some open grassland they call Lu Bugna beside the river around 4800 metres. A woman with long hair and a conical hat was carrying a bundle of twigs. She came to greet us. She looked like a witch. Haka was about forty and had five children below the age of fifteen. She gave us tea in a tiny stone and turf house, amongst the poorest I had ever seen. Haka was a widow and also two years ago had lost her eldest daughter. 'She was killed by mistake by a relative,' Pasang said. What had happened was that Haka's nephew and her daughter had been herding yaks. They were throwing stones at them as they always do. A stone intended for a yak had struck her daughter in the neck. Her throat had swelled up and over several hours she became unable to breathe. She died the same day. Haka and her family live here all year long. I suppose it must be below zero at night for eight months and in snow for six. She has nine yaks and four sheep. She grows no barley and no other crop. So we bought firewood and dung. Pasang asked if he could cook in the house because it was raining. He made noodles with lamb and onions. Then we cooked ribs on the fire and gave everyone meat. Pasang felt this family was so poor that we should not simply pay them for fuel. He gave them from his own money a present of 50 *yuan* – five days pay for labour in this region. We followed his example with more. So breakfast today was *tsampa* and tea, + two eggs; lunch was a slab of Chamdo bread with a little peanut butter and dinner above. We were moving fast today, bouncing down the valley and overtaking the horses. Torrential rainstorm this evening; flooded my tent and I moved to higher ground. Elliot's guts seem better. We're in the Hidden Kingdom at last.

From any point on Gya Lam, which now lay to the south and west, it is a two-day journey into the Nagru region. To the north the valley weaves down to reach a tributary of the Salween which it feeds and leads to the road near Pengar, close to the expedition's roadhead at Khinda; it is perhaps a week on foot. This is a region that is isolated even by Tibetan standards. In all the places we passed on the trek from Tsoka few visitors were ever seen. We presume these valleys had never been visited by foreigners. The very few had simply travelled along Gya Lam. Grass gave way to forests as we descended the following day, which was to be our last with Nima and Po Thondup. We had all grown fond of each other. Elliot and I wished they would stay. 'Our families will be worried if we do not return and the people of Nagru will be angry,' Nima told Pasang that evening. We camped, again in the rain, at a village called Dorputang around 4300 metres. I felt the final mark of friendship was Po Thondup's action that night. He scooped in his hands a warm pile of yak dung from the entrance of my tent. '*Yakpato* (good),' he said with a smile. Perhaps it was good luck. A day's march below we would turn south-west up the Tashi Lung valley which seemed to lead on the Russian 1:200,000 map towards the Sa La, and Sepu Kangri. Elliot continued to remind me on a daily basis that I had tried to abandon the map in Lhasa.

We had already fallen into the rhythm of a long mountain journey. There were the chores of packing each morning and loading horses but, being a small party, these were trivial. Sometimes we would talk, animatedly, about this or that, and at other times prefer silence. It is as important to respect a companion's space in the open air as it is in a crowded office. Moods go up and down. We seemed to remain equable, and were dominated by interest, anticipation, a love of the landscape, and travel itself. There was also the hard and tedious work of electronic communication, but the exercise was useful for the future. I think I prefer a pencil, a notebook and no satellite phone. The usual highlight of each day was lying in front of a fire towards dusk drinking tea, tired and happy with a day's progress nearer our goal.

There was something a little eerie about the Nagru valley. The people seemed to have a reserve, though this never bordered on hostility. We felt a sense of faint unease. We were however welcomed by one person, a nun who was Nima's relative. Dorputang village seemed lifeless and the people moody. Horses would be difficult to obtain, they said, and their price increased. It rained almost continuously through the night. Dogs stole the entire supply of eggs. There were no fables of the past, and no shrines here. We were depressed and disappointed by the Hidden Kingdom. It transpired later that our romantic vision of Nagru may have stemmed from a tiny fragment of history. Prior to the seventh century the region had indeed been independent. King Songsten Gampo (613–670 A D) who first unified Tibet had conquered the area. Perhaps the stories we had heard simply reflected this. Songsten Gampo's reign had been the start of an era of Tibetan expansion; a century later it was a Tibetan army which invaded imperial China – and even occupied the capital Xi'an in 763. There was however no feeling of former prosperity and no remnant of this golden age gone by.

Despite our misgivings, fresh horses arrived next morning. After tea and *tsampa* we said goodbye to Nima and Po Thondup. 'We have never had such pleasure travelling with strangers,' Nima said to Pasang as he rode off. We returned the compliment. Our new horsemen were silent and glum. They seemed to lack the love of travel of our previous companions. We tried to be jolly but found little response. We spent another day in frequent showers descending through woods, and reached the junction of the Tashi Lung valley where we turned left, to the south. Wherever there had been bridges here they had been swept away. The river of the Tashi Lung was substantial, about fifty metres wide and a frothing torrent. 'All the bridges in this region have been destroyed in the rains,' the horsemen said. 'We cannot even reach Pengar (downstream, to the north) by the path by the river.' They had had the worst summer in living memory. To reach their road at Pengar they would have to follow a route that crossed several passes. This was irrelevant to ourselves because we were heading upstream and south, but we took heed of the river and wondered about the state of the bridges for the main expedition's approach march. This was to begin near Pengar.

As we began to ascend the Tashi Lung we saw a fine monastery on the opposite bank. 'That's the Channa *gompa*,' Pasang announced. The story he told was that centuries ago a lama was looking for a place to found a monastery. He had laid his rosary on a rock beside this very river: a blackbird stole it and flew off. I wondered if it had not been a magpie, a frequent companion here. 'No,' said Pasang, 'it means a *blackbird*.' He continued: 'You see the high rock beside the prayer flags. That's where the blackbird left the rosary. The lama found it there and built the monastery.' We'll never ford that river, we thought and walked up the hill beside it. A monk shouted and gesticulated wildly on the opposite bank. We left the *gompa* unvisited. 'Don't worry about monasteries,' I mentioned to Elliot. 'We'll be at Samda in a week, you'll see.' His diarrhoea had returned and he looked thin. I felt well and I could now tighten my belt to its furthest buckle.

This was a short and otherwise miserable day. 'We camp here,' announced the horsemen early in the afternoon. Again we camped in the rain and next morning paid porters and horses for another day, moving for less than an hour to the village of Nag Su Do at 4500 metres, around the tree line. We could already see our destination as we set out. Here we met the village headman and tried to butter him up with a watch as a gift. I bought an old Chinese coin from him for 50 *yuan* that was probably valueless. We misjudged the meeting completely. 'Maybe there will be horses, maybe not,' was all he would say. The Sa La, he said, was two days away. 'And be careful,' he added 'there are bad men here,' indicating two youths who were hanging around the camp. Pasang discovered that the father of one was in prison, having murdered his neighbour; the death penalty is unusual in Tibet.

This short day was 28th August, the date of the London press conference. We had conserved battery power for this occasion. The Libretto PC had been out of action for a week, but with a struggle and using the solar panels continuously we had enough power for the satellite phone. During the late afternoon, mid-morning in London, I dialled the press conference continuously. There was no reply. Chris had given us the wrong number. Eventually we tracked down the meeting and made contact. It didn't seem to go well: but perhaps it was me. Here we were in the middle of nowhere and, I felt, on a great journey. No one seemed interested. 'It is often the way,' I said to Elliot. We slept uneasily that night, awaking to find that the remains of the precious lamb had disappeared. The two youths skulked about.

Two miserable new horsemen arrived, even more surly than the last.

They were young men who looked as if they had been despatched on an errand neither relished. We tried our best and occasionally a glimmer of a smile would appear. Their horses were thin and looked sad. One had been attacked recently by a wolf; the wound had been neatly patched by a six-inch square of cotton material stitched into the haunch. A nice job, but the horse limped. At least these people knew the way to the Sa La, or so it seemed. Anyway, why should they come with us? I tried to feel optimistic, and grateful. We trudged up the valley in the rain. In the early afternoon at around 4700 metres a magnificent ice and rock peak soared out of the valley to the south-east, a local Eigerwand. This was Kok-po. On the map it was over 6500 metres high. Doubtless in years to come this peak will become a major objective for a future generation of mountaineers. We had had glimpses of the massif from the Sa La the previous year.

The clouds closed in again and we pressed on in driving rain. The two horsemen indicated uncertainty and, on closer questioning, it emerged that neither had crossed the Sa La nor knew exactly where it was. We felt hesitant and despondent. The path along the valley floor had all but disappeared. We camped in the drizzle and cloud in a barren valley close to 5000 metres and built a tarpaulin shelter for cooking in the pouring rain. A man in a deep red robe loomed out of the mist, sat and had tea. He fingered a rosary constantly. He was interested in our journey. He provided a ray of hope and some warmth.

'Would he come with us?' I asked Pasang.

'No, he must look after his yaks.'

But the nomad gave explicit instructions about how to reach the Sa La. As he spoke the clouds parted and we could see a col, the lowest point on the ridge at the head of our valley on the left.

'That is not the Sa La,' he said, 'but it is close by that place and above it to the right.' This began to make sense. I remembered that the pass crossed the rock ridge at a point higher than the col. Chris and I had reached the southern slopes of this col in July 1996 and had not liked what we had seen on the other side. There had been a precipitous gully, out of the question for an ascent with horses. In June 1997 Jim Fotheringham and I had climbed the southern slopes of the pass above the col with some difficulty and had looked across north to a feasible snow slope. It was this slope we needed to reach.

The man pointed to a band of red rocks that arched down to the river. 'From here you follow the river,' he said, 'until you reach the red rocks. Cross the river and climb the rocks and you will find a path leading to the

Sa La.' The mists closed in again. He left us. In the night I wondered if
this visit had been a dream. My diary written the following day tells the
story:

Next morning, we could see but a few hundred metres through the mist.
We set out in rain, and with our horsemen becoming gloomier by the
hour, we climbed up the trackless valley floor. Where the hell were we?
We really did not know. The 5000 metre mark passed, and then to our
left, there rose a red scree slope. Compass and Garmin Global
Positioning System were of little use here – we did not know the co-
ordinates of the pass. We crossed the river and plodded up the red slope.
To our amazement a track appeared out of nothing and led to a cairn.
'We build these stones for good luck,' said Pasang as he built another.
Out of what had then become driving snow, a route snaked upwards,
and in the distance were two prayer flags like goal posts on the pass
itself. We were there by 2 p.m. and peered over the pass towards Sepu
Kangri. A precipitous slope of loose rock on ice lay below extending for
a few hundred metres. We each took a horse, and coaxed each frightened
beast a step at a time. We slithered down, falling in heaps with the
horses, sliding down ice and sending boulders trundling down the
slope. We were too exhilarated to be scared. The end was near. Below
this the terrain eased. Within half an hour we were on easy scree. A
patch of blue appeared, the sun peeped out and the north face of Sepu
Kangri suddenly unfolded before us. The day became gentle. We saw a
nomad tent several hundred metres below us.

'That's Karte's *ba*!' shouted Pasang. Elliot was out in front. Familiar
figures appeared from the tent, grasped his hands and beckoned him
in. Pasang and I hurried on down. Karte and Tsini stood outside holding
their palms outstretched in welcome. We rubbed foreheads as family
members greet each other. 'We thought you would never come,' they
said and gave us milk, yak-butter tea, fresh cheese, *tsampa* and yoghurt.
We were back among friends. Even the dogs seemed to welcome us. It
was an emotional moment. Tears of happiness came to everyone's eyes.
Elliot said, 'I was beginning to think we would never meet friendly folk
again.' He gazed longingly at the snow face of Sepu that rose 2000 metres
from the valley floor. We dropped to the campsite by the lake, paid the
two horsemen and thanked them. They left without a smile or a
goodbye, but in fairness they had done a job that many would have
baulked at.

The news was good in parts. Everyone we knew was well and Tsini was back working with the yaks after her illness of 1997. But we learned from our friends in these meadows below Sepu that the two bridges on the expedition's northern approach march had been washed away. These had been at the roadhead at Khinda and below the Samda monastery. Both were important. Karte told us that he had been unable to reach Khinda at all earlier in the summer. There seemed several courses open. One was to move west of Sepu Kangri and investigate a new southern approach march to the mountain, following part of the 1996 recce. Another was to explore towards the Yanglung Glacier, north-west of Sepu, to see if there was a mountaineering route there, whichever approach march was to be used. The third, rather dismal option was simply to travel north to look at the remains of the bridges and investigate river crossings. There was however insufficient time for all three journeys unless we split up.

The notion of Pasang leaving either of us was at first untenable. We had become entirely dependent upon him. But why not separate? We were all fit and ready for more. We spent an idle day by the lake, washed and thought about it all. We decided to go south. We would all follow the same route to the Yam La, a pass west of Sepu, to reach the Yang valley. From there Pasang would ride with Jayang, Karte's nephew, to reach the road to the south, near Jiali, where we had been in 1996. These places were perhaps seventy or eighty kilometres away over several passes. Elliot and I would look at the Yanglung Glacier. A man named Puh, one of our base camp neighbours, would come with Elliot and me. We hastily assembled a Tibetan phrasebook of about ten words, and a vital phrase to use when we phoned the Khada Hotel: 'Please call Chris Bonington quickly.' The team would soon be passing through Lhasa. We could say in Tibetan where we wanted to camp, and secure basic necessities and horses, and count from one to ten. We began to feel proud about beginning to communicate ourselves.

Next morning, 1st September, Pasang and Jayang rode off on horseback towards the Yam La en route to Jiali and were soon lost in the clouds. Puh, Elliot and I followed carrying heavy loads. The weather deteriorated and a vicious snowstorm swept in as we crossed the 5600-metre pass. Puh was poorly equipped and I gave him all my extra clothing. We hurried down to the Yang valley, forded the river and camped on the grass. To the west rose the Yanglung Glacier, the first time we had seen this side of Sepu Kangri. We climbed up the valley to 5000 metres that evening. The upper reaches of the glacier and the west face looked reasonable mountaineering terrain, even at this distance some eight kilometres away, but the icefalls below them dictated that this was no valley from which to gain access to the mountain.

Perhaps, I wondered, the route that Jim Fotheringham had suggested in 1997, which approached Sepu Kangri from the north, could cross over from base camp to those upper slopes. This would be a decision for the climbing team. Elliot made a foul evening meal. The remaining noodles had been soaked in washing-up fluid. They tasted repellent alone and worse with tinned fish. He decided he was not to be disturbed by me getting up to pee in the night and chose to bivouac instead of sharing the tent. I zipped up the door of the green Voyager and went to sleep. Rain pelted down in the early hours and woke me, and there was a spectacular thunderstorm. After this I was dead to the world.

I woke next morning to find the snow was over a foot deep. The light-weight trekking tents had been flattened. Elliot emerged from his snowy cocoon outside. Puh was frozen, despite having my socks and gloves. I had already given him a sweater, leaving me a T-shirt, a pair of underpants, a fleece, overtrousers and one pair of socks as my entire wardrobe. There was little need for anything else. Puh walked over to a *ba* a quarter of a mile or so away to try to buy some milk and borrow a blanket. He returned after an hour, empty-handed, but we could see he had been in animated discussion with a woman outside the *ba*. No problem, I thought, I'll find out what that was all about with my Tibetan. Elliot laughed. We decided to write down our translations and ask Pasang to adjudicate on his return. Elliot wrote: 'I had a bad night and it was very cold. Can you lend me a blanket?' I was reading more into Puh's description and decided he was trying to explain that the woman had been bitten by a dog in the night and required a bandage. There was no answer to the contest, and no milk.

The route back to the lake over the Yam La now looked difficult. We would wait for Pasang and Jayang, whom we expected back the following day. The snow thawed during the afternoon and we went for a stroll. We saw several horsemen ambling up and down the broad valley. There were groups of laden yak on the move. Late August is the season for the yak-herders to descend to lower pastures. I had asked why they did this when the weather seemed mild, if wet. The reason is that they prefer the cattle to feed on the grass shoots when these are young. 'It makes the meat taste better,' they said. Around 10.30 a.m. we saw in the distance two figures riding with determination, breaking into a gallop when the ground allowed, trotting when it did not and rarely moving at walking pace. Pasang and Jayang waved, forded the river and jumped off their horses. Their saddle blankets were soaked in sweat. They had ridden for over 150 kilometres.

'The road south of Jiali is blocked,' Pasang announced, 'and the leader was unhelpful. We'll never get fifty yaks there. We must go north tomorrow.' We sat and had tea. We asked him to judge on the matter of Puh's visit to the *ba*. Elliot had won.

'Why don't we leave now?' I asked everyone suddenly, trying to take the initiative. 'It's only eleven o'clock. Let's drop down the valley to Samda and stay there.'

And so descend we did. Towards nightfall we were putting up tents in the meadow beside the monastery. 'Welcome,' said the caretaker monk with a smile, his only word of English. I tried to answer in Tibetan. Two days later we reached Khinda, the roadhead. I took to Word for Windows again:

Landslides have changed the face of the Khinda valley. Its fine wood and stone bridges have been washed away, and have been replaced by strands of yak leather, wound taut on wooden poles, temporary crossings for the local people. We have had to swing across on climbing harnesses. Initially, I had a restless night thinking about dangling above the torrent, but soon these river crossings became routine affairs – though never to be undertaken lightly. An hour or so before Khinda, we were tired and dusty. Elliot and I were separated by a few hundred metres. I saw him talking to a woman who was driving her goats down the valley. I stopped and they caught up. She was in her twenties, attractive with bright red cheeks. She was called Alo. They both looked animated. She seemed unhappy that Elliot's hair spread like the top of a carrot; she was shouting at him and pointing to it. A romance was in the air, but it went no further than glances. 'You should see how she throws a stone,' Elliot said with pride. I felt just slightly uneasy that someone else had spoken to 'my friend', and teased him mercilessly about his lover.

Towards dusk on Saturday, 5th September we arrived exhausted at Khinda, another village where we have friends from previous years. We met Tembe, the man with three fathers, and were welcomed as old friends. Our tents were soon up on the river bank. Elliot and I gazed across the river, a swirling muddy torrent across which last year there had been a fine footbridge. Now it was washed away. When I had last been there engineers and a construction gang were about to build a bridge for trucks and a motorable road to Samda. The funds had run out; two concrete pillars either side were all that remained. A single wire spanned the river. An old truck was parked on the opposite side.

Soon the expedition would arrive. We were suddenly conscious that our journey through these mountains was over. Our small and close-knit duo would soon be enveloped. A man I scarcely knew has become a close friend. This expedition will be a great endeavour too and I'll be seeing old comrades again. Perhaps we will be better fed, better housed and usually carry less heavy loads; but we will not enjoy again the isolation, the daily anticipation and wonder of the last three weeks.

We waited at Khinda for several days. One morning there was a cloud of dust in the distance far past Senza, the district headquarters up the valley. The boys were coming! Within minutes there were trucks and Land Cruisers on the river bank opposite. People leapt out and shouted instructions. Huge tripods appeared, with legs spread like lunar landing craft. Still cameras flashed and filming began. Elliot and I waved and slid quickly across the wire bridge on harnesses to return abruptly to the twentieth century. The first words we heard were, 'This is Chris Bonington for ITN, central Tibet,' as a news broadcast ended. Another life began.

11   Tortoises and Hares

1st – 20th September 1998

CHRIS BONINGTON

In September 1998 the landscape was so very different from the previous spring, more as it had been on our 1996 reconnaissance. The country was a subtle mixture of brown, sienna, purple and blue, the rivers full of swirling evil water, with muddy puddles on the beaten earth road. Blushes of green from the sparse grassland of the plateau stretched, undulating, towards distant hills, the green merging into varying shades of brown, grey and purple with tinges of red and black – signs of the geological origin of the rock and the chemical deposits in the Tibetan soil. Yak were dark dots scattered over the landscape, a flock of goats and sheep, guarded by a couple of little girls, moved slowly parallel to the road, browsing the thin shoots of grass. *Bas*, the yak-hair tents of the nomads, formed bigger splashes of brown in the distance.

I was sharing the Land Cruiser with Graham Little and Scott Muir.

Scott was in the front passenger seat. He had just changed the Tibetan pop music cassette in the Land Cruiser's player for one of his favourites he had borrowed from his father – The Doors, a 1970s group he had borrowed from his father.

'This must have been your kind of music,' he commented with a grin. I didn't like to tell him that I was probably considerably older than his father. His lower face was concealed by a bandanna, as were mine and Graham's, in an effort to exclude the pervasive dust of the Tibetan plateau. We looked like a trio of cowboys out of a B movie. Scott could certainly fill the part. Twenty-two years old, he has film star looks, with penetrating grey eyes, a broad smile from large, gleaming white teeth and regular features topped by a shock of blond hair. If Scott was the young cowboy out on his first round-up, Graham was the seasoned veteran. In his late forties, he is tall and lanky, with an often severe, even ascetic expression. They had first met when Scott, as a lad, attended one of Graham's lectures and it was this that had inspired him to take up climbing. They met again when Scott was already gaining a reputation as a forceful young climber, made several routes together in Scotland and Graham then invited him to join Jim Lowther and himself on the Kulu Eiger.

Graham commented ruefully on the way that Scott tended to vanish over the horizon when they were walking up to a climb in exactly the same way that Graham did with me, when we were climbing together.

For them, it was a first impression of the Tibetan plateau.

'I had no idea it was going to be so fertile,' commented Graham.

I had been just as surprised on my first visit and even now, although I was more familiar with it, I still couldn't help wondering at the huge empty beauty of the scenery, with the great arch of the sky dotted with fluffy clouds.

The three-man media team was in the first Land Cruiser. Martin Belderson, the director, was anxious to stay out in front to film us in suitably dramatic or beautiful spots as we rolled over the Tibetan plateau. Of the three, I only knew Jim Curran and was very happy that we had him along again. We had done so much together in the past. He had filmed with me on Kongur in 1981, on Rangrik Rang in 1994; we had been climbing, playing darts or drinking together in the Avon Gorge whenever I had lectured in Bristol over the years. Jim had taught at the local art college until 1993 when he took early retirement to base himself in the Sheffield he loves and concentrate on his writing and film-making. He has written a powerful yet sensitive account of the 1986 K2 tragedy, when thirteen climbers, including one of his best friends, Al Rouse, died. He went on to write an excellent history of K2 and was now embarking on my biography. It is not often that one has the official biographer on an expedition.

For our present trip, Jim was the main cameraman. There were originally to be two, but Rob Franklin fell ill in Lhasa and returned to the UK. He was working for Northern Films, a small independent company with whom I had worked before. I had never met Martin Belderson before we started planning the expedition, but was impressed by the way he mucked in with us, was always ready to help, but most of all, by the very genuine concern he seemed to have for us as a team. The third member of our media group was Greig Cubitt from Independent Television News. His role was to send news stories of our climb back to ITN by satellite. Quiet and affable, he was like many ITN cameramen I have met, self-sufficient, unflappable, completely professional and yet very easy to get on with. We had already become a single team rather than being a group of climbers watched and filmed by the media.

A last tortuous road over the pass and we were dropping into the Salween valley. The previous year the route had been paved with ice. Now it was clad in grass with a shallow river tumbling at its foot. The Salween came into sight, brown, turgid and full, swirling its way towards Burma and the Bay of Bengal. Before long we started passing strings of horsemen and women dressed in their best, all heading down the valley. We soon came across their destination, a line of gaily marked white tents by the roadside selling every kind of ware from clothing and harnesses to food and transistor radios. The stalls were just below the first big *stupa* of the valley which was so gift-wrapped in prayer flags you could barely see it. We joined the throng of people making towards it, old women telling rosaries or spinning prayer wheels as they walked, young bloods, their long hair interwoven with bright red cord, the mark of a Khamba man, swaggering around, some of them obviously the worse for drink. There was a happy, holiday feel to it all. We discovered it was the religious festival, Kama Dunpa, when the Seventh Star is seen in the sky and all troubles and problems can be washed away, yaks become strong and the grass lush and green. We made a contribution to the *stupa* and continued on our way to Diru.

Like Nakchu it had changed in the intervening fifteen months since we had last been there. The bridge had been swept away and there was a diversion in the centre of the little town, and right in the middle of the village they had built a modern-style shopping mall with stainless steel shutters and lock-up shops of the blue, semi-opaque glass the Chinese seem so fond of, and the shiny plastic facing that becomes shabby almost before the building has been completed. Even the compound where we had stayed on our two previous visits was being up-graded with the open-corridor balcony on the first floor having been filled in with glass and the muddy courtyard paved with rounded stones from the river embedded in concrete.

But there was still no sewage system or running water. The modern flashy buildings seemed an empty façade, almost a cinema set, imposed upon this old Tibetan town. That night we went to the little Chinese restaurant we had used on the two previous occasions. This also had moved on. As I opened the door I was greeted by the blare of western pop music churned out from a giant television screen. The outer room that had been empty the previous year had been turned into a night club, with booths round the walls where shadowy hostesses waited, but the rooms where we had eaten were unchanged, with their incongruous pictures of tropical beaches and the sailing ship around the walls. The food was still remarkably good even if the music was overwhelming.

Next morning we set off up the final pass, zigzagging over into the Yu-chong valley. It was like coming home as we drove past the empty school buildings just short of the roadhead. I had never seen any children studying there but, as it was now the height of the harvest, presumably they were all excused school to help their parents. The fields were golden with the ripe barley.

Charlie had warned us on the phone that the bridge was down. The entire base on our bank had been swept away. The two tall concrete plinths of the new bridge stood sadly to one side. Now there was no footbridge, as this too had been washed away. There was just the steel cable.

I could pick out the tents on the other bank. Suddenly I saw Charlie, suspended upside down from the wire over the river, partly pulling and shinning, partly being hauled up towards us. It was wonderful seeing him again, though I couldn't help feeling envious. He and Elliot had had the same kind of adventure that I had enjoyed in 1996. I had had a flavour of it from his reports for the website. They had certainly achieved a great deal, not only in their exploratory approach but also in their recce of the western approaches to Sepu Kangri. I was longing to hear their story but now there was much to do. Apart from the beard, Charlie looked remarkably similar to when I had last seen him at our packing weekend at the beginning of August. I had somehow expected him to look much leaner.

We had two lorryloads of gear to transfer across the river. I left the others to it, while I accompanied Dorje and Tachei Tshering, our new liaison officer, to see the district leader to arrange for the hire of some yaks. Tachei, a quiet man in his late thirties, spoke no English but had already shown himself to be eager to help. We gathered that he had been appointed liaison officer, with Dorje acting as his interpreter, because of Tachei's greater seniority within the CTMA and that they wanted him to check out the potential of the area for commercial trekking expeditions. We drove to the district headquarters but were told that the leader was down by the river. We returned to find him by a pavilion-like tent pitched close to the bridge. There had been a change of district leader since last year which was a pity, for his predecessor had broken his leg and been treated by Charlie. The new leader was a plump smooth-looking man dressed in a suit. I presented him with a Victorinox watch and knife, which he initially refused but was persuaded by Dorje to accept.

Unfortunately, it didn't make him any more helpful. He told us that we had come at a very bad time – it always seemed a bad time – that all the yaks and horses were being used to bring in the harvest and we couldn't possibly have any for another week. After some persuasion, he relented and agreed to write a letter to the village headmen in the valley leading up to Samda. At this point, one of Tembe's fathers entered the discussion. It was Tembe who had found us our yaks back in 1996 and we had become good friends. This father was the headman of Khinda, the village on the other side of the river. We thought he was going to be an ally but quickly discovered that he had his own agenda. He told the headman that no one would be able to spare any horses or yaks until the harvest was in but that he could then provide us with all the yaks we would need all the way up to base camp – good business for him!

I said how important it was to get away as quickly as possible, but matters were all left very much in the air. That afternoon we shifted about half the loads. It wasn't just the time it took us to haul them across but, as this was the only means of crossing the river, we had to give way to the constant flow of locals also wanting to haul themselves, their packages and even their bikes over. They used a little slider made of hard wood, that fitted over the wire and was attached by a yak-hair rope that they made into a harness, so they could sit comfortably and haul themselves hand over hand. We finished shifting the loads the following morning and the next three days were spent negotiating for yaks, with plans being made and changed on an almost hourly basis.

On the night of 9th September we were assured that we would have thirty horses the following morning, not enough to shift all our gear and food but at least we could move the entire team, leaving behind some of the big communal tents, a lot of the food and our fuel. Elliot, on the grounds that he had already had an adventurous time and that we needed Charlie as our doctor, was nominated to stay with the rear party. Next morning only fifteen horses turned up with the warning that this was all we were going to get. All change. I felt we needed to get the climbing team up as soon as possible but the others could wait, except for Jim Curran who set out straight away so that he could film our activities. We started to re-adjust all the loads to fit the new plan, and half an hour later another twenty horses turned up. This meant we could take more loads and as we laid out our kit it became evident that we could carry with us most of the gear we were going to need in the next few days. However it was now so late it was obvious we weren't going to get far that day. So I opted to stop at Bakrong – the first village, just three hours' walk from Khinda.

That raised another problem. Jim had already set out and was bound for a spot we had stopped at the previous year. Graham Little came to the rescue, offering that he and Scott Muir would push ahead and catch Jim up. It was characteristic of Graham to want to be out in front and in some ways a source of worry. We already seemed to be developing into two separate pairs rather than being a team of four. Graham and Scott shared a restless energy that had earned them the nickname of 'the hares', with Victor and me picking up the rear as 'the tortoises'. Victor and I talked about it as we strolled up the track leading out of Khinda. There were more differences than that of speed and fitness. We detected in Graham an impatience, indeed intolerance, of the ways of Tibet and the tempo of an expedition, the delays caused by the harvest and possible manipulation by Tembe's father, and yet, even as we discussed it, I think both Victor and I became aware of how paranoid we were becoming. This could be potentially divisive.

We stopped for a leisurely packed lunch, provided by Pemba, only to find that our campsite was just round the corner. A slightly disgruntled Jim Curran was waiting for us. He had made good progress and Graham had only overtaken him when he was well beyond Bakrong. Graham and Scott had opted to press on to Samda and wait for us there, while Jim, who did not have his sleeping bag with him, returned to Bakrong.

We caught up with the hares the following day just below Samda, where another yak-hide rope provided the way across another river. The cantilever bridge we had used on previous occasions had been swept away in the recent floods. Graham and Scott looked decidedly sorry for themselves. The previous day they had failed to reach the crossing point. It was even further than I remembered, and they had walked until it was dark and slept under a tree. It was only after Graham's Therm-a-Rest airbed deflated, that they realised it was a thorn tree. They had crossed the river the next morning and walked to the Samda monastery but had received a cool reception and been unable to get anything to eat. They were finally offered some *tsampa* but had not found it to their liking.

'Serve 'em right for rushing ahead and being so fit,' was the general if unexpressed feeling.

We had another full day's stop at the crossing, waiting for the yaks to arrive from the villages further up the valley. It gave us plenty of time to haul over all our loads, charge up the computer and phone batteries and generally catch up with ourselves. It was warm and sunny. We were con-gratulating ourselves on choosing the right season and doing our research on the weather: crystal clear nights and fine days.

We finally reached base camp on 13th September. The warmth of the greeting that Tsini and Karte gave me was truly heartening. I was invited up to their house and given Tibetan tea and yoghurt. It was as if we had never left, although we had also come full circle. On our departure the previous year, Sam Tso Taring, the Sacred Lake, had still been clad in ice, the ground covered by freshly fallen snow. Now it was like going back to the summer of 1996 with the water of the lake, as it had been then, an opaque grey-brown from the glacier sediment fed from the glaciers. The grass was still a lush green and though it was mid-September summer still seemed very much with us.

We were faced with our first crisis almost immediately. It had nothing to do with climbing. The previous day I had noticed our yak train had forded the river just below Sam Tso Taring, perhaps to call in at one of the *bas* that were pitched on that side of the river. I had thought nothing more about it until the yaks arrived at base camp and were unloaded. Several of the loads had been soaked, including the alloy box containing the Toko computer, a vital piece of equipment for downloading the news reports by satellite back to ITN. Greig Cubitt was amazingly laid back about it all. He gave it a day in the sun to dry out. Next morning when he tried to power it up nothing happened. He took it apart patiently, using the satellite phone to talk to technicians at home. It still wouldn't work. We started planning how to have another machine sent out. But on the third day, presumably having dried out completely, quite miraculously it started to work. Greig had saved the day. Charlie, too, found his calm resourcefulness a godsend:

I had more than a little problem and began to seethe. Nothing worked. All I wanted to do was send an e-mail. But I found there was no power for the Mobiq (the satellite phone), none for Chris's Apple Macs, and none for my own Toshiba Libretto PC. The solar power and wind power systems hadn't really worked since we'd arrived; and I had been rather sheepish about it all. They had all been my baby.

Outside it was dusk after a sunny day had blazed non-stop at two banks of solar panels. It had begun to snow, and a fresh breeze across the lake was turning both, not just one of the wind generators. One, an Ampair, was whirring silently, and working well. The second, an Airwind, wobbled uncontrollably and looked as if it might fly off its pole. At speed it resembled a Stuka divebomber, delivering a package of fear to anyone nearby, despite an attractive power output.

Also, our custom-built rechargable battery power unit, christened 'the Magic Box', was dead, despite the full day of sun, and the present wind. I had also been trying to charge its back-up, an encased 12-volt battery, for three weeks. This too had zero voltage output. The hours went by in frustration, fiddling with switches on 'the Box', and measuring voltages.

Greig Cubitt and I were alone at our base camp beside the lake. I just wanted to throw everything into the water, scream and go away. I had spent about six months planning the various power units for our communications systems, around £3000 (of our sponsors' money), and, I guess, £1000 transporting it all here. It doesn't work. 'It'll never work, it's too fucking complicated,' Ruth, my wife, had said, months ago. 'Why don't you take a proper generator, or someone who knows what they are doing?' I had stormed off into the garden. 'I'll show her . . .' I told Gemma, the ageing retriever, who, having been listening attentively, skulked under the table.

Eventually, I asked Greig if he'd like a whisky, and if all was well with his family. I think he knew what was coming. He was so organised. His two Honda EX500 generators purred away quietly, produced live three-pin sockets, powered a TV editing suite, and transmitted film to the world apparently with no difficulty and no cursing. He seemed to know exactly what he was doing. After the second scotch I broached the subject of the generators. 'Of course, but you can't have them all the time,' he said in his kindly way. 'It's only a question of fuel.'

Wish I had brought them myself, I thought. They weigh less than a yakload. High octane fuel had been available in Lhasa. The local children even know how to start them now.

The blame, it must be admitted, was mine. I had tried to organise a system which was too complex, and despite the months of preparation, there had been little time for real testing, particularly of the base camp equipment. Some of it all worked well, some of it didn't, but we muddled through, though we were entirely reliant on Greig's generators.

For the attempt on Sepu Kangri we adopted a different philosophy from the previous year, favouring a more alpine-style approach rather than fixing a lot of rope, and therefore decided to take acclimatisation steadily, making a series of training climbs that could also ensure an effective reconnaissance. I wanted to have a much better look at the possibility of getting round the side of the Turquoise Flower to reach the western approaches of the mountain. This was the route that Jim Fotheringham had favoured and which we had reconnoitred but had failed to push through to a satisfactory conclusion. Elliot and Charlie's recce over the Yam La had also helped. We had their digital photos of the upper slopes of the western flank of the mountain. Graham and Scott wanted to have a close look at the route we had used the previous year – the Frendo Spur, as we had named it. Victor and I decided to walk up the hill immediately south of base with a view to looking at the head of the valley and the route round the side of Sepu Kangri on which we had made our abortive foray in 1997.

First we had to cross the isthmus between the upper and lower lakes. There were more icebergs than on the two previous occasions, the result perhaps of the heavy rains. Some were shaped like ships and submarines and one of them was just like the classic pictures of the Loch Ness monster. The stream between the two lakes was running fast and deep but fanned out at its entry into the main lake. Victor took off his boots while I relied on the waterproof quality and length of my Yeti gaiters to stay dry as I picked a way from one stream to the next in the shale delta. I crowed about how dry my socks were when Victor complained that his feet were frozen, ignoring the fact that my own were decidedly damp, too. We moved on up the winding path through dense shrubbery of willow, catkins hanging from their slender branches. It was as if we had never been away.

It took us past the home of Sam Tsen Tsokpu, the hermit. He was waiting for us in front of his house with Graham and Scott, who had set out earlier. He hadn't changed. The same sense of tranquillity emanated from him and long dark ringlets of hair framed a face in repose that broke easily into a smile as he offered us hot water. Without an interpreter I tried to communicate in sign language my pleasure at seeing him again and being back in this beautiful spot. He gestured us inside, sat on the bed intoning a prayer, blessed us, gave each of us a pill containing nutmeg and tied a bunch of coloured wool strands to the thread I already had around my neck. I tried to explain that the Akong Rinpoche, high lama of Samye Ling in Scotland, had given it to me. I couldn't make myself understood: he just smiled benignly.

I felt happy and relaxed as we walked across the flat-bottomed valley and then very slowly, through willow and azalea, up the grassy slopes towards the spot that Charlie and I had reached in 1996 on that very first recce. I was feeling the altitude, the back of my throat was sore, but I still delighted in the green of the grass, the blue and purple gentians peeping out. Above, the curving sweep of the Frendo Spur dropped down from Seamo Uyl-mitok, the Turquoise Flower, the Daughter of Sepu. We stopped for lunch by a tumbling stream of clear water. Pemba our cook had prepared a packed lunch of peanut butter and marmalade sandwiches. We were spoilt indeed. I pointed out to Victor the route we had taken the previous year and the sites of our camps. He commented on how unstable the upper séracs seemed. They certainly looked more pronounced than they had seemed the previous year.

We traversed the slope towards a broken rocky ridge from where we hoped to get a better view of the ridge leading round to the back of the mountain, where we had had the cursory reconnaissance the previous year. Victor shared my growing enthusiasm for the potential of the outflanking route. From this point the way up to the crest of the Frendo looked even more inhospitable than it had in the spring of 1997 when it had been snow-covered. It was now a dark talus slope below crumbling rock. We carried on, Victor gaining ground as we picked our way across the steep yak pasture. To my relief he stopped on the top of a craggy spur for another gaze at prospective routes.

We could see no sign of Graham and Scott. They had walked up the far side of the glacier, a mile or so away, intending to investigate the route to the crest of the ridge and, at close range, the state of the old fixed ropes that we had left. We now had sufficient height to get some tantalising views of the mountains to the north, behind and above base camp. They were much lower than Sepu Kangri and, according to the map, all below 6000 metres, but we had glimpse of glaciers and jagged rocky peaks over which Victor enthused – one always has the dream of further climbing once the main objective is disposed of, and so rarely has the chance to realise it.

We wandered back down to base during the afternoon, chatting about future plans, at ease with each other and well satisfied with our preliminary reconnaissance. Next morning I was down with a heavy cold – my Achilles' heel on so many expeditions. Illness had been going the rounds. Graham had been struck down in Lhasa, spending most of the time there in bed. Rob Franklin, the cameraman from Northern Films, had been so ill we had left him in Lhasa to recover and catch us up later, but he returned to Kathmandu and then to Britain. Victor had been sick at Khinda. Now it was my turn.

I resigned myself to resting whilst the others set out on a series of energetic day walks. The very afternoon that Victor and I returned from our first foray, Charlie set out alone to climb the peak behind the camp; he left at about three and was back just in time for supper, having managed a height gain of nearly a thousand metres in a couple of hours, which showed how he had benefited from his long exploratory walk. He bounced into camp at dusk, proud of the modest 5700-metre rock summit, the first of the trip. I just wished I felt as strong.

The following morning, the hares, Graham and Scott, tackled a higher summit just beyond Charlie's peak, reaching the top after crossing a shattered ridge of alarming tottering towers that gave warning of the quality of the rock on Sepu Kangri itself. They came down, full of elation too and with a discovery. Graham was convinced that the big rounded summit of Sepu was the highest point, and not the slender spire, Sepu's Eldest Son, marked as highest on the Chinese map.

The next day Charlie and Victor set out to climb the peak immediately behind and west of base camp. Charlie wrote about it:

I was absolutely bubbling with energy. I felt embarrassed to have left Elliot out of it, he was still somewhere down the valley with the loads, but Vic wanted to come. We had explored the approaches previously and had been to see Puh and his family in their tent on our way down, feasting on fresh sheep cooked in the cauldron of cheese he was making. It wasn't a major summit, but a snow dome of about 5800 metres on top of a rock ridge. I was quietly conceited that I was moving faster than Victor on the approach. To hell with guides, I thought. I can do this. I'm faster than him.

We scrambled up the rock ridge unroped and reached the base of the snow a couple of hundred metres or so from what looked like the top. I suddenly didn't like the snow. It looked easy enough, but to the south the face on top of which we were standing descended at an increasing angle. 'This is all going to go,' I said and whimpered. I was very very miserable, like a child. We had a fine view, and to go to the top would simply be peak-bagging. Victor was confident and took me firmly in hand.

'Look, you silly twit, this is my job. I know this slope is fine. It's granular snow on ice, well formed and there isn't a chance of it avalanching. I'll solo it with pleasure.' He made as if to untie. I continued whimpering and followed on the rope, trying not to look down. It was, of course, perfectly easy. After less than an hour the ridge fell away in front of us. We were on the top. Sepu and its satellites stretched across the southern horizon. A fine 6000-metre peak stuck out in the southwest, somewhere around Lharigo. I felt equally scared on the way down but then, as always happens, it was all forgotten. We dropped back down the rock ridge, walked down the scree and stood beneath the snow face.

I almost wanted to crampon up it. Victor called our summit Charlie' s
Peak. I thought it was a name which would never stick and wondered
about *Amchhi Inji-ne*, The English Doctor. We dropped in again at
Puh's. He had *momos* cooking. I over-ate and had another of Pemba's
vast evening meals at base. God, he can cook.

One morning after a warm spell several days later, Victor was rather
silent. This was unusual. There was something shifty about him. I
pottered about and quaffed a gargantuan breakfast, and then glanced
up at *Amchhi Inji-ne*. A grey nearly horizontal line now ran just below
the summit crest. Our footsteps were still just visible through the
binoculars. The entire face had avalanched below our tracks. I decided
I had better stick to trekking and carrying loads from base. Bugger
guides, and serious climbing, I thought . . .

Meanwhile I had dosed myself up with vitamin C on Charlie's advice and
caught up with e-mails, crouched over my computer in the comms tent. It
was much busier than in 1997, with sometimes twenty messages coming in
the e-mail daily. This, combined with downloading digital pictures for the
website, could take much of a day. It was certainly a high-tech expedition
with a worrying hunger for electrical power. The team had four computers
and the two satellite phones, with all of them on the go for much of the
time. Greig had his editing suite, the big Toko computer that was now up
and running as well as the high-speed data terminal, all of which gobbled
electricity. He had brought with him two Honda two-stroke generators, on
which, as Charlie has related, we had become increasingly dependent. We
discovered that there was barely enough wind to turn our two windmills.
The array of solar panels could barely keep up with the demand on a sunny
day, let alone when the cloud rolled in. I worried that the fine weather of
the approach march had vanished. It was often cloudy and there was the
occasional snow shower at base.

Elliot at last caught up with us on 17th September, having escorted the
baggage and food we had left behind at the roadhead all the way up to base
camp. Victor and I had already decided to ask him to join us on our recce
of the approach to the western flank of Sepu Kangri, though at this stage
we had no plans to consider him as part of our serious climbing team, as
he was still comparatively inexperienced. Graham and Scott were planning
to attempt Chomo Mangyal, the Wife of Sepu, a peak of 6236 metres at the
far eastern end of the Sepu Kangri massif. It looked the easiest of the Sepu
peaks and would make a good training climb and a fine first ascent Scott

and Graham set out early the following morning, planning to camp just below the peak.

I left most of the preparation for our trip to Victor and Elliot, while I worked with Greig to complete our first real report for ITN, finishing it off with a piece to camera, while two of our young neighbours held up the reflector to light my face. So it was two o'clock before I was ready to leave, having hurriedly packed all my gear. I felt harassed and ill-prepared, though my head was less full of cold. The other two had waited for me, and we walked together across the isthmus at the head of the lake, weighed down by huge packs. We trailed slowly up through the willow wood, past the hermit's home and on up the valley beyond. The previous year we had struggled up the side of the glacier but Charlie had found a much better route on the way down, staying on the crest of the moraine. I now took over the lead, trying to remember our route in reverse but ended up going much too high. We had to lose precious height to catch the end of the moraine that led easily to the head of the glacier. Victor and Elliot followed, joking about my memory and route-finding ability, but it was good-humoured stuff: I felt at ease with our little team.

There was hardly a path and our route switchbacked along the crest of the moraine and over piles of rock slide debris, but we were making good progress in reasonable weather. However, in the late afternoon, the clouds that had been steadily building up finally burst in a deluge. By the time I had unpacked my sack to dig out an anorak packed near the bottom, the other two had vanished.

I was beginning to feel tired and prayed that they wouldn't have pressed on up the long slopes leading to where we eventually hoped to camp, in striking distance of the ridge. So I felt an immense sense of relief when I rounded a corner and saw Victor and Elliot erecting a bright yellow tent under a rocky overhang. It had stopped raining by the time we had the tent up. But I didn't like the look of the block of rock that was hanging like the Sword of Damocles over it.

We had a look round the corner where the valley opened out into a pasture with a stream of gritty brown water tumbling through it. It was altogether more pleasant and less threatening and so we shifted camp a few metres, re-pitched the two tents and started to prepare the evening meal. It was an idyllic site, the grass still green and lush, for this was beyond where the yaks grazed. Some small droppings indicated the presence of chamois or small deer.

There was a rumble from the Wall of Death, as we had named the huge sérac wall at the head of the valley where the upper Thong Wuk Glacier was forced over the retaining wall of the ridge we were about to investigate. A shaft of sunlight broke through the clouds to light the hills down the valley, just above base camp. I felt happier than I had been at any time on the expedition. Worries about e-mails and administration, about my own fitness and whether I could keep up with the others just slid away. Victor cooked a soup-like mess of dehydrated potato into which we mixed a tin of mackerel. We had settled into the usual sparring rapport. There was no sense of competition, though I sometimes wondered whether Elliot, who we referred to as 'the porter', Victor being 'the guide', became fed up with having his junior and youthful position constantly brought up. I was very much the old man of the party.

That night the rain hammered on the single-skin tents. They were an experimental design, much lighter than the tents we had used previously, but being single-skin there was condensation inside, though it didn't seem to be excessive. Since we only had a few hundred metres to climb the next day, we didn't bother to set the alarm, started brewing once it was light, and relaxed in the early morning sun.

At the morning call Charlie told me that Graham and Scott were back from their attempt on Chomo Mangyal. They reckoned they were within 200 metres of the summit on the north ridge when they were forced to turn back because of the avalanche risk. The snow had been appalling. They had camped the previous day at the toe of the glacier footing the north flank of the peak and set out at 7 p.m., planning to climb through the night, a tactic that Graham always favoured. They had hoped to climb the west ridge but the route to the crest proved to be much harder than they had anticipated and they spent most of the night floundering up unconsolidated snow lying on steep very hard ice. In the dawn they found that the west ridge was covered in dangerous windslab and therefore they traversed across to the north ridge below a sérac wall, only to find steep bottomless snow. Graham wrote in his diary: 'At a height of 6000 metres we both agreed that to press on would be to risk too much. There are many good reasons not to die.'

At least they were rewarded with some superb views of the north-east ridge and the face of Sepu Kangri and the peaks immediately to the east.

We couldn't help having that naughty little bit of satisfaction, combined with the glow of virtue at our own role in carrying out a worthy recon-naissance, that the hares had had their comeuppance. It put an extra spring into our steps as we set out for the top of the moraine, some 300 metres above.

It was so different from the previous year. Then we had climbed this route in the dark up snow-covered slopes that had a thin crust which broke under our weight every two or three paces. Now we could see where we were going and I set off first, picking my way across the slope trying to find a grassy path through the scattered scree and boulders. My sack felt lighter and I was exhilarated by the prospect of finding a way round the side of Sepu Kangri. I'd even pulled far ahead of the others. I sat and waited for them and then started up a ramp poised over a deep moraine valley with a small lake in its bottom, to reach a broken buttress. Scrambling led us awkwardly yet enjoyably to the top, Victor and Elliot making ribald comments again about my memory and route-finding ability. I explained how different it had been all covered in snow and in the dark.

A final stretch and we were on the crest of a moraine at the side of the glacier sweeping down from the ridge which bounded the west face of Sepu Kangri. This was where we had camped on our way down last year. Then it had been covered in snow. Now it was a rocky moraine with a few fairly flat gravel-covered areas on which we worked to make tent platforms. We had finished by two in the afternoon, had our third brew and first dissension.

Victor suggested he showed Elliot how to shorten a rope. This entails putting coils round your shoulder to reduce the length of the rope when moving together. It was all good stuff, and I told Victor I was quite sure I, too, had a lot to learn. As a self-taught climber, as most of us are, you muddle along a bit with methods that might not be quite as efficient as they should be, but they work for you. Then somehow, I'm not sure whether it was the guidespeak voice that I felt Victor was adopting, or perhaps my own difficulty in accepting the systematic and very efficient way he made the loops and tied the knot, but I found myself going into a diatribe about guides and the fact that we were just three climbers together and not two clients. Concern about my age and whether I could keep up with the others and contribute my bit undoubtedly made me more edgy. It was all rather unfair and definitely over-the-top on my part, but it was to be a recurrent theme in what was otherwise a very happy climbing relationship. Victor commented in his diary, 'Chris has taken strongly against mountain guides, which is a pity, for I am one.' I wasn't the only one to be strangely unreasonable about mountain guides, as it turned out.

I think it was I who first suggested we should try to reach the crest of the ridge, some 400 metres above us. Whether it was me trying to assert my amateur energy or just to clear the air, I'm not at all sure, but we all quickly forgot about the minor bust-up as we clipped on crampons and started plodding up the dirty gravelled ice leading towards the ridge.

The previous year we had made for the lowest point, a rocky notch, whose approach had been covered in snow. This now seemed more rocky and unattractive. Victor had picked out a line while making the first ascent of Amchhi Inji-ne. It was close to the point where Fotheringham's Ridge, as it soon became known, reached the upper Thong Wuk Glacier. We were hoping there would be a corridor into what we christened the Western Cwm of Sepu Kangri. But that afternoon we took the line of least resistance just to get a good view. We kept to the ice and later the snow slopes that led to a little peak well to the west of the corridor.

I felt good, was out in front picking the route, zigzagging up the ice and crossing a snow slope of porridge-like snow to the crest of the ridge. It was a magnificent situation. One side of the ridge dropped away steeply to the Yanglung Glacier far below, whilst on the other side towered the shapely pyramid mass of Lhallum Tamcho, whose steep ice-veined walls Charlie and I had admired in 1996 when we had made our recce to the south. The pointed summit was crowned with a huge overhanging cornice. A sheer wall barred the head of the glacier, like that of the Thong Wuk, with even bigger séracs poised above it. Fotheringham's Ridge offered the only safe approach to this aspect of Sepu Kangri and the line that Victor had picked out would enable us to avoid traversing the knife-edged crest of the ridge.

We traversed along the ridge, letting ourselves down a little cornice which reminded me of the one on top of Number Four Gully on Ben Nevis, the easy way back down. Then we strode easily back down to camp, well pleased with our day out. The weather seemed to be clearing. Maybe this was the start of the post-monsoon settled weather. Poised high above the Thong Wuk Glacier in our moraine camp, we were almost level with the site of our previous camp II at the foot of the Frendo Spur. We were already in shadow, but the west face of the Turquoise Flower was bathed in the golden sunlight of the late afternoon. It slowly changed from gold, to pink, to a purple that crept up the face until all was black against the darkening sky.

We set out an hour before dawn the next day and were delighted to find that wet porridge snow had frozen into firm névé. The ink-black sky glittered with stars as we stepped up the crisp snow in little pools of light from our headtorches. As we gained height the horizon to the east lightened with a band that turned from red to gold, a reverse of the spectacular light show we had had the previous evening. It was daylight when we reached the shallow gully between the end of the rocky wall of Fotheringham's Ridge and the sheer sérac walls that stretched all the way to the Thong Wuk icefall. It was the only break and looked feasible. I was determined to have my share of leading – doing my bit, not being guided. Nothing to do with ego, I thought. Victor happily agreed and was already hammering in a peg for the belay while Elliot uncoiled the rope.

It started with an easy plod up knee-deep, soft snow. The gully's walls guarded it from the rays of the sun so that snow hadn't consolidated. The angle steepened, the ice beneath the snow was steel hard and I felt progressively less secure. I was about twenty-five metres above the others, dug out a trough in the snow, screwed in an ice piton as a runner, and worked my way crab-like back into the corner where I could secure a good rock belay.

It was Victor's turn to lead. I felt greedy. I would have loved to have led the next pitch. It was steeper, more exciting, a vertical wall of ice abutting sheer smooth rock. Victor moved steadily. His tools were sinking into the ice with a reassuring thwuck. He disappeared over the bulge. The rope ran out, there was a long delay and then a call to come up. By the time I had jumared up the rope that we planned to leave in place, Victor was already traversing a boss of ice to a platform on the crest of the sérac wall. He let out a yell of triumph. It was easy ground beyond. The route he had spied from a distance had indeed proved to be a winner.

We were now able to move together on a single rope, taking turns to go out in front. We were working well as a team on this lovely cloudless morning, plodding across slopes of névé below the crest of the ridge, until near its end we climbed up on to its rounded top. We were looking down on the icefall that spilled into the Thong Wuk Glacier but the glacier above looked reasonably straightforward, winding round the side of Seamo Uylmitok, the Turquoise Flower. This led up into the upper basin Elliot and Charlie had seen three weeks or more earlier leading towards the summit mass of Sepu. There were threatening séracs high on the west face of the Turquoise Flower, and ice walls and crevasses stretching across the glacier, but these looked negotiable.

We strode down the slope towards a broad shoulder on the side of the glacier. We were revelling in the beauty, in the discovery of what seemed a good route up the mountain and the sight of more peaks on every side, which we could explore and tackle once we had Sepu Kangri out of the way. We were enjoying that heady optimism that comes so easily on a perfect day.

We sat and brewed a pan full of tea and talked over plans. We joked about Elliot's probationary period as team porter. Victor particularly enjoyed rubbing it in, which I suspect Elliot was finding irritating by now, though he hid it well. He was a delightful companion, very steady and moved well on snow and ice. I felt it high time that we made him a full member of the team and invited him to join. He gave a slight smile and bowed. We then turned round and started back down, dropping all the way back to base camp. We were content, were going strongly, got on well together and, best of all, we thought we had found the route up Sepu Kangri.

12 The First Attempt

25th September – 1st October 1998

CHRIS BONINGTON

There was no time to wait. I just had to have a crap: there wasn't even time to put on any clothes. I crawled out of my warm sleeping bag, frantically unzipped the tent door and scrambled, stark naked and bare foot into the dark. I hardly noticed the cold or the sharp rocks hidden under the freshly fallen snow. I couldn't get far from the tents before the diarrhoea wracked me. Oh, the misery of it! I could feel the cold of the wind on my bare skin and the sting of spindrift. I fled back to the tent. I had been up four times that night. I crawled back into my sleeping bag, prayed this would be the last attack, and eventually dropped off to sleep.

We were at camp I on the moraine, on our way, we hoped, to the top of Sepu Kangri. The hares, Graham and Scott, had left a day early to re-rig the climbing rope Victor, Elliot and I had left in place on 20th September. It was now nearly a week later. The rest of us, with Martin Belderson to film our departure, had set out on the 25th. Just before we left Pasang had produced a flag that had been given to him by Sam Ten Tsokpu. On the flag he had written a prayer and asked that we should take it to the summit. I found this endorsement of our plans very reassuring. We were carrying food and fuel for five days and were so confident of success that we were already planning what peaks we were going to try once we had Sepu Kangri out of the way.

Victor and I had walked up together. My cold had just about vanished and I was feeling sufficiently fit to be able to chat amicably as we traversed the moraine to the meadow before the final slog up to camp I. Victor had pulled away from me at this point, but I still felt I was going reasonably well. The cloud had been building up throughout the afternoon and a flash of sheet lightning, followed by a rumble of thunder, gave warning of the storm that was about to engulf us. There wasn't too much wind, but it started to snow in big fluffy flakes.

It snowed heavily most of the night. We had originally planned to set out at 3.30 a.m. and reach our previous high point before dawn to be poised to make as much progress as possible up into the corridor of the upper Yanglung Glacier that day. However, it was still snowing at 3.30, and I suspect I was not the only one to feel a sense of relief as I settled back down to sleep. It was light when I next woke and we carried out a shouted discussion between the tents about what to do. The cloud was still down and intermittent snow flurries swirled around us. Although only twenty centimetres or so had fallen during the night, Victor and Graham were concerned about the risk of avalanches. So was I. In addition, the gear and spare food were in a mess, partly buried in the freshly fallen snow. We had left a cache of food under a cairn but all of this, with the exception of a single can of salmon, had vanished. Could this have been marmots, the smaller pica, a fox, or perhaps even the *yeti*?

We decided that we would probably stay put that day, then considered going down to avoid using up the food we had so laboriously carried up. Finally, we agreed to keep two people at camp I so that they could work on the camp, while the rest descended to get more supplies. It was Graham who suggested that we really needed to turn camp I into an advance base as a sound jumping-off point for the summit attempt. Then Elliot reminded me it was time for the eight o'clock radio call to Charlie at base camp. I struggled into my clothes and boots and ploughed up to the boulder just above the camp, from where we had found we had the best reception, to discuss our plans with Charlie and ask if he could organise a carry to camp I and some animal-proof food containers.

I wandered back to the others and immediately sensed a tension among the little group standing by the tents. Victor, with a scowl on his face, was muttering about bloody waste and irresponsibility. One of our Coleman stoves was lying rather sadly in the snow. Apparently Graham or Scott had hurled theirs out of the tent in a fit of exasperation, after struggling unsuccessfully to light it. The rest of the team were standing around, looking subdued and embarrassed. I realised I couldn't let this fester, so asked Victor what the problem was.

'Let's sort this out once and for all,' I told him. Then addressing the team as a whole I said, 'Come on everyone, you'd better be in on this,' and I invited Victor to air his grievance. It all came tumbling out, that Graham never listened to any of Victor's suggestions, that he rubbished everything

Victor said. Then the final straw was that Graham had never taken our route round the back seriously but had always ridiculed it.

I felt I had to intervene on this one: 'Hang on, Victor, that's not fair. Graham agreed to this route and he's been really enthusiastic about it.'

At this point Graham said he was sorry he had offended Victor. But he didn't sound very sorry, and spoilt it all by going on to point out that Victor was quite fond of making jokes at other people's expense, so this had just been a case of the boot being on the other foot.

I finally exploded. 'For God's sake stop behaving like children. This is a bloody fabulous mountain and we're here to enjoy ourselves and climb it. Can't you give each other a chance? Come on, shake hands and let's get on with the climb.'

They shook hands without much enthusiasm. I had put a lot into trying to bring them together and felt myself almost on the point of tears. I walked away just to regain my own sense of balance. On returning, to brush the whole thing away, I suggested that, while the rest of us returned to base for the night, Victor and Graham should stay up at camp I to get to know and appreciate each other a little better. It raised a welcome laugh when I announced this; Scott, looking downcast, said he'd like to stay on up as well.

'I hate these arguments,' he said, 'and I can't stand all this waiting around.'

'I'm sorry, Scott, you'll have to come down with us. We need you to carry a good big load back up,' I explained firmly. It was time to be assertive.

'I'm going to find it difficult to be motivated if I've got to go all the way back down,' he muttered, as much to himself as any one else.

'Look, it's you that's got to motivate yourself on an expedition like this,' I replied. 'You have to face loads of setbacks on a mountain and it's just a matter of coming through them, of not letting them get you down. That's what expeditioning is all about.'

As we descended we met Charlie and Minchi, our local helper, carrying between them a plastic barrel and a box to keep our food safe from four-legged thieves. It was always good seeing Charlie. He was very much my confidant and we had a laugh over the altercation between Victor and Graham. He also promised me some diarrhoea pills when we reached base. Once there, I had time to sort myself out and prepare for the climb ahead in a way that I had been unable to do before. There had been too many external pressures with ITN reports, answering e-mails, worries about my cold and whether I was getting too old for it all. Rupert, at home, had picked up on this, e-mailing me:

Dear Dad,

Hope you're feeling a bit better and the weather is clearing. One of the pics you sent through (Martin, viewing rushes) did not open. The other two opened no problem so maybe there was just a glitch in that one. I'm sure once you've had a good rest and you're feeling better things will look a lot rosier, you definitely sounded a bit flat this morning. We all send lots of love and if this is going to be your last big trip, don't let things get you down as you're on your holidays and should be enjoying yourself and you'll be better soon any way.

Big smiles and lots of love,

Rupert and Ann

P.S. The kids at Ann's school want to send you another good luck e-mail because Ann has been taking in your ITN news reports and they've really enjoyed them.

My last trip? What on earth is he talking about? I thought.

That night we had a relaxed game of bridge, though we missed our mentor, Graham. We wondered with some mirth how he and Victor were getting on. Next morning it dawned fine and that afternoon we stormed back up to camp I in three and a half hours. It was a lovely clear evening and this time we really did feel confident. The camp had been tidied up, a stone table built and that morning Graham and Victor had made a carry to the end of Fothers' Ridge to establish a dump of gear at our high point. They seemed to have reached a degree of accord. In the meantime two of our Tibetan porters had brought up more rope so Victor climbed the slope, for the second time that day, to extend the fixed rope over a potentially dangerous section just beyond the top of the gully we had already fixed. We set the alarm for 4.00 a.m.

We were away by 5.30. Martin wanted me to do a piece to camera by the light of our headtorches as we set off for the mountain, as my signing off for the latest *News at Ten* piece. I was on edge to get going as I could see the little pools of light from the headtorches disappearing up the slope above, while Martin struggled in the poor light with the focus of the video camera. Eventually he was satisfied and I set out on what proved to be glorious firm névé. It was just getting light as I caught up at the start of the fixed rope. It was a lovely cloudless dawn with Chomo Mangyal, the Wife of Sepu, and Gosham Taktso, the Prime Minister, etched sharp and black against the lightening sky to the east. By the time I reached the top of the ropes, the others had all pulled out of sight and the sun had climbed from behind the north ridge of the Turquoise Flower to shine on the upper slopes of Fothers' Ridge. I was going slowly but steadily and couldn't repress my irritation when I saw Victor's head peer over the top of the ridge. He'd come back to see if I was all right. I snapped at him that I didn't need guiding, but immediately apologised. It was friendly concern that had brought him back.

We had a brew at the end of the ridge and examined the route through the glacier leading into the Western Cwm. The only worry was a line of huge séracs high on the west face of the Turquoise Flower. If they came away they would sweep the route but we should only be in the danger zone for an hour or so. Victor had ferried up our three pairs of snowshoes the previous day. These had been his idea. He'd phoned me a few days before our departure suggesting we took them. I'd never used snowshoes in all the years I'd climbed, but I agreed and said I had a couple of pairs in my climbing store. We had tried to buy some more in Kathmandu but had only found one pair, so we had three between the five of us. Victor suggested we should take all three with us on this attempt, but we were sceptical and it ended with Victor just bringing a pair for himself.

Scott was first off, roped to Graham, and we three tortoises followed. Victor had a cold and said he didn't feel too well. Nonetheless he took the lead and I was very happy to follow at the back with the best-consolidated footprints to step into. We dropped down to the glacier and followed the line of steps made by Scott over the broad snowfields, avoiding what were obviously very deep crevasses. We then weaved our way through sérac walls towards the top of this first step. Scott led most of the way, but near the top he faltered briefly and Victor surged into the lead, taking us to an ice ridge in front of a huge moat-like crevasse that stretched the full width of the glacier.

While Elliot put on a brew, Victor and I made a recce, first going left, then right to find a way through. I was feeling stronger than at any time on the expedition. It was good to have the energy reserves to take an active part in finding the route and making decisions. We chose the right-hand route, following the ridge to a point where the ice wall on the other side of the moat had become lower and the crevasse below it choked with snow. This enabled us to cross gingerly and reach the entrance to the Western Cwm which suddenly opened out in front of us to reveal a wide easy-angled basin stretching towards the massive bulk of Sepu Kangri. This was indeed a back entrance to the mountain, the vindication of Jim Fotheringham's hunch the previous year.

It was only two o'clock in the afternoon and I suggested we have another brew and then get as far up the basin as possible; but by the time the water had boiled, the sun had come out from behind a cloud and in the scorching heat glacier lassitude took hold and we decided to stay where we were. We had made good progress that day, having climbed about 800 metres to reach a height of 6170 metres, above the high point of the previous year. After we had rested, Victor suggested to me that it might be a good idea to recce the start of the route up the Western Cwm in preparation for the next day. He's a very good mountaineer, always thinking ahead. We kept a lot of rope between us, mindful of the potential size of any hidden crevasses, and picked our way cautiously towards the southern wall of the cwm to get round another huge lateral crevasse that barred the route. Having found a way round, we returned to the tent. Elliot, Victor and I were squeezed into a two-man Quasar that we had learnt on our attempt on Panch Chuli V in 1992 was just big enough for three. Indeed, it was comfortable and cosy with all the advantages of having a double skin and a good bay front and back for cooking and a porch. We also knew that the Quasar would stand up to almost anything the mountain could throw at it.

It was a superb sunset with the shapely dark pyramid of Lhallum Tamcho silhouetted against a fiery cloud. At the head of the valley the summit of Sepu Kangri was at last clear. It was a huge dome guarded by sérac walls, lit golden pink in the setting sun. We must have been tired for, in spite of our plans for an early start, I delayed cooking next morning, preferring the warmth of my sleeping bag whilst the others slept. Scott and Graham in a single-skin lightweight tent had been cold all night, which perhaps helped them make an earlier start on breakfast. We had barely finished our first brew when they were away in the dim cold light of dawn. Feeling guilty, we skipped breakfast, crawled out, got ourselves packed and away to follow the tracks left by the hares.

It was a long easy plod in the chill shadows as we walked under the walls of Lhazo Bumla, the Thousand Buddhas, with Lhallum Tamcho behind us, gleaming white in the early morning sun. It was a relief when at last the sun climbed over the north-west ridge of Sepu Kangri to warm us. We stopped for tea and a discussion. Victor was still feeling rough and had been happy to bring up the rear. He had fought his cold and pushed himself hard at the same time. He was now paying the price. None of us had helped ourselves by missing breakfast. We also had to decide which ridge to go for. Should it be the north-west ridge which linked Sepu Kangri with the Turquoise Flower? This was the ridge for which we had been heading the previous year when we had tackled the Frendo Spur. From our present viewpoint it looked less attractive. It started with a knife-edged snow arête leading to slopes that had the tell-tale marks of windslab avalanche. These led up to a sérac wall that stretched across the top of the mountain. The west ridge, the right retaining arm of the cwm, looked steeper initially, though there were also danger signs in the snow. But we could pick out a route through the sérac walls at the top.

We wavered between the two routes. It was so easy to read into either advantages and threats, and we finally came down in favour of the west ridge. Graham was still going strongly and set out in the lead. To my surprise, he was heading for a steep slope to the side of the sérac wall guarding the crest of the ridge. It looked quite unnecessarily steep and I started probing round to the left to try to find an easier route. Elliot, a keen off-piste skier, makes up for lack of mountaineering experience with a good knowledge of snow conditions and a strong streak of caution to offset my *sang froid*. He protested about the state of the slope, which indeed was unstable with deep soft snow under a very thin crust. I retreated and we watched Graham, whose progress had slowed to a crawl. It looked steep and difficult.

'To hell with this,' I said. 'There must be an easier and quicker way.'

'But what about the snow?' said Elliot. 'It looks bloody dangerous to me.'

'It's not that bad,' said Victor in support. 'There's no signs of avalanche around here.'

So I started out once again, ploughing round towards a little prow of ice on the corner. Once there I could see that there was an easy route all the way up. Graham was now at the top of the steep part, but yelling that it was desperately insecure. I thought we were on the right route. I also thought it was time to let the youthful greyhound and ex-porter, Elliot, off the leash. He was never really a tortoise at all, he just indulged us. So I stopped, brought him up to me and suggested he took over the lead.

'Head over there,' I said. He did so, and promptly half-disappeared into a bergschrund. I heaved on the rope, he wallowed and in a few minutes equilibrium was restored. Although easy, it proved to be a long way round and the snow was even deeper and softer. I had surrendered the lead at just the right moment.

The weather had been changing insidiously, a few clouds at first and then suddenly we were in the cloud with some flakes of snow gusting around us. A shout ahead, and we saw Graham and Scott pitching their tent on a broad shelf the other side of a crevasse.

'We might as well camp here. It's flatter than over there,' suggested Victor.
'I think we should camp with them,' said Elliot.

'We don't have to be on top of them the whole time, this is a miles better campsite,' I said.

'That's not the point,' replied Elliot. 'If we're close together it's easier to make plans together. We're getting into too much of a them-and-us attitude.'

'All right, we'll go over there,' I agreed. 'It's only a few feet anyway.'

And so we did, digging out a campsite close to theirs. Once we'd put the tent up, Victor, with renewed energy, suggested we climb to the ridge again to prospect the next day's route, but this time I decided to conserve energy and stayed in the tent. Elliot joined him and they set off, wading through deep snow past a small bergschrund and on up the slope beyond. There were still breaks in the cloud, but there was an ominous build-up to the west. The summit of the Turquoise Flower across the basin seemed very accessible and only a little higher than us, which helped to confirm the height of 6350 metres shown on my altimeter watch. We had 600 metres to go to the summit, a distance we should be able to make in the day.

Victor and Elliot came back an hour or so later, elated and reassured. They had not been able to see much because the cloud had closed in, but they reported that the snow on top of the ridge was firm. That evening on the radio call Charlie reported that the e-mail forecast from Bracknell was good, predicting clear weather for the next day. We were all set for a one o'clock start to climb through a star-studded night to summit in the dawn.

I set the alarm for midnight but hardly slept. I was so excited I lay there listening to the snow patter on the tent. But where was this fine spell in the weather? Midnight came and it was still snowing. We crept deeper into our sleeping bags. Two o'clock came, then three. I dropped off and didn't wake again until dawn. Everything was silent. Could it have cleared? I gave the inside of the tent a shove, and there was a swooshing sound as the snow slid off, followed by the gentle patter of more snow falling on the tent. I peered out to find we were in a whiteout. I couldn't even see the sérac wall immediately behind camp.

At that moment a woebegone Graham arrived to tell us that they had been soaked with condensation during the night in their single-skin tent so they had decided to dig a snow cave. Scott was already out there burrowing away. We got up and helped them, taking turns with the single shovel. At the morning radio call Charlie told us that the high pressure ridge that should have given us clear weather had vanished. I suggested he should phone Bracknell to see if he could get something more detailed.

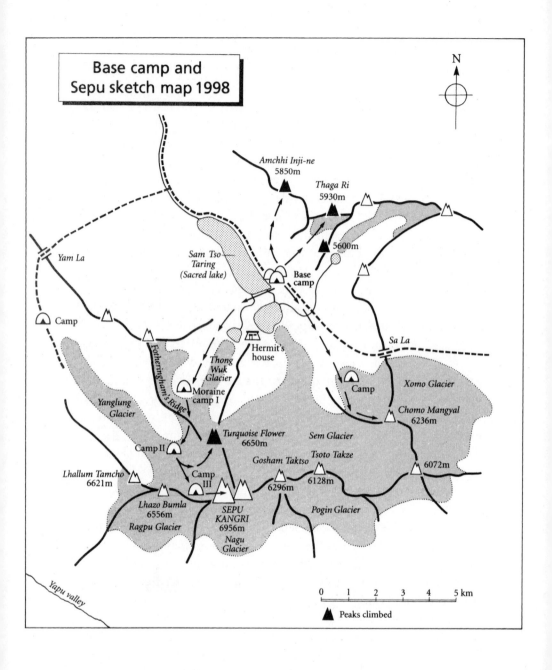

Base camp and
Sepu sketch map 1998

N

Amchhi Inji-ne
5850m

Thaga Ri
5930m

5600m

Sam Tso
Taring
(Sacred lake)

Yam La

Base
camp

Camp

Sa La

Hermit's
house

Fotheringham's Ridge

Thong
Wuk
Glacier

Camp

Xomo Glacier

Yanglung
Glacier

Moraine
camp I

Chomo Mangyal
6236m

Camp II

Turquoise Flower
6650m

Sem Glacier

Lhallum Tamcho
6621m

Camp
III

Gosham Taktso

Tsoto Takze

6072m

Lhazo Bumla
6556m

SEPU
KANGRI
6956m

6296m

6128m

Ragpu Glacier

Nagu
Glacier

Pogin Glacier

Yapu valley

0   1   2   3   4   5 km

Peaks climbed

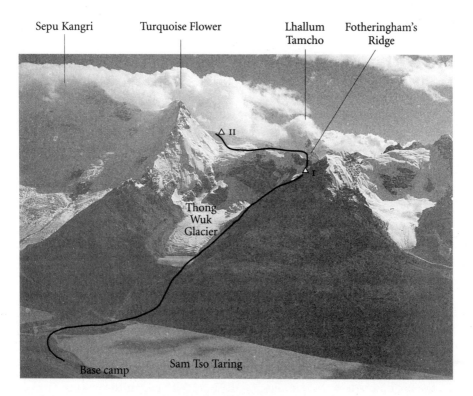

1998 ATTEMPT: SEPU KANGRI FROM THE NORTH

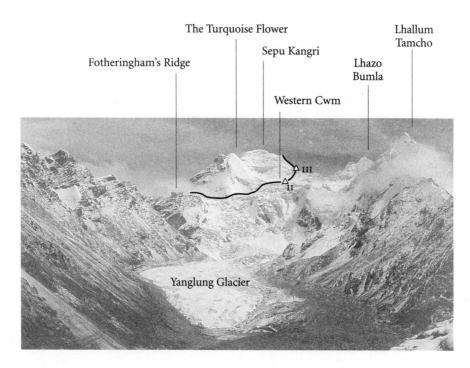

1998 ATTEMPT: SEPU KANGRI FROM THE WEST

That afternoon Graham and Scott piled into our tent and we played bridge, my highest game yet, although we had a dream of playing a round on the summit when and if we got there. In a final radio call with Charlie he told us that the Met Office at Bracknell had been very helpful. They said that the high had collapsed but there might be a short spell of fine weather next morning. We were worried at this stage about getting down in heavy cloud. Our rations and, more seriously, our fuel were getting low and there had obviously been a massive fall of snow, which meant that the avalanche danger was high.

I cursed as it snowed again through the next night and we all began worrying, not so much about our chances of reaching the top, but of escaping from what might well prove to be a trap. Graham woke us as it dawned at 5 a.m. He told us that he and Scott had gastro-enteritis probably from eating a can of fish that had been blown. He was fully dressed, looked ill and cold, and was ready to start down. In the comfort of our tent, we took another couple of hours to get ready. It was obvious we had to retreat, but none of us was looking forward to it. Outside there was a total whiteout and it was gusting hard. Finding our way down the Western Cwm, round the big crevasses and then picking the point of descent through the icefall below camp II was not going to be easy.

Victor and I talked it over and agreed it would be best to use Graham's direct ascent line for our retreat. With a bit of luck we could get down in two long abseils. I suggested to Victor that he went with Graham and I'd bring up the rear. He asked Graham to go out in front as he knew the way, although it was difficult to recognise anything in the driving cloud and snow. I was the last to leave and joined them on the brink of a steep drop which vanished into the whiteout. Victor had cut a bollard in the snow and lowered Graham over the drop. He was swallowed into a swirling white maelstrom. Victor just kept paying out the rope until it became taut. The cloud thinned momentarily and through the clearing we gained a glimpse of the floor of the basin with the broad moat-like lateral crevasse which we needed to outflank on its left-hand end. I quickly took a bearing with my compass. It was just about due north. We could also see that Graham had reached the end of the rope. The others followed.

Victor volunteered to climb down the steep part of the slope if I belayed him. I was all too pleased to agree. The cloud had rolled in again and we were picking our way blindly. At the end of the rope I waited for the others. Victor pulled out the snowshoes that he had insisted on carrying and once again suggested that since the going would be easier for him, he might just as well take the lead. I no longer had any hang-ups about being guided, I was just happy to surrender the position of stepping out into the void and the prospect of falling down a hidden hole.

Victor was able to make a dramatic demonstration of just how effective snowshoes are. He hardly sank into the snow, while Scott, following behind, was sinking up to his knees, so although Scott was second on the rope, in effect he was the trail-breaker as the snowshoes failed entirely to make steps for the next person. We hadn't gone far when it became obvious that Scott was struggling, weakened by his gastro-enteritis. Elliot volunteered to follow Victor and stayed there for the rest of the descent, trail-breaking all the way. It seemed interminable as we fumbled our way through the blank snowfields in thick cloud. There were no points of reference, no sign of the walls on either side of the cwm and no sound. I was at the back and checking the compass, I could see that Victor was aiming slightly off his bearing to ensure that when he came to the big lateral crevasse he would know he had to turn left to reach its end.

We duly hit it and followed left for what seemed a long time. You always start doubting your judgement in these circumstances. As we came to its end, we started peering for the marker wand we remembered leaving. A shout came from Elliot, that he'd found it, but we couldn't see the next one. We discussed the direction and geography of the next crevasse system and started off tentatively once again. Another providential break in the cloud and we glimpsed the vital marker. We had found camp II and the start of the route back through the icefall.

It was only midday and we certainly had time to get to camp I, and maybe all the way to base camp, although the icefall immediately below us could well pose a serious avalanche risk. Once again it was going to be difficult to navigate. Graham was first off. I think he wanted to take his turn out in front. I was on the rope immediately behind him. He went gingerly into the moat that we had crossed on the way up, but was going very slowly, almost fumbling. I was getting impatient when Victor, who was now at the rear, suddenly pushed past, saying to me, 'We've got to do something. This is taking too long.' As he overtook Graham, he murmured something about giving him a rest, and just kept going. This was tactless, perhaps, but necessary. Graham, weakened by the stomach bug, was not only going slowly, but was being slow in taking route-finding decisions. So it ended up with Graham at the back and Victor out in front, with all five of us on a single rope for safety.

We made good progress to the top of a steep chute of deep soft snow which looked very unsafe. Victor tried it in a couple of places and finally opted to go straight down. We had at last come out of the cloud, or it had lifted, so we could see the beginning of Fothers' Ridge. The snow, although deep, seemed surprisingly safe. The last threat was from the big sérac walls above on the flanks of the Turquoise Flower. We ploughed on down to Fothers' Ridge and felt we were just about out of danger. All that remained was a short climb, followed by a careful descent on the deep snow the other side. We were then at the top of the fixed ropes.

We were at camp I by 4.30 p.m. and reckoned we could just make it to base by dark. Graham considered staying that night at camp I because he felt so ill and tired. I wondered if I should volunteer to stay with him but to my vast relief he decided to come down. I left practically everything at the camp and travelled down very light. I noticed that Graham and Scott were taking all their kit, and wondered if they had decided they had had enough of the route.

I was very tired and yet at the same time satisfied, feeling that I had performed reasonably well and that our threesome of tortoises, or perhaps one tortoise (myself) and two Ninja Turtles (Victor and Elliot) had formed a good team. I was certainly looking forward to getting back to the climb. Our different feelings were captured by Greig Cubitt on our return to base. When he asked me how I felt about it all, I laughed and said that it had made a good trial run for the summit, while Scott described the experience as absolute hell. But then stomach upsets are murder at altitude.

13 *Amchhi Inji-ne* – The English Doctor
1996–1998

CHARLES CLARKE

'You're going to do WHAT?' gasped Jim Curran, as we walked down from base camp to Samda one afternoon in October 1998. '*You* can't write a whole chapter about *medicine*. There wasn't any, was there? I thought you had to be Tibetan, young, female, and pretty to get any treatment at all on this trip,' he added. 'You fat old bastard,' I murmured in reply, and we laughed. But I was goaded by this indictment of my attitude to the sick. I felt I had a story to tell, both because practical expedition medicine has been an interest for over thirty years, and particularly because I had come to know the local people so well.

On expeditions I have had to deal with life-threatening high-altitude brain and lung oedema, lobar pneumonia, frostbite, kidney stones, amoebic dysentery and, on two terrible occasions, fatalities. These major issues have been in settings far from the support of a hospital, medical colleagues, intensive care wards and nurses – the expertise one comes to rely on at home. On every expedition there are also the common and medically less serious problems – diarrhoea and vomiting, coughs, chest infections and toothache – and the inevitable acute mountain sickness, as the body acclimatises to lack of oxygen above 3000 metres. Psychological issues, depression or anxiety are frequent in these settings, too. Expedition medicine offers other special circumstances. For example, the relationship the doctor has to patients is unusually close; there are the practical difficulties of examining people in tents and issues which arise when treating local people. Decisions are made using criteria very different from those of the ward round or clinic, when an X-ray, scanner and a surgeon are nearby.

Preparations begin long before the medical box of drugs and dressings is assembled, with some cold hard thoughts which are difficult to share. I speculate, trying to answer imponderable questions: what if there is a major accident? What rescue facilities will be available? How would we deal with a death? My management of most of these issues is pragmatic. On Sepu Kangri we would not, for example, take either intravenous infusions, bottled oxygen or life support emergency equipment, mainly for reasons of weight, but we would have a wide variety of drugs. I had discussed this with the team, and put it in writing. (Immunisation, medical insurance and the medical kit itself are dealt with in Appendix 7.)

The rescue question was easily answered: on Sepu Kangri there would be neither helicopters nor rescue teams, other than ourselves. The transmission home of possible bad news presented a real problem, because of our regular satellite telephone communication system, but the issue it raised had to be faced. In the past, expeditions would withhold news about possible accidents or fatalities until the facts were established. We decided that we could only have a transparent policy of making any information available as soon we received it. Usually such anxieties would come to nothing; a late arrival back at camp, a bivouac or a failed radio call are commonplace, but they assume a different meaning when a friend or relative has been anticipating a telephone call from 6000 miles away.

So what really happened on these three expeditions? They began with something I had never really considered, being seriously ill myself. It is still salutary to look back on my own illness in 1996 at the end of the recce. I mention the story again not to be self-indulgent but to illustrate dissociation, the strange state in which sick people fail to recognise the severity of their illness. It is frequent at sea level, having some protective value, suppressing fear. In a distant setting, on a mountain, or when colleagues fail to recognise the situation, dissociation can be disastrous. One wonders how many mountain accidents have happened because of it. Particularly on expeditions, patients often say they are fine when they are not. You have to watch like a hawk.

This leads to a second issue. On an expedition, patients are usually friends. Like many doctors, I try to avoid treating friends or family. Critical judgements become blurred. But as a doctor in a camp or on a climb I eat with people who may become patients, I sleep next to them, laugh, play cards and argue. Occasionally, I may not like them, and vice versa. Coupled to this, there are no fixed hours of work. Consultations occur in a haphazard way, before breakfast, in the company of others or, typically, at bedtime, usually when I have packed away the medical box and it has begun to snow. All these things conspire against clinical accuracy: it is vital to distinguish the difference between medical triviality and major illness. It is all too easy to be caught out. One has to be aware of one's own disposition, whether one is a tut-tutter, suspecting everything could be serious, or the opposite, too casual. It is clear from Jim Curran how he sees me: laid back. I learn from this. We remain friends.

On these three expeditions to Tibet we were lucky. Our teams only suffered the routine ailments. During 1997, Tsini's dramatic illness had a profound effect on me and changed my relationship with our lake shore neighbours. I was drawn very much more into their lives. I received confidences and was treated in a deferential way. Then, as a direct result of my treating Tsini in 1997, patients from far and wide came to base camp for an opinion and treatment in 1998.

Whilst medical facilities in these remote areas are very far from the better aspects of what we have available in the west, hospitals and doctors do exist. It is easy to decry local practice; physicians and surgeons in these places are sometimes dedicated and highly skilled. Unlike in many Himalayan settings in the 'free world', there are government medical services in this region of Tibet, though they are not free of charge. In the state hospital in Lhasa complex surgery is carried out. There is a hospital in Nakchu, and a smaller thirty-bedded hospital in Diru, as there is in each county town. In villages, there are Tibetan doctors or paramedics, practising a mixture of western and traditional medicine. We would sometimes see a doctor on horseback, a red cross on his leather bag, the Christian emblem of medicine and symbol of his profession. I always felt his logo should be Buddhist, the swastika perhaps. In the smallest shops, antibiotics were on sale, modern drugs for stomach ulcers and rheumatism, vitamins, iron tablets, bandages and painkillers; the multinationals have endlessly long tentacles.

Traditionally, the relationship between an expedition and local people has often been distant. In *The Mystery Rivers of Tibet* written by Kingdon Ward in 1923, the caption of the frontispiece photograph are the stark words 'Tibetan Woman wearing Jewellery'. The woman bears no name and we learn nothing more about her. Kingdon Ward was a British botanist and explorer who visited the Mekong–Salween divide on several occasions and wrote extensively of the wild terrain on the Burma–Tibetan border, travelling through country much the same as ourselves. His work resounds with details of geography and travel but I felt as I read on that the writer had not really met a Tibetan, nor had he enjoyed that sense of welcome in a yak-herder's family tent. Perhaps it was that Kingdon Ward was constantly on the move, or perhaps that he felt some native British reserve in grappling with the lives of people who were often regarded as inferior. A second book of the era gives some insight into the latter perception. *Kamet Conquered* was written by the prolific mountaineering author Frank Smythe. His party reached the summit of Kamet (7758m) in Garhwal, northern India in June 1931, the highest mountain then climbed; a fine achievement. But one short passage gives insight into contemporary views. It is about Indian independence. 'India is not, and cannot be for centuries fit to rule herself, and to abandon her would be equivalent to putting all the animals of the Zoo into one cage,' wrote Smythe in 1932. Happily, a view that is unprintable and for most unthinkable today.

For me it is the characters I meet in remote places who provide an important focus for an expedition. In the valley beneath Sepu Kangri we were welcomed into this small community of some thirty people with whom we felt free to discuss almost anything, to such an extent that the very intimacy was sometimes irksome. We were drawn close to people for several reasons other than Tsini's illness. Chris and I, and later Elliot and I, had been the first westerners to penetrate these valleys: people were thus interested in *us*. But they were an inherently friendly bunch anyway. In these small communities one soon senses hostility, dishonesty or reserve. The families who lived around Sam Tso Taring, the Sacred Lake, were hospitable, helpful and immeasurably honest. Pasang was invaluable; his skills as a translator were vital, but he also enjoyed his work and was often the first to initiate meetings.

Our neighbours were members of several families. Our base camp tents of many colours that decorated the grassy shore intruded on several small stone houses and *bas*. We saw this exquisite landscape during the spring, summer and autumn over three years. The hillsides were at first harsh, snow-covered and windswept, changing to faint green, grey and brown before bursting into summer plumage of rich grassland, studded with primulas, saxifrage, poppies, azaleas and juniper. There was a slow start to summer in this place of legend. In May 1997, the surface of Sam Tso Taring was still frozen solid. We began to know who it was that crossed the ice in the distance. We would recognise the huddled figure of Dorbe, yak-herder and stonemason, bent under a load of wood, the gaunt profile of Orsa, Karte's mother, or which children were holding hands, skipping and laughing. We would know who was driving yaks or whose dogs were barking in the early morning. The scale of the scene before us was vast. The lake is over five kilometres long and over a kilometre wide, with the cirque of ice peaks rising from its eastern and southern shores some 2000 metres above. Here were frozen waterfalls, cascading like *kataks* into the lake from the glaciers above. Here were the nine snow-capped peaks from which snow plumes streamed in the wind like manes of galloping white horses. As if to complete the simile our neighbour Karte's pure white stallion was a frequent visitor to the camp, feeding on the new grass and tripping over guy ropes. All our neighbours were frequent visitors and we were made welcome in their homes.

This was the land about which an elder statesman at the Alpine Club in London had made the sarcastic comment before we left in 1996, 'Really, there are no mountains of any interest in *that* area of Tibet.' While a British Chamonix guide had commented, 'Off to climb some bumps on the Tibetan plateau, are you?' In reality surrounding us rose the sacred peaks of the White Snow God, the Turquoise Flower, the Daughter in Disgrace, the Thousand Buddhas and other satellites of the Sepu massif. Beneath these summits were people I came to love.

Karte was a tall thirty-five-year-old with traditional long hair tied up with a bright red hairband. His winning smile concealed a mind that was sharp for business. He had married Tsini, who was thirty-four, some twelve years previously. She was from a village lower in the valley. Whilst Karte wore a mixture of Tibetan and more modern dress – trousers and a shirt and sometimes a long-sleeved robe, a *chuba*, Tsini like the majority of Tibetan women wore traditional clothes, a long black skirt, *chuba* and a multi-coloured apron. She tied her long plaited hair with a silver and turquoise clasp and wore a lavish necklace. It is so often women rather than men who are the guardians of a culture. She was an attractive and vivacious woman. Also in the house was Orsa, her sixty-four-year-old mother-in-law, a gaunt, gentle and distinguished figure. 'Here she comes, looking like an Italian contessa,' Jim Curran would say as Orsa would sweep gracefully into base camp.

The household was completed by Orsa's husband, Tsering Sonam, a quiet tall man with a shock of unruly short hair, and Tsesum Dolma, Karte's divorced sister, her two boys, Jayang and Pala, and her daughter, Choezo. Jambo, the mischievous six-year-old daughter of Puh the yak-herder who lived nearby, often stayed there. In the muddy yard outside goats scampered about. Jambo would cradle one of the kid goats in her arms: an inseparable companion, the living equivalent for her of a Barbie doll. She would cuddle and kiss it, while in return the kid suckled her tongue.

There were other members of the family who lived away from home. The eldest son, Tashi Sedar, worked on the Nakchu–Diru road. Another daughter, Harko, lived with her husband and children across and down the valley, while a third, Soton, who had learnt to read and write, worked in a government office in Amdo. Whilst all the men who lived here were literate and it seemed, self-taught, no other women had learnt to read and write. I suspected Soton no longer wore a coarse sheepskin *chuba*, necklaces, dagger and the silver hair and belt decorations of her sisters. She lived in another world. She had travelled by jeep to Senza in the winter of 1997 to take her mother to Amdo for a holiday.

A hundred metres further up the valley lived Dorbe the stonemason. A slight man in his mid-thirties with large ears and an opaque right eye damaged by previous infection, when we first met in 1997 he stood shyly beside the kitchen tent. He was filing a large nail, nervously, on an oilstone grooved with time. We gave him a meal. 'Do you carve stones?' I had asked him through Pasang. 'Yes,' Dorbe had replied simply, but no more. Whilst Karte's large family had obvious wealth in yaks and goats, and stability and confidence, Dorbe had a different tale. He lived with his two daughters, Shonzo and Tsokdung, and Linga, a son about ten who was the image of his father. Their mother had died in the winter of 1995. Dorbe lived in extreme poverty and had just enough yaks to sustain his family. He owned two male yaks and eight *dis*, females. His stone house was tiny and sparse. He had built it himself eleven years ago when the local community had given him grazing rights.

Dorbe was devoted to stone-carving. He sat outside his house and chipped away each day. *Mani* stones and carvings of Buddhas lay around, as if for no purpose. He did not make them for sale, nor was masonry a family tradition. 'I wanted to be monk,' he once said, and then gazed lovingly at Linga his son and stroked his head. Unlike his neighbours, Dorbe was a Buddhist, rather than a follower of Bon, but he would join in the *pujas* at base camp, read the prayers and beat the drums. Sometimes he took yakloads of *mani* stones to the monastery at Senza. With his retiring manner, he did not mention an entire three-metre high wall of stones he had carved nearby. Like the other residents of the lake shore, Dorbe stayed in his house all the year round, through the harshest of winters at the head of this remote valley. 'Would you like some stones?' he had asked. When we left each year he would bring each of us a small *mani* stone. His neighbours laughed at his misfortunes in a kindly way. 'It would only happen to him,' Karte had said when Dorbe had been bitten by a dog.

Looking down on us was the hermit, who acted as a second opinion on matters practical and medical. I visited him on several occasions. He produced from his house some handwritten parchment about Sepu Kangri, and at my request made a copy. Pasang had some difficulty with the translation. When we returned we sent the pages to Samye Ling. His words explained the place of Sepu Kangri in local lore:

Smoke-offering Ceremony to the White Protector Deity of Sepu

In the limitless expanse of So-Mu there is the perfectly pure celestial palace in which resides the Sugata Lord of Peaceful and Wrathful Deities, along with those who fly through space and the Bon protectors and the special protectors of sacred places. Please come here, without one exception and with your entourages, to this smoke-offering feast of compassion for the six classes of being. Please come to this place of offering.

Offered are torma made of the finest jewels and grains, along with red and white offerings, flesh and blood and the golden brew. Offered are substances representing yak, sheep and goat, powders, oils and medicinal plants. The blue smoke rising from these offerings is consecrated with mudra and mantra and thereby becomes transformed into inconceivable quantities of wondrous goods and wealth.

Smoke is consecrated for the lineage from Samantabhadra all the way down to my guru.

Smoke consecrated for the three worlds.

Smoke consecrated for the white deities of the three worlds.

Smoke consecrated for the overall lord of the three realms, Tonpa Shenrab and his entourage,

Smoke consecrated for the one who differentiates good from bad, Tsangpa Tarjo and entourage . . .

Kye! We offer the finest of all smoke offerings, empowered with mantra and mudras, therefore bestow the finest of what is wished for, in unimaginable ways, fulfilling each persons heartfelt desires. Protect the Bonpo teachings. Befriend those good people who perform virtue. May I, the yogi, and those near me, be freed from falling ill, may our livestock not be stricken, please ensure this, lords of wealth. May friendship not be lost through quarrel. Destroy the hosts of enemies and defeat the hosts of demons. Help us at the time of death. Hoist the banner of the teachings to the sky. Bestow every accomplishment. May all be auspicious.

Our other immediate neighbour was Puh and his wife Kokor with her long gentle face. They lived in a house a kilometre or so west of base, overlooking the lake, with a summer *ba* nearby with a view even more spectacular than our own. They had six children, one of whom, Jambo, usually lived with Karte and Tsini. Puh was stocky, tough and generous. He had travelled with Elliot and me across the Yam La to the west of Sepu. Rarely did he come to base without a present; usually it would be yoghurt. On one occasion he brought a fresh shoulder of lamb and on another a pair of hand-knitted yak-wool socks, a reminder perhaps that I had given him clothing on our journey and ordered him new People's Liberation Army trainers from Lhasa because his own were too small. In the summer *ba*, he and Kokor would feed us lavishly when we passed by on recces on the northern side of the valley. As well as tea and yoghurt I remember well Kokor's *momos*, and lamb cooked in the milk she was making into cheese.

Finally, there was a small settlement at the mouth of the lake, some five kilometres below base, an easy walk along the shore, or across the ice in spring. Here was one of the houses of Norge, the jolly wizened 'old lady' who was the same age as Chris. Beside her lived Seka. 'She's Dorbe's girlfriend,' announced Pasang with a smirk. Seka was a widow of about forty with a grown-up daughter.

We had one other local friend. Minchi lived two hours below camp and had decided he wanted to work for us in 1998. He was about forty and had a long-suffering wife. 'What is her name?' we asked, as we always did. '*Woman* is what we call her,' he replied with a laugh. We bullied him about this and told him it was politically highly incorrect. Jim Curran thought that Minchi looked as if he had just completed his Harvard PhD, with his long hair, spectacles, intelligent face and an infectious laugh. The post of kitchen servant seemed somewhat menial for this owner of a substantial house, herds of yak and goats and several horses, but he stayed with us throughout most of 1998.

These families were the only permanent residents of the Sa valley. They moved to *bas* during the summer, driving yak into the highest pastures up 5500 metres, and made cheese. They were thus not true nomads. No one else visited the valley often. An occasional traveller would cross the Sa La to the north-east of base, usually en route to Samda monastery, or to hunt for the caterpillar fungus, a medicine of great value and an important source of income. These latter visitors were unwelcome.

The hunting of caterpillar fungus was an important annual event each June, policed by local custom and rules which would allocate certain hill-sides to each family. The caterpillar fungus (*cordyceps sinensis*) is an extraordinary hybrid about three centimetres long. A thread of fungus grows beneath the soil looking like a charred matchstick. As it does so it is eaten by a caterpillar about the size of a cabbage white larva. Poisons in the fungus kill the caterpillar: all that remains of the caterpillar's suicidal conquest is its dry stiffened effigy from which protrudes a single brown fungal stalk a centimetre or so long. This stalk pierces the ground and releases spores to propagate itself. Local family groups, small and large, set out with little picks, like miners departing for a shift to seek this priceless harvest. When the daily rate for manual work is 10 *yuan*, about £1, a successful day's hunting will yield hundreds of caterpillars which are sold on to traders for several thousand *yuan* a kilo.

Jim Curran and I had joined Minchi and his two daughters on a caterpillar fungus hunt in 1997 and spent a tiring afternoon plodding up steep grassy hillsides above 5000 metres. It was exhausting work, bent double near the ground searching for a tiny brown speck a centimetre long. A sighting is followed by a shout and a blow with the pickaxe which roots out a sod of turf; this is dissected carefully and the dry caterpillar complete with stalk placed in a bag. I spent the entire afternoon on one hillside and found one caterpillar. Minchi's sharp-eyed daughters dug up fifty or more. 'A good day's work,' Pasang announced. We found it difficult to ascertain the precise use of the product. 'It is good for health,' we were told. This elixir from the central Tibetan highlands is exported far into China where it is particularly prized, to appear in the street markets of southern Asia far from its mountain home.

In 1997 Jim Curran and I had stayed at Minchi's house on our way to Samda, out to the roadhead and on to Nakchu. I had been consulted frequently as we descended the valley, but there was no one who needed much medical help. However on the road journey back to Lhasa I was asked to see another patient who presented a difficult and insoluble problem. I did little to help him. In the back streets of Nakchu, Pasang found the way to a house through a maze of alleys. A man called Tsering lived there. He was the nephew of a woman from Samda village whom I had treated for backache. Tsering had suffered from an obscure illness that had continued for some ten years. Breathlessness was a prominent feature. I went carefully through the history and examined him, but I was at a loss to explain the problem. I would need the results of 'special tests', I said. 'But here they are,' replied his uncle, reaching under the bed withdrawing a folder of X-rays, and CT scans from Chengdu hospital where the patient had been studied. I soon joined the company of the Chinese doctors, quite unable to reach a diagnosis, but I assured everyone that he had been thoroughly investigated. I mention the case because it showed me how available medical technology was in such distant settings, even though in this case it did not seem to have solved the patient's problem. Jim and I had pressed on to Lhasa.

We were able to spend a few days in the capital in 1997. I took the opportunity to visit the museum of traditional Tibetan medicine, which added quite another dimension to my own experience. The old medical college, once adorned with golden *stupas*, used to stand on the hill opposite the Potala. The building was razed to the ground in the troubles. Now still close to the Potala, but in a more modern home, is the traditional Tibetan hospital. On the top floor there is a small museum housing a set of eighty *tangkhas*, historical paintings of Tibetan medicine.

As a medical student and during my continuing education, I have hardly heard a mention of the skills of ancient physicians and surgeons. These historical aspects tend to be put to one side as the mumbo-jumbo of the age before science had enlightened us. In the Lhasa medical museum I was introduced to this ancient world. I came away wiser and eager to learn more.

In the late seventeenth century, shortly after the time when William Harvey discovered the circulation of the blood, Tibetan medicine was far advanced and its practitioners famous. Whilst being unaware of the causes of most diseases, like their European counterparts, the Tibetans were experts at diagnosis, the recognition of disease patterns. They also had clear understanding of how to approach symptoms, noting that there were psychological, behavioural and environmental aspects of ill-health. In Tibet the emphasis was upon a holistic approach, upon taking a careful clinical history, and physical examination; assimilating the two would lead to a diagnosis and decisions about the many alternative forms of treatment. In Europe at that period physical examination was almost unknown.

Tibetan traditional medicine was held in the highest esteem between the eighth and seventeenth centuries, and much of what was happening in Lhasa was mirrored in the ancient practice within the courts and cities of India, China and the Middle East. Several factors have conspired to leave a peculiarly clear picture of how Tibetan physicians carried out their work. The first was Tibet's isolation which produced a continuous medical training curriculum that was maintained into the early twentieth century. Secondly, Tibetan medicine was above all pictorial. The series of some

TOP Scott and Elliot at the end of Fotheringham's Ridge, where it leads into the Upper Thong Wuk Glacier. This showed there was a route round to the west side.

ABOVE The team climbing through the glacier leading into the Western Cwm of Sepu Kangri.

OPPOSITE TOP Victor, moving up through the heavily crevassed area of the icefall. Lhallum Tamcho in the background.

OPPOSITE BELOW Lhallum Tamcho at sunset from camp II.

PREVIOUS PAGE Chris leading towards the crest of Fotheringham's Ridge, on the reconnaissance to find the western approach route to Sepu Kangri.

Scott (left) and Elliot, brewing on the way to camp II.

TOP Graham leading up to a steep sérac wall on the west ridge of Sepu Kangri. camp III was just beyond the skyline.

ABOVE Camp III at 6360 metres, the Turquoise Flower in the background. The storm that was to defeat us rolling in.

Graham and Scott decided to make a better shelter by digging a snow cave. The Quasar tent which Elliot, Victor and I slept in is above.

The comfort of a snow cave. You can dig shelves at will, in a temperature that is always just below freezing.

Retreat in the storm.

The second attempt, setting out for the crest of Fotheringham's Ridge; note the snow is much deeper than previously.

Graham Little on the second attempt, just above camp 1.

The final day, setting out on a
perfect morning from camp II.

The west ridge of Sepu Kangri.
Scott and Victor are climbing up
the west ridge above camp III.

TOP The view from the summit of the Turquoise Flower, looking across to Sepu Kangri.

ABOVE Victor's view of the Turquoise Flower with Graham a tiny dot just below the summit.

OPPOSITE Victor at the high point, radio-ing base to say they had decided to retreat.

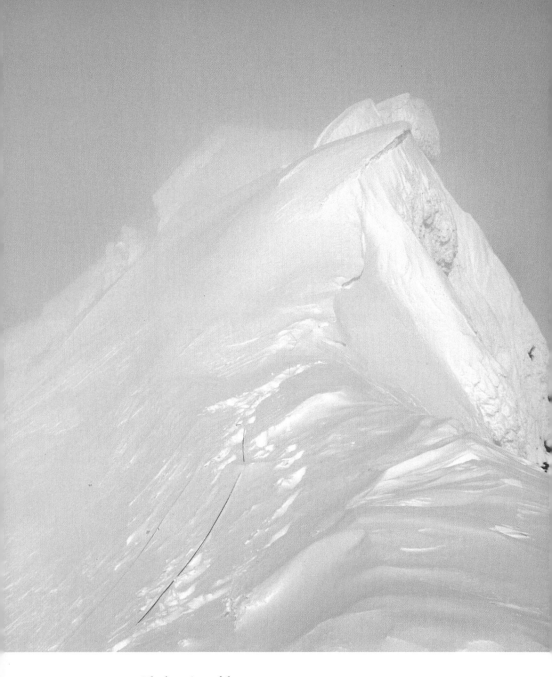

The last view of the
summit of Sepu
Kangri, 150 metres
above Victor and
Scott's high point on
the west shoulder.

Elliot, Graham and Scott
battling it out at bridge.

On the return, Dougal our
mascot, a very mangy
mongrel. Our supper, a freshly
slaughtered sheep just above.
He is ever hopeful.

Bouldering, Victor in action.

TOP RIGHT On the return, Elliot (and Charlie) decided to travel on horseback.

RIGHT (& OVERLEAF) The autumn colours, just short of the roadhead at Khinda.

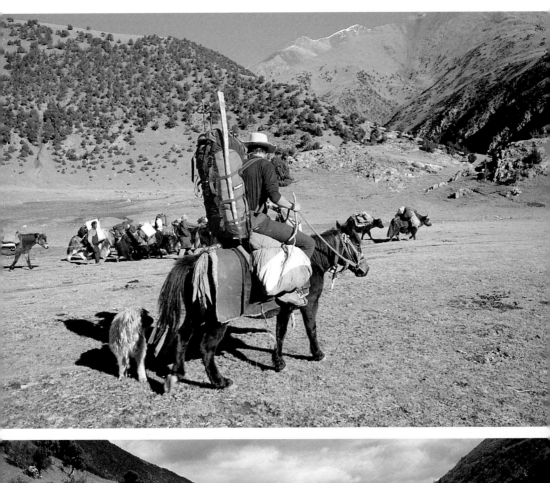

eighty medical paintings or *tangkhas* was assembled in the late seventeenth century by the physician and regent to the fifth Dalai Lama during the Qing dynasty. Three sets of these *tangkhas* survive today and have been used for teaching aids for many generations. One is preserved in the Lhasa museum. Their clinical illustration and imagery is especially unabashed and lacking in reticence. This may be partly because the Tibetans deal with their dead by chopping up the corpses before exposing them to nature, to be devoured by vultures, dogs and wild animals – or, I suppose, to be scrutinised by anatomists. Also, of course, vivid images are memorable for students.

The leaders of the Tibetan medical world were intimately related to the courts of the Dalai Lamas; the borders between medicine, public morality and law were indistinct. Physicians regularly held senior positions in the religious state. The preservation or, through different eyes, stagnation of Tibetan Buddhism into the twentieth century undoubtedly encapsulated traditional medical practice. The *tangkhas* capture this, showing anyone today with a vestige of interest in medical history a vignette of how doctors behaved and practised 300 years ago.

Even by the twelfth century, anatomy was highly developed and the skeleton understood and documented. The Tibetans already had an armamentarium of surgical tools for wounds, for abdominal operations and eye surgery. There was an understanding of arteries and veins, being the division between pulsating and non-pulsating vessels, with rudimentary diagrams of the circulation of the blood with the heart at its centre. Fertilisation of the ovum by sperm was understood; and there are paintings of the developing foetus within the womb.

Many of these *tangkhas* resemble religious paintings with a central figure leading allegorically to the different parts. Others follow the form of a tree whose stems and branches lead to individual leaves, each bearing a name and a picture. It is however the less anatomical or factual aspects of these paintings which provide special insight into the physician's art.

The Tree of Diagnosis is the third *tangkha* of the series. The tree has three stems: Interrogation, or asking for the clinical history; the Stem of Inspection, the initial observation; followed by the Stem of Palpation, the detailed examination. Within Interrogation there are twenty-nine leaves depicting symptoms. There was recognition not only of physical pain, such as the crushing chest pain of angina, but also psychological symptoms such as restlessness and anxiety. This gives the *tangkha* of the Tree of Diagnosis a deeper meaning, with a breadth far beyond the detailed artistic extravaganza of the Leaves of the Stem of Inspection which portray the appearance of the tongue, urine or faeces. In the Stem of Palpation it is however pulsology that really stands alone. There are nine *tangkhas* devoted entirely to the study of the pulse at the wrist. Rate, waveform and character need to be interpreted, as they are today. There is also quite exquisite attention paid to *how* the pulse should be palpated.

Another *tangkha* is devoted to Treatment. The tree has four stems: Dietary Therapy, Behaviour, Medicaments and External Treatments. The latter included cupping, branding with red-hot iron, blood-letting, cold-water baths and enemas, of which there are lurid illustrations. Each of these therapies develops into a detailed artistic treatise. It is however in the Stem of Behaviour that we see the insight these ancient physicians had into human suffering. The behavioural treatment for depression, called *rlung* disease, is pictured in the Leaf of Having Delighted Friends, while for fatigue, *mkhris-pa* disease, there is the Leaf of Leisurely Rest.

Moral values and their preservation in society assumed a major importance for these doctors, with their close relationship to the ruler of the land; they would even seem to have had an unhealthy preoccupation with the obscene. To deter the population from excessive sex, from sexual abuse of the young, especially of young monks, from masturbation and sexual encounters with animals was felt to be part of the remit of preventative medicine in Lhasa at the turn of the seventeenth century. Each is vividly displayed in the *tangkhas* showing the Causes of Disease.

The Tibetan medical establishment also had firm views about the Conduct of Physicians, as one might have expected. Wisdom, experience, benevolence and mercy are each extolled, often with memorable epithets. For example: 'A doctor without basic knowledge is tantamount to showing something to a blind man.' There was also the arrogance clearly recognisable in any medical era: 'A physician must have good lineage, otherwise it is like giving the throne to a fox.' These *tangkhas* continue with guidance to doctors about those patients who should be excluded from treatment, for example, 'those who despise the doctor, those who violate religion, those too ill or too old to treat, [and with a certain familiarity] those who will not pay.' But the clearest confirmation that doctors in seventeenth century Tibet behaved as many do the world over today concerns communication with patients: 'In explaining a disease, when the case is thoroughly understood one should announce the diagnosis either like unfurling a banner from the rooftop of your house or blowing a conch. But when the situation is confused one should talk ambiguously like a snake with a forked tongue.'

Announcing the diagnosis: detail from a seventeenth-century *tangkha*.

My eagerness to discuss these issues was greeted with some disrespect when I returned home in 1997. The children had come to have dinner. Rebecca, our twenty-six-year-old, turned to Naomi, her younger sister, and said quietly: 'Noo, I'm afraid Dad's gone all Buddhist. But I expect he'll get over it.' Naomi replied, quick as a flash. 'Mmmm, I know, Bec, but he's just been having his gap year. They always go a bit odd.'

Despite the Islington mocking-birds, my studies, albeit as a novice, taught me how to approach patients in Tibet and particularly to take time and care whenever I felt the pulse.

In 1998, once again the team was relatively healthy, though Jim Curran fell wretchedly ill with gastro-enteritis at Samda. In October, while the climbing team was resting after the first attempt on Sepu Kangri, Jim, Martin Belderson and I had left base for a short holiday to see the Devil Dances at Samda monastery, some hours below camp. Samda is a mediaeval place. The monks' quarters are mostly simple first-floor rooms. Behind each protrudes a wicker, mud and lath privvy, the hole in the wooden floor discharging from two metres into the muddy street below. Beneath each privvy yaks take cover from the snow, dogs skulk about, and ravens scavenge. Passers-by give these areas a wide berth. We reached Samda and drank Tibetan tea, at which point Jim became pale, a shade which turned to grey-green. He spent the next two days groaning at hourly intervals in the privvy, looking more sickly each time he returned to his simple bed. The yaks below were showered with an evil effluent of diarrhoea and vomit. Gifts of more tea, raw yak meat, and twists of bread fried in rancid butter, all well-meant, turned him greener still. He lost his sense of humour, almost entirely.

'Why are all these people here?' he wailed, as yet another group of Tibetans came into our little room, smiling and unannounced.

'Just to have a look at you,' I replied. It was true. There was not a lot I could offer, as I had brought not as much as an aspirin with me: another error. One must be prepared anywhere for trouble – to be separated from the medical kit simply will not do.

Meanwhile, Martin had work to do, filming the Devil Dances and I wanted to write and photograph. The three-day stay gave me an opportunity to experience the place, to wonder at it, perhaps reflect a little. We were warmly welcomed and any problems of the previous years seemed forgotten. We wandered around freely, were given tea and food in the kitchens and were housed in a room for visiting high lamas – a rough wood, lath and plaster shell, decorated with garish *tangkhas*, some snapshots of other monasteries, and incongruously, a battered photo of Deng Xiao-Ping. There were four rough wooden bunks with a stove. What a powerful place Samda was. Many monasteries are built in commanding situations. This one is like a citadel perched on an isolated plateau nearly a kilometre long that rises at the junction of two rivers at 4300 metres. The old shrine, the *lhakhang*, stands like a prow at its western end, a two-metre *mani* wall below it, looking out to the mountains. Some of the lower *mani* stones bear orange lichen which takes centuries to grow. In the centre of the meadow is the new prayer hall, the *dukhang*, an imposing two-storey structure, while surrounding it and connecting it with the *lhakhang* are monks' quarters, single rooms at first-floor level. Alleys criss-cross the site, making Samda a village in itself.

To the north is an open meadow with old squares of stones buried in the grass, foundations of buildings long forgotten. Yak and sheep graze there; dogs skulk about; ravens and magpies feed. This had been our campsite on several occasions. A high path surrounds the entire *gompa* with a near complete *mani* wall beside it. Some of the walls are simple slates but others are massive granite boulders, age old, every one too heavy for a man to move alone. On each of these stones was carved a single letter of the *O mane padme hum* prayer. Locals from houses below the monastery and yak-herders travelling to and from the high pastures encircle the place morning and evening, chanting prayers and clutching rosaries.

Samda is a *gompa* without great present splendour, apparent wealth and obvious relics. Its forty monks seemed to be largely construction workers who have been rebuilding the site for some ten years, following its destruction in the Cultural Revolution. History will rightly forget that two Englishmen, Jim and I, helped place the massive coping stones on the *dukhang* roof one afternoon in June 1997.

The monks knew little of their home's more distant history. We pieced together something of the story from a book we were shown; the hermit also helped us. As for many monasteries, the earliest history is fragmentary. It is said that Samda was founded by a Bon high lama named Yung Dung Lichung in the eighth century. It was destroyed in the twelfth century during the Sok Mongolian invasion and was refounded in 1465, the Year of the Bird, and flourished until the 1960s, when it had again been destroyed. Today rebuilding is nearly complete. The *lhakhang*, some fifteen metres square, has an entrance hall decorated with wall paintings of the four guardian deities of the north, south, east and west. Within the central shrine are two new golden Buddhas each a metre high, and books bound in red wood covers. New *tangkhas* hang on the walls. By 1998 the reconstruction of the *dukhang* was nearly complete. Golden effigies of deer called *rida-pomu*, each some two metres high, adorned the new roof and were visible a kilometre away.

At dusk, when the temperature often fell to freezing, the setting was like a vignette from *The Name of The Rose*. There were furtive movements of robed lamas, nomads and a sinister-looking, bearded kitchen servant, a man with an evil laugh, but a heart of gold. Deals were struck in the small tented market that had grown during the afternoon. At dawn next morning the deep bass horns and wailing conch shells sounded from the *dukhang* roof. At 9 a.m. we walked to the courtyard, cleared of snow from the day before. Within the *dukhang*, it was like peering backstage at the theatre. Amid the butter-lamp shrines, *tangkhas*, silk hangings and incense, the dancer monks put on the massive devil masks, took red, gold, green and blue sashes from wooden chests, strapped on embroidered boots, and tested dance steps. Others practised drums, timed the clashes of cymbals and blew their conches. Outside, the crowd assembled in the crisp morning, after an icy, crystal moonlit night.

By 10 a.m. two clowns arrived, armed with horsewhips and lurid masks. They mock-whipped the crowd into silence, terrifying little children, and beat in earnest a dog which strayed on to the dance floor. There is no mercy for dogs here. The crowd laughed. Storytellers introduced the Devil Dance, a tale of the triumph of good over evil, but neither they, nor even a visiting monk from the Drepung monastery in Lhasa, could explain how the dance related to it. The vast red awning parted, and from the *dukhang* the monks processed into the courtyard, the chief lama leading Shon Ta, the eldest, a seventy-six-year-old who had been a novice at Samda some sixty years previously.

Cymbals clashed, the drums and horns began. The eight devil dancers swept into the square; children gasped. The crowd remained rapt in silence as the masked dance began. Slowly the dancers beat their drums, feigned death, rose, and circled the square, until the tempo changed, rapidly rising to a frenzied crescendo; each swirled back into the *dukhang*, leaving the two clowns, who, as if to emphasise the make-believe, continued a mocking dance, miming steps and movements as the horns and cymbals fell silent. Other dances followed, but none held either the crowd or ourselves.

As we rode on horseback back to base, a familiar figure hurried past; it was Minchi from base camp. One of his yaks had been attacked by a wolf near his house the night before: we had slept peacefully on a pasture only a few minutes away.

Our visit to Samda was a privilege but we could not help noticing the four small poor dwellings beneath the monastery itself. Each was a single room lit by an open fire. Here lived farming families, some of whose sons were monks. One can look at this homely squalor as part of a mediaeval idyll, but compared with these homes the quarters of the monks above were spacious luxury, and the prayer hall large enough to house two dozen families. Perhaps if Samda is to survive far into the third millennium its prelates will have to look more towards the material needs of those who support it. 'They've got it made, those lamas,' Elliot had mentioned with some disgust when he had first been there.

Jim recovered gradually, but he had looked deathly. It took a week or so before he seemed to have forgiven me for taking no drugs with us to Samda. It was only then did I feel confident enough to say, 'Good try, Jim. Nearly had to go home, didn't you?'

'Bastard, you really are an absolute bastard,' he gurgled. And we both laughed.

When we returned to Tibet in 1998, I had little work for several weeks until Elliot and I had crossed the infamous Sa La and reached valleys we knew, and where I was known to the locals. We were welcomed warmly by Karte and Tsini. It was good to see them all looking so well. News of our arrival soon spread down the valley, provoking an epidemic of health screening in this hardy population. Whilst this would have delighted BUPA, like most physicians I distrust screening, unless people have problems. Well people came from far and wide. 'Please, check them all,' Pasang would say, as a group of nomads approached. I became practised in pulsology, and soon learnt to say in Tibetan that all was well. 'I've learnt so much,' said Pasang, 'if I'm ever out of work I'll travel around and be a doctor here. Nothing to it, is there?' However, the real test of my technique came when I had to conduct these proceedings from horseback, leaning from the saddle to grasp the outstretched wrist to feel the pulse of a horseman who had trotted alongside me. The people of the valley were wholly unable to understand that *amchhi inji-ne* had not been born in the saddle like themselves. I had examined the man's pulse from my perch only because I was too frightened to dismount.

These routine check-ups usually seemed light-hearted rituals for both patients and myself, but, as it always is, the work was punctuated by difficult, interesting and unexpected problems. At Samda I saw two monks. The first was Shon Ta, the senior member whom we had met at the dances. He had had a slight stroke which had made his speech slurred but was recovering well. He seemed to be the only person at Samda who pre-dated the Cultural Revolution.

'Those were terrible times,' he said. 'I do not want to think or speak about them. They were times when all the people took sides, either with religion or with the government.'

Pasang was quite rightly cross with me for having raised the subject at all, and I felt I had abused my position. He mentioned to me later that the old lama had told him that in this valley it had been the local people who had destroyed the monastery. It was so in many others, we gathered. This land has known great suffering, but I always feel that one needs to try to understand the Cultural Revolution, its duration and its devastation throughout China before making isolated judgements about Tibet. Those times had indeed been terrible for many people.

The second monk was younger, and more difficult. He was twenty-two and had been ill for three months. 'He is just weak,' they said. I looked at him carefully and found nothing wrong. This well built man had not however moved much from his bed for weeks. I gave him some vitamins and said I would return to see how he was in a week or two, when we would be passing on the way to base camp with the climbing team. When we did return, he wasn't around. A month or so later a tent decorated with embroidery was pitched beside base camp, surrounded by a retinue of followers. The young monk was inside, reclining on a carpet, the picture of health, I felt, after examining him again. We were able to discuss the problem with him, somewhat unusually in private. I said I thought he had become rather exhausted and there was nothing serious afoot. He seemed relieved. I gave him some more vitamins and suggested he do a little more each day. Another month later we heard he was back on duty in the monastery. Chronic fatigue is a worldwide problem.

In a tent at a river crossing I was shown a man of fifty whose home was further down the valley. 'He's gone mad,' announced Pasang. 'He gets on his horse and rides around the valley getting lost. He talks rubbish and can't remember where he is.' I saw a calm but bewildered man who, it seemed to me, was becoming demented. There was little to do, but I suggested he would be better at home with his family. Weeks later, he came to base camp, not to see me, but to consult Sam Ten Tsokpu, the hermit, who gave the same advice.

It had become dark and I was about to leave the nomads' tent. 'But you have to see the boy who can't pee,' said Pasang firmly. Gyatha was seven. A membrane covered the end of his penis, like a tightly stretched condom. Through a minute hole in this membrane sprayed a fine jet of urine when he peed. This was a phimosis, a developmental problem that in theory could be solved easily by a circumcision. I thought of Nelson Mandela's autobiographical story of village circumcision with a stone. I felt uneasy. A surgeon is what we need, I thought, or a rabbi. I spoke to Gyatha and Yinsu, his mother, and said that I could see them at base camp but suggested it would be better to go down to Diru to seek advice at the hospital. The yaks and ourselves were moving up the valley the following morning, so I would be unable to help immediately. A month later Gyatha and his mum came to base camp.

'Now you can do the operation. They want you to,' Pasang announced. I thought about this, about bleeding and infection, and decided against it. I am not a surgeon, and a DIY circumcision in the dining tent was not a good plan. 'We'll take you and your mother to Nakchu when we go,' I said.

Gyatha's eyes lit up. 'Nakchu, Nakchu,' he said and jumped up and down with excitement. The second opinion of Sam Ten Tsokpu was sought; he agreed with the proposal.

A second embroidered tent appeared near base camp at the end of September 1998. It housed shy people who had come from far away. The women wore different jewellery from the people of the Sa valley. They lacked the inquisitive confidence of the locals. They hung around for a day and then consulted Pasang. 'One woman is going blind,' he said, 'and there is a man with a face problem.' Two stooped figures bent with the gait of very ill people walked towards us. They had come with their families from near Pelbar, a journey on horseback of some two weeks from the east. Yeshi was thirty-two. She was certainly losing her sight because of a devastating infection in both eyes. The right eye was a dull white ball of pus. The left was heading that way. This looked like pan-ophthalmitis, infection throughout the chambers of the eyeball. She was otherwise relatively well and there was no disease elsewhere. I gave her the largest doses of antibiotics I dared, suggesting she stay several weeks to continue the course. She improved gradually over the first week, but I looked out one morning: their tent was gone.

The man was also gravely ill. I never knew his name. He was thirty-five. His face was distorted and he kept the right side covered with a blood-stained scarf. When he removed this I could see he had a hole below his right temple which was ten centimetres across, and several deep. It was black, and rotten. He was in constant severe pain. Each nerve that issued from the skull base had been destroyed; he was blind in the right eye, and the right side of the face was swollen and dropped. Pasang winced at the sight and then as the stench caught him, he rushed out to vomit. The patient had, I thought, a skin cancer which was now eroding the skull. The cancer had been growing for over two years. It had begun as a small sore which would not heal. If treatable at all, he would now require the most major surgery. I suggested Chengdu or Lhasa, but said I would try to help his pain. We worked on a mixture of drugs over the week, and at the end he succeeded in having a night's sleep. 'The hermit told him to go home and stay with his family till the end,' Pasang said. It was no bad advice, I thought. He would die soon. He left for Pelbar with Yeshi's family.

Shortly before we left base camp I turned to dentistry. 'Wow,' said Jim. 'She's lovely, too.' I reminded Jim of some ethical issues in medical practice. His reply is unprintable. Deshi and her husband had come up from Samda. She was twenty-two and finely dressed. Her husband was a pleasant, tall, aristocratic-looking man. They had only been married a month. She had asked me to take out the tooth when she been one of the visitors to Jim's bedside at Samda. At the time I had hoped she would not follow up the request. The tooth was broken and the socket was filled with green pus. The remains of it wobbled a little, which I thought was hopeful. Pemba boiled the instruments in the cook tent, while I gave Deshi some heroin and explained to her and her husband that despite my efforts the root might splinter, and pieces remain in her jaw. We set to work. Deshi sat on a crate in the dining tent wrapped in my towel. Jim filmed the procedure. I was distinctly nervous. Quite where the local anaesthetic went was a matter of some good fortune but after several injections her mouth became numb. I grasped the tooth with the forceps: a fragment snapped off immediately. I cursed, began to sweat and wished Fotheringham, the proper dentist, had been around. I dug deeper into the gum, and squeezed hard on the pincers. Deshi winced: I heaved. The entire remnant, roots and all, came out in one followed by a gush of blood. We all sighed with relief. She walked away groggily. Later that afternoon her husband rode off to Samda, while Deshi walked behind him. All had gone well.

Shortly before we left base camp for the last time I was ill again, much to Jim Curran's delight. Minchi's fourteen-year-old daughter had popped up to see her father one day and had 'flu, or a migraine. She had looked dreadful and clearly needed to stay at base camp. A tent was easy, but she had no bedding so I lent her my spare light sleeping bag. She was fine next morning and scampered off down the valley. I retrieved my bag and used it one afternoon for a snooze. It smelt of yak, but it didn't bother me. A day or so later I began to itch betweeen my toes. I began to scratch like an angry cat. The itching spread up my legs; there were little spots and lines. I thought it was some allergy for a few hours until I saw a scabies mite on the sleeping bag. *Sarcoptes scabii* is an elegant beast. It looks not unlike a miniature scorpion, and it is just visible to the naked eye. I had never seen the creature in the flesh before. Scabies is an intensely itchy skin disease caused by the female mite burrowing into the skin and laying eggs.

I leant out of my tent and said softly to Jim next door, 'Guess what? I've got a touch of scabies.'

He roared with laughter. '*You've got what? Scabies!? Scabies!?*' he bellowed across the camp, making sure that even Bonington, in his distant tent, could hear clearly. '*From that fourteen-year-old Tibetan girl in your sleeping bag.*'

An application of benzyl benzoate is the treatment of choice; the bottle was in the medical box. Jim had some louse powder from a Sheffield pet shop (I never thought to ask him why). I dusted my sleeping bag thoroughly, bathed myself in benzyl benzoate, and was soon cured.

14 So Near, Yet So Far

8th – 12th October 1998

CHRIS BONINGTON

I felt tired and jaded in spite of carrying a light load. It was almost as if we hadn't had the week's rest. It was 8th October and we were on our way back up the mountain. I fell behind almost immediatley and the others pulled away out of sight as we followed the familiar way along the moraine. Back at base the others had been ice-bouldering on the lower part of the glacier where it flowed into the lake. Graham had led a continuously overhanging ice wall which he described as the hardest thing he had ever climbed. I had used work as an excuse to rest, but it didn't seem to have done me much good. I couldn't help wondering about my chances of getting to the top.

The others had rested and waited for me at the meadow just below the final slopes leading to the camp, but, as I arrived, they immediately started off again – the tail-end Charlie syndrome. I wasn't quite the last. Victor had stayed behind to up-date the web diary which he had been sending on a regular basis to *Scotland on Line*. He caught me up in the meadow. I always enjoyed Victor's company and as we plodded upwards, chatting about the trip and future plans, I forgot my fatigue. The last leg, with the 400-metre climb, went surprisingly easily.

We agreed that night that we'd start brewing at four the following morning to get away by six, which would give us plenty of time to reach camp II that afternoon. I slept through the alarm, as did every one else, a sign of just how tired we all still were, and it was nearly five when I awoke. I was sharing a tent with Graham and he volunteered to cook breakfast. I was all too glad to let him but we were in a hurry and just had some apricots with a brew of tea, something I later regretted.

We were ready to leave around 7.00 a.m. I was last, but initially felt I was going reasonably well, dreamt of what it was going to be like reaching the summit and even mentally rehearsed my 'piece to camera' for the benefit of ITN. I caught up with Elliot at the bottom of the fixed ropes but once I started jumaring up the steep little gully, my energy oozed away. Scott had been the first up and it must have been much harder for him, for a huge amount of fresh snow had accumulated in the gully. Once again the tail-end Charlie syndrome operated. As I reached the top of the gully the others had had their rest and were ready to leave. Victor and Elliot were away first and Graham asked me whether I'd like to tie on to their rope. My first impulse was to decline, saying I wanted more of a rest and doubted if I could keep up, but Graham pointed out the risk of avalanche. I agreed to tie on.

It was slow going. The snow was soft and deep and felt dangerous. After a few hundred metres, about half way to the crest of the Fotheringham Ridge, Victor stopped and waited for us to catch up. It was time for assessment. The weather had closed in and it was starting to snow. I asked everyone in turn how they felt about what we should do. Scott looked glum and said he was very tired. Graham and Elliot were worried about the snow conditions. Victor was the only one who was upbeat, commenting on the fact that, although the snow was deep and soft, we had seen no tendency to avalanche at any time. He felt we should keep going and make use of the bad weather to get in position to take advantage of the good spell we anticipated. We decided to continue as far as the end of the ridge and then come to a decision.

I felt more and more tired. The rope pulled at my waist. I couldn't even keep up with Victor trail-breaking through deep snow, so I untied the rope connecting me to Graham. The gap between us widened quickly. I just plodded on in their wake, trying at the same time to analyse our prospects. I was beginning to have serious doubts about my ability to reach the summit, let alone keep up with the others. I didn't want to slow them down but, beyond that, felt that I hadn't anything in reserve in the case of an emergency.

In addition I realised that we really did need Victor's snowshoes but we only had three pairs at the dump at the end of the ridge. The couple left without would be at a big disadvantage and would almost certainly travel more slowly. One solution would be for two of us to drop out, leaving a fast snowshoe team to head for the summit. I would certainly be happy to be one of those to descend. Not only was I going slowly but I had lost all my drive and fire. I simply wasn't enjoying it. I'd always been aware that I probably only had one good try in me and my recovery rate wouldn't allow me a second. By the time I reached the crest of the ridge, the others were already assembled at the dump. At least when I caught them up, the stove was going and a brew was on.

We talked around it once again. It was now one in the afternoon and we had been on the go for six hours; on the first attempt the same stretch had taken only two. At the present rate of progress it seemed very doubtful if we would reach the site of camp II before dark. Graham suggested the possibility of digging a snow cave at the dump and carrying on the next day, but no one seemed very keen. It was at this stage that I made my suggestion.

'Surely, with only three pairs of snowshoes, it makes sense for the three strongest to push on using them, while two of us must go back. That way it should definitely be possible to get up to camp II this afternoon and be in a better position to push for the top. I'm knackered and would be happy to stand down. What about you, Scott? You were saying you felt pretty rough?'

'I don't know about going back down,' said Scott. 'I'm tired, but I think we all are. If I went down I wouldn't come back up again. I just haven't any enthusiasm for this kind of climbing again.'

'If Scott goes down, so shall I,' said Graham. 'We've worked well as a team and I want to keep it that way.'

We continued discussing the different options and then Victor stirred things up.

'You know, Graham, you were going pretty slowly last time. You did hardly any trail-breaking. Wouldn't it be an idea for you to go down with Chris?'

Graham showed great restraint saying, 'I think it'd be useful, Victor, if you remembered what the hermit said about avoiding conflict and uncharitable thoughts on the mountain.'

I felt I had to wade in to Graham's defence, reminding Victor of Graham's lead up to camp III.

'Look, stop arguing,' said Elliot. 'I'm the junior member and came in at the last minute, I don't mind going back down. Chris's idea certainly seems to make sense.'

So that settled that. The other three started fitting snowshoes to boots, strapping them on awkwardly with bits of string and tape, while I tried to do a piece to camera for ITN explaining what we'd decided. The first time I tried I couldn't control my emotions and slumped down and cried. The others patted me on the back, muttered reassurances and then, once they were ready, we all hugged and they plodded slowly off into the driving snow while I managed to do my piece to camera with Elliot.

As they vanished into the cloud, he and I turned round and started on our return journey. In spite of my emotion I had no regrets. It seemed the only sensible thing to do and I hoped gave the other three a real chance of success. I felt sorry for Elliot. He had volunteered to come down with me out of a sense of duty but it was obvious that he longed to be up there with the others. We reached base in the late afternoon. I was incredibly glad to be back but was also worried about the others. We didn't hear anything from them that night, but it dawned a perfect cloudless morning, one of the very few we had on the expedition. At the 8.00 a.m. call Scott's voice came through.

'It's a fantastic view we're having. We're up in the Western Cwm. You can see for miles. Lhallum Tamcho is all golden. It's great up here.'

'What about snow conditions?' I asked.

'Diabolical. Getting up to the camp yesterday was desperate, even with snowshoes. We were totally knackered and it's really deep and slow here today. We'd be pushed without the snowshoes. Anyway we'll keep going.'

Elliot, was standing next to me, silent. After the call he walked away from the camp with his Therm-a-Rest, laid it out and settled down on his back in the morning sun, hand over his face, as if he couldn't bear to look up at the mountain any more.

Later that day he wrote:

The contrast between the singularity of purpose and the dam-burst of emotion and 'otherness' that have taken over has shocked me utterly. It is as if I have been lurking deep at the bottom of an icy lake, only fully registering details directly connected to the mountain. This focus has carried all the significance and purpose of being here. It is all that has mattered. Base camp has, of course, pleasantly involved conversation, stories, card games, food. But all that has been ambient noise, filtered by the omnipresent focus upon climbing the mountain.

Shockingly, I have burst through the surface of this lake and deeply gasped a lungful of arctic air. With the realisation that I will not reach the summit, suddenly there is noise everywhere. Reality has come into stark and unwelcome clarity, there is no longer any filter to mountain and non-mountain matters. There is a crackle of conversation that I don't want to hear. The everyday life at base camp, rather than the comfort it was, is now something I don't want to know about. It is hard to grasp the significance of anything.

Instead, bruises and aches make themselves felt, sunburn starts to sting and I am more aware of my numb frost-nipped toes. Awakening this morning, I cursed that my boots had frozen solid overnight, something that previously hadn't been of concern. I so desperately want to go back to the dream in which I was submerged.

There is a certain amount of irony in my feelings. From within the insular depths of concentration, the sense of being so very alive pervades your whole being. There is a heightened sensitivity to your situation and circumstance and, more importantly, to how they might change. Even from 6500m, Tibet stretches away to an unbelievable distance. Autumn shades of tans and browns colour the lower hills. The chilled blue sky has an army of white cumulus advancing across it, creating a patchwork of dappled shadows racing up and down the valleys kilometres beneath us. With this there is a constantly swirling vortex of questioning. Have I drunk enough liquid? How strong do I feel? Will I be able to dry my gloves? When did I last check that loose screw on the crampons? Somehow the cold makes you feel more alive.

The simple process of clipping into the fixed rope and making sure the karabiner closes securely, of placing one cramponed foot in front of the other, even of the process of taking steady, deep breaths – the simplest actions are painstakingly regulated with precision and control. The clarity of each action is almost hyper-real. Even now, I can see each motion with a peculiar sharpness.

However, in this reawakened state, with the full array of ongoing, everyday actions, there is a dullness: the edge has been taken off perception. I feel like a spoilt child denied what an infant's expectation of sole attention most clearly expects. And this makes me even more frustrated.

Today dawned possibly the clearest day we have had. Glistening ice and snow brightly reflects the mountain light onto base camp, forcing me to shield my eyes as I scour the summit ridge for the other three. The weather window is perfect and they will be inching their way to the summit, as I watch, from base camp, almost unbelievably jealous. I try to comfort myself by diluting this jealousy with the immense relief that at least Chris and I are now safely back on level ground.

I was reminded of how I would have felt at his age if I had volunteered to come down. Elliot was just one year older than I had been on my first ever expedition, which was to Annapurna II in 1960. I remember the agony of worry that I might not be selected for the summit bid. I wonder if in similar circumstances I would have volunteered to turn back out of a sense of fairness to the others. I suspect not. My ambition at that age was too hungry. But I also can't help envying Elliot that agony of longing for, intense though it is at the time, he has so many more years of hard climbing in front of him. Even more poignant for me was Elliot's driving freshness of enthusiasm, when everything is a discovery and that all-abundant energy carries you up the mountain with such pleasure, even when the going is tough. I had had a taste of that all-embracing drive on our first attempt but this last time it had been a struggle all the way, with no promise of recovery. I was glad to be at base and found it easy to hope for the success of the others. It would be a genuine vicarious enjoyment, but that is never quite as satisfying as being there yourself.

Meanwhile, the other three were out of sight in the Western Cwm. Graham described their start earlier that morning, from camp II:

Packing sacks and gearing up takes an age and the first slanting rays of the morning light are already kissing the mountain tops by the time we get moving. I'm out in front, coaxing stiff limbs into reluctant trail-breaking activity. Even wearing snowshoes, the thin surface crust collapses under my weight, forcing an endless series of high steps until I can pass on the lead with a clear conscience. For me, following in the trail of Scott and Victor is nearly as tiring as breaking trail, as they are both lighter and shorter in stride!

The consolation for this gruelling activity is the vast panorama spread behind us, top-heavy corniced peaks framing an endless perspective of mountain ranges, some holding snow, making them distinctive amongst the anonymous grey and brown ridges of the Tibetan plateau. Ahead is the complex white world of the upper west face of our mountain with its hanging séracs, hidden crevasses and problematic route-finding.

Victor hogs the trail-breaking, taking some perverse pleasure out of ploughing through the bottomless snow on the steepening slope leading up to camp III. The parting base camp words of Jim Curran suddenly flash before me: 'Sepu Kangri is only a mountain – loved ones back home are much more important.' Why am I on this dangerous slope I ask myself? How much does climbing this mountain really mean to me? A very clear voice inside my head says that to continue is folly, this mountain is not for me. I tell Victor and Scott of the bad vibes. Victor says that he has sensed my increasing concern but does not consider the slope to be dangerous. Scott agrees. It is the parting of the ways.

This is how Victor saw it:

By 10.30 a.m. the advance party, as Scott persisted in naming us in the radio calls to Chris, had reached the worrying slopes below camp III. In spite of the deep fresh snow, we had made such good time in snowshoes that Scott and I had begun secretly to entertain thoughts of turning our journey to camp III into a summit push. But Graham had other ideas.

'What do you think about the snow?'

This is the usual code for expressing deep concern. Scott and I thought the slope was safe, at least this morning. Graham remained unconvinced. He untied, added his best wishes to those of our base camp staff, the film team, the hermit, his pilgrims, Chris and Elliot, and ploughed back alone into the Western Cwm, and thence towards the Turquoise Flower. Graham was unhappy about the sub-camp III slopes, but he showed an extraordinary bravery that day. Not only did he set off alone to climb a peak of 6650 metres, but also did so circumnavigating crevasses big enough to chuck aircraft carriers into.

Graham is usually a silent, apparently slightly stern man. He describes his push for the Turquoise Flower:

As I turn to descend my eyes fall on the snow dome that forms the western summit of the Sepu Kangri massif. It is known by the beautiful name, Seamo Uylmitok, the Turquoise Flower or Daughter of Sepu, and at 6650 metres is a significant summit in its own right. To the north it presents an elegant spur, by far the most impressive feature of the whole massif. As a parting shot, I mention my newly planned short diversion – an ascent of the Turquoise Flower before quitting the mountain!

Being free from the rope and the decision-making process of a team of three, gives me renewed energy and I snowshoe across the great snow basin towards the col that separates the Turquoise Flower from the central and highest peak of Sepu Kangri. Avoiding the long gash of a crevasse, I swing round to gain the lower slopes. Dumping my sack, I start to ascend, still wearing snowshoes but carrying crampons just in case I should encounter that rare phenomenon, firm snow! Fifty steps at a time is my self-agreed rate, with a short rest between sessions.

Before long the surface of this east face starts to firm up. No more sinking, just wonderful crampon crunching! A mounting wave of sheer pleasure flows through me, all my negative feelings are replaced by positive ones, that unique mountain joy kicking in as I approach the summit. Suddenly I'm there. The Sacred Lake and the tiny splash of colour that is base camp are a vertical 1900 metres below me. I am alone on my summit, yet share my wonder at this flawless perspective, at this moment of perfection. I look over to the bulk of the main peak without envy. If Scott and Victor do climb it I will have lost nothing, for mountaineering is not just about what we do but what we feel, about the balance between risk and responsibility, about a very personal profundity.

I can understand Graham's actions, the seeming contradiction, pointed out with a hint of irony by Victor, between a decision to turn back based on caution and one to tackle, solo, an unclimbed peak, admittedly a fairly easy one, across a basin and up a snow slope under whose surface could be concealed any number of crevasses. The key to understanding his reasoning was the fact that he was now his own master, free to make his own choices. Graham and Victor never really bonded at all. They are so very different in personality and in their approach to climbing.

I got on with both of them individually and thoroughly enjoyed climbing with them as well, but I also have been in situations where I have felt uncomfortably carried along, as Graham did here. Victor seemed to have taken the initiative, as Graham observes with his comment about Victor hogging the trail-breaking. So Graham withdrew from the attempt on the summit for what to him were sound reasons of caution, and then went on to take what were probably considerably greater risks, but ones that he felt were of his own choice and within his own control. But then climbing and the interplay of humans have never been based on logic.

Scott and Victor pressed on towards the summit. In Victor's words:

Scott and I ploughed on and up to the snow cave at camp III. I felt part of a very strange creature indeed, part tortoise, part hare, a true chimera. At camp III, we spent just over an hour and a half making tea and digging out the snow hole. So much snow had fallen since our last visit that the entrance was now a metre deeper than before, and the ceiling had sagged alarmingly, provoking horribly claustrophobic thoughts.

It had begun to cloud over by 1 p.m., by which time Scott and I had re-hydrated ourselves and excavated the snow hole enough to satisfy our craving for a secure retreat. We watched Graham, a tiny speck, reach his summit and turn down for camp II.

It was thirty-odd metres to the crest of the west ridge above the camp. The Looming Buttress, which seemed an awesome and steep barrier before, proved to have almost perfect cramponing snow. Gone was all the deep soft powder of the Western Cwm. The west ridge had been blasted over the past days, the snow was compact and firm, and formed of the wind-carved waves that the Inuit call *sastrugi*. It was enjoyable, the views were opening out, the snow was good, we were moving fast. This was a perfect day. Scott turned to me and said, 'I love the mountains!' And he meant it.

Across the top of the Looming Buttress was a Smiling Gash, a crevasse slice which we followed in one easy but spectacular pitch, and above that a pair of small basins to the west ridge. Suddenly we were on the corniced ridge leading to the summit.

'It's like the view from a plane!' said Scott.

Below our feet, the south face of Sepu Kangri dropped in one huge ice-sheathed cliff to the valley floor, bouncing up on the far side with ragged-edged horizons topping each other far away towards Burma and Bhutan. Over all this southern sky battalions of dark clouds were lining up.

The wind, from which we had been protected till now, was battering the south face, vibrating with the force of the impact. Above us, the rest of the ridge was shrouded in the cloud cap, which we finally understood to be a natural product of the fierce wind. It was orographic, lifting up the moist southern air and forcing it to condense out as vapour, the cap was filled with mist and stinging ice driven up the mountain by the wind.

As we stood, braced and leaning, the clouds began to arrive, and brought more winds with them. We had been so engrossed we did not sense the impending storm.

It was now 5.30 p.m. We radioed Chris who said that the Bracknell Met Office predicted minor showers this afternoon, and good weather tomorrow. Scott and I needed at least two hours of good visibility to reach the top, and this had now gone. We would have to follow the ridge with some accuracy. To our right overhung the cornice above the south face, to our left, avalanche-prone slopes waited at the head of the north-west face. There was not much room for error.

The little wooden wands I had cut at base camp would soon be our only means of navigation. Even with these, we would have serious difficulty returning from the summit in a night-time blizzard. I quickly ran a list of names through my mind, people who had failed to do just that. As Scott and I battled with the impulse to go forward and the rationale to turn back, at least till tomorrow, the distance of visibility had shrunk to the distance we could prod our ski pole.

There was no choice. We turned down, and then failed to find our next marker wand, just metres, a cricket pitch distance away, till a momentary lull in the wind brought a thirty-second clear spell.

Back in the snow cave we were protected from the weather. We were happy, the forecast was good, we knew the way, the route was clearly climbable. We would need six hours to do the return trip from the snow hole. We set our alarm clocks for 2 a.m., and by the time we had brewed a couple of litres of tea and eaten a handful of Jordan's Crunchy, and pulled on our boots and clothes and harnesses it was four. We stood outside the hole unable to believe what we found. The ridge just above us moaned as the spindrift arched high into the night sky. We went back to the claustrophobia of the snow hole.

Back at base camp we were undergoing that all too familiar feeling of helplessness as we waited for the next radio call. The mountain was swathed in cloud and there was snow in the air. I was worried not only about Victor and Scott, but about Graham as well. He didn't have a radio at camp II, so we had no means of knowing whether he had returned there safely, whether he was staying or coming all the way back to base, a course of action that would be even more dangerous on his own than his ascent of the Turquoise Flower.

It was a moment of profound relief when we saw Graham descending the waterfall across the lake. He soon walked through the mess tent doorway. He had become fed up with waiting for the others at camp II and decided on a solitary descent. He described it as harrowing, having triggered a series of powder-snow avalanches on the way down. At least there was now one less person to worry about.

We got up at six the following morning to get a forecast from Bracknell. This was earlier than the regular e-mailed one so Charlie, who had been handling all the calls with Bracknell, gave them a ring to get a tailor-made forecast. The Bracknell duty officer was still optimistic, talking of a clear patch of sky that was heading in our direction. We passed this on to Victor, who takes up the story:

At 8.00 a.m. I crawled out to radio Chris who said the weather today was forecast to be fine. I felt the blizzard tearing the air to shreds and looked at the radio incredulously. 'But it's just like the Cairngorms here!' I said.

By 10.30 a.m. Scott was heating his Berghaus Baltoro boots over the stove. I'd been out again, and a certain depression was engulfing our mood.

We had more brews and ventured out at noon to find there was no change in the weather.

'What is the most important thing in bridge?'

'I don't know, Scottie, what is?'

'Be bold in your bidding! We should go for it.'

So at 2.00 p.m. we tried the bold approach, standing in the blizzard on the ridge above the camp. Shouting into the wind Scott mouthed the words, 'Let's get the hell out of here!'

The descent was now beginning to worry us. The camp III slope was ready to slide off in one big mass and, as the spindrift settled on it, hour by hour it was become increasing unstable.

The previous night we had slept badly, we had hardly eaten, we were running out of things to brew (we had been very enthusiastic in that department and dehydration was not a problem, though frequent pee stops were becoming one) and the stale air inside our deep freeze was giving us mild but constant headaches.

I dreamt a dream of geometrical ghosts. A pair of curiously triangular figures, carrying perhaps scythes? The first figure was beckoning. I woke with a bitter taste in my mouth, and ghosts in my mind.

By the time we descended on the camp III slope, the blizzard had been blowing for thirty-six hours. The moaning sound it made over the ridge was now a dull roar, a jet turbine noise. The slopes below us were going to be loaded.

'That slope is humungulous, it's just Russian roulette,' said my friend. I knew. I thought that the slope needed another name, the sub-camp III slope did not convey what I felt then about it. A more suitable name, at least for me, would be the Slope of Abject Terror. The thought of it gave me asthma, and I pulled a large gasp on my inhaler before ploughing down into it. Scott carried the snow shovel. You cannot dig an avalanche victim out with an ice axe, and fatality is exponentially proportional to burial time. So speed and shovel. My only chance.

The Slope of Abject Terror curved away like an upside down bowl, after fifty metres it dipped to forty-five degrees, the optimum sliding angle, and a crevasse appeared on the right. This feature, three metres wide and indeterminably deep, was our island of safety. Scott and I hoped that it was wide enough to swallow avalanches from above.

I kicked a ledge inside and made a safe snowy stance, and strangely, at that moment I sensed one of the triangular ghosts fade away. Scott looked a bit disconcerted as I counterbalanced him over the edge of the crevasse.

The rest of the Abject Terror, unseen in the whiteout, ran out to the Western Cwm like that eighty-metre ski jump thing. Though he tried, Scott failed to set off the next part of the slope, and by the time I joined him on the glacier the second geometrical ghost had also faded away.

Our legs were tired and the rest of the day went by like a marathon long after you have hit the wall: ploughing our trench back to camp II, the Corridor, the Fotheringham Ridge, that awful crusty snow down to camp I, where dear kind Elliot had volunteered to come up with the Sherpa staff and help us clear the camp.

The news from base was of failing generators and Charlie's windmills finally coming good, and also the good doctor had been tending to a minor epidemic of tummy bugs. Elliot asked how we were feeling.

'No bother! Our bugs are well dead of starvation and altitude sickness!' said Scott.

Our sense of humour was returning, but as we passed under the hermitage, I found time to stop. Sam Ten Tsokpu's flags were fluttering, a white smoke billowed for a second in the breeze – a sign? Can he make black smoke? I asked myself. I sat down on a red granite boulder half-buried in the water. The stream trickled like Buddhist bells. I looked up at the storm-veiled mountain and, well, I was happy. Happy to have been so close, and happy to be alive. And happy because, like Scottie, I too love the mountains.

15 Leaving Friends

16th October 1998

CHRIS BONINGTON

It was time to go. The jet stream continued to blast across the top of Sepu Kangri, swaddling it in a permanent cap of wind-blown cloud. Winter had arrived. We all had jobs and families to go back to. We ordered the yaks and on 16th October started back down the valley.

The farewells were sad. It was unlikely that we would ever return to that lovely valley. Our neighbours sensed this too. Tsini especially was silent, yet stoical, standing with a distant look in that strong, intense face, watching our preparations for departure. We had distributed all surplus food, fuel and rope to our neighbours. The yaks were loaded and to calls and shouts of their herders, we set out for the last time along the shore of the Sacred Lake. No doubt Sam Ten Tsokpu, perched in his eerie on the other side of the valley, watched us leave.

Our journey back to the roadhead had a bitter-sweet quality, highlighted by the gold and red of autumnal leaves shining brightly against the dusty brown of wind-seared grass. Charlie and Elliot rode down on ponies, Charlie having his narrowest escape of the entire expedition when the girth of his saddle slipped. He fell off, plummeting down a steep scree slope above the river, but was unhurt. The wooden frames outside the villages were laden with raised stacks of golden barley, the husks still on the stems. The villagers were preparing for the long cold winter. By the roadhead the level of the river had fallen and a makeshift bridge of branches and logs had been built across the islands of gravel. The entire population of the village came out to help us carry the loads across to the truck and three Land Cruisers that were waiting. Elliot's lady friend, Alo, who had fallen for him during his stay in Khinda at the start of the expedition, had dressed up in her best blue *chuba*, coloured her cheeks with rouge, and blushed when she saw him. Dougal, a doleful yet rather lovely brown mongrel who had adopted us at base camp, had followed us all the way down. He was now curled up in the dust, unaware that this short spell of regular meals and kind words was over. Within an hour we were across the river at Khinda. We hugged old friends and thanked them, threw the loads into the transport and drove off. Somehow it was better to leave quickly.

Our next stop was at Diru, with its pretentious administrative buildings, the brand new shopping mall with shiny aluminium shutters, but still no sewers, street lighting or running water. That night we ate in the restaurant owned by the district leader. There were small partitioned rooms, each with a big round table with its lazy Susan in the middle keeping the dishes circulating. The food was excellent and course followed course. Not only was it a restaurant but also a night club with three heavily made-up Chinese hostesses and a huge television set blasting out western pop videos. The floor was empty until Charlie invited the prettiest hostess to dance, giving us a bravura performance of slinky ballroom dancing. Soon our inhibitions were driven away by quantities of beer and we all joined Charlie on the floor. Pasang, a little drunk and tearful, was apologising for we knew not what, while the young lorry driver was rivalling Charlie in ballroom skills.

Sitting in the darkened room with the music hammering, I couldn't help wondering about the contrast between the village where we had spent the previous night, by the Chih-chu, the rushing torrent of a river and this brash onslaught of western music and values that had invaded this outpost. How long would it be before this influence affected the beliefs and way of life of the Tibetans who, at least here deep in the country, probably existed in much the same way as they had been before the Chinese came?

I was tired and about 11 p.m. I decided to walk back to the other end of town to the compound where we were staying. I had gone about a quarter of a mile along the pitch-black street when suddenly a pack of dogs growled and snarled out of the blackness. The rain poured down and the mud of the road was slippery underfoot. It was so dark I couldn't even see the gleam of their eyes. I sensed a rush of bodies from behind, swerved round and with a reflex action kicked out, but my kick hit nothing. It was all so sudden. My mind registered that I was being attacked and that I was in real danger. They were snapping and barking all around me. I felt a bite in the back of my calf, kicked out again, lost my balance and sprawled in the muddy road. I was terrified. I scrambled up to my feet and edged across to where I sensed the houses were at the side of the road. I propped myself against the wall to guard my back, and my snarling tormentors hemmed me in.

There were no lights and not a soul around. I seemed to be in a deserted town. It was ironical that I was in one of the most frightening and dangerous situations that I have ever faced, after making the sensible safe decision a week earlier to leave the mountain. I was backed against the wall for I don't know how long and was desperately wondering when Charlie and the others would finish their junketing, when a light came bobbing through the darkness. A Chinese couple were returning home. The man flashed the light around him enabling me to catch glimpses of the snarling dogs. They were intimidated, held back by the light, as I rushed over to join the couple and be escorted across the bridge out of the dogs' territory. The couple turned off to the left and I went on alone, apprehensive in the dark, but there were no more dogs. A few metres further on I reached the locked gates of the compound, shouted and banged until a sleepy caretaker let me in.

Back in our room I took off my drenched clothes and bathed the incisor wounds on the back of my leg in cold water. The deep tooth marks already looked red and angry. I wondered if my rabies inoculation was still effective and waited impatiently for Charlie to come back. It was a long wait and when he did arrive, he had been dancing non-stop for three hours and the beer had flowed freely. But he was immediately full of concern and started to search for the antibiotics, rabies booster and syringes. He and Elliot had to delve in the dark through the mountain of baggage in the truck outside. The waiting seemed endless. He emptied the medical bag all over the floor of the room and fumbled in the debris but couldn't find syringes or needles. The team, now all returned and relatively sobered up, watched the performance with interest; Charlie had also lost his spectacles. He ended up emptying some drug from a full syringe, substituting an antibiotic and jabbing it firmly and accurately into my buttock. I was so worried by this stage that it was an immense relief to have any kind of treatment.

Next morning the inflammation had settled, although the wound was still sore. We had a breakfast of delicious dumplings in a one-room café by the bridge, nearby where I had been attacked. Mangy dogs, most of them strays, skulked in the gutter by the side of the road. In daylight they posed no threat and were the abused rather than the aggressors. It was under cover of darkness that they could assert their territorial rights and get their own back on their two-legged enemies. Charlie, as he relates, had also had some more work that night:

After trying to sort out Chris, I wandered outside into the yard for a pee and a stroll to find Pasang, also worse for wear, and clutching his right wrist. Not another casualty? It's like Saturday night in A&E. Blood was dripping from his hand and the wrist was deformed and swollen. He had fallen over in the street. The wrist looked fractured. I bandaged it up, made a makeshift splint from some wood and crashed into bed exhausted. We were all grumpy next morning.

Medicine never quite ends. Gyatha, the little boy who needed a circumcision, and Yinsu, his mother, had travelled with us from Samda. Gyatha wore a traditional robe and new shoes, his best clothes, and was excited at his first journey outside the valley. He had sat proudly in a Land Cruiser while Yinsu huddled uncomfortably in the truck. We looked in at the hospital at Diru, next door to the compound where we stayed; the doctor advised us to take the child on to Nakchu. I was glad I had not embarked on the circumcision myself in the hills.

That night we were installed in the garish cold Nakchu Hotel. The road had seemed endless. Chris appeared to have forgiven my performance the previous night with the antibiotics. His leg was less painful, thank God. Pasang's arm was in a sling, but no worse, and he was moving his hand. What will Yishi his wife think? I shared with Elliot, and feebly we tried to look back on the last few weeks, until he suddenly looked a nasty grey colour and began to vomit. He puked the night away – I really had picked the wrong room-mate.

Early next morning I made arrangements for Gyatha to be seen at the hospital. Yinsu looked bewildered by the noise and traffic of the city but her son was loving it. We left them with the Nakchu family we had met in 1997. 'They'll charge double if they see you at the hospital,' Pasang had warned. Gyatha stood to attention and bowed. We shook hands and rubbed foreheads. Tears came to his eyes. I left some money for them and we headed for Lhasa. Graham Little, the treasurer-in-the-field, wrote faithfully in the accounts book: '500 *yuan* [about £50] – to Charlie, for boy's penis.'

We ended with an anxious drive through patchy fog along the tarmac road. Back in the busy Lhasa streets, we drove to the Khada Hotel, exhausted the hot water supply and slept, tired and happy. The afternoon before we left I visited the Norbu Lingka zoo to see the mysterious *temu*. We were disappointed: it was a honey bear.

Our stay in Lhasa ended with formality. The farewell dinner, as guests of our hosts, was a banquet in the old style. The menu ran: eel fillets, celery and chilli, smoked duck, gelatinous corn soup, deep-fried fish in sauce, roasted cashews, spinach soup, pears with sweet rice, prawns and melon, chillied noodles, sweet buttered peanuts, honey-glazed chicken, whole eels, clam kebabs, sweet pastries, chicken kidneys, *momos*, beef slices, chillied langoustines, crab in chilli sauce, peacock-shaped *chocktoi*, chicken slices, rice, real tortoise soup, diced vegetables, beer, *moutai*, turtle-blood liqueur, Bordeaux, Coca-cola, Tea.

We live in a world of strange contrasts. Not a month previously dinner had been *tsampa* and raw dried yak meat in a place where the income per capita is around $250 a year.

Returning is a curious phenomenon. I had been away for over eighty days. If one misses home greatly, long expeditions are impossible. I was suddenly conscious of my absence from Ruth and the children and longed to see them again. Then I thought of work and money, and realised quite suddenly that I had not thought about either for as long as I could remember. The hospitals which had granted me leave had barely crossed my mind. I had not seen a bank statement for three months. Now it would be back to work and the politics of the National Health Service. I found I looked forward to seeing patients again but found little joy at the prospect of the administrative battles and the jockeying for position that are part of daily life. For these three trips, above all others, had made me feel that I had enjoyed a life that had been truly my own, that no one can take away. I think I shall remember them when I die.

And what of my own feelings? I had dearly wanted to reach that summit. I had, perhaps mistakenly, perceived it as the end of a personal era. I have found climbing at altitude, carrying my share of the loads increasingly demanding in the last few years. I was aware that I was no longer able to pull my weight fully within a team where I was always the oldest member. I had decided, and talked to others about the decision, that this would be the last peak of such a height that I would tackle. It wasn't a matter of giving up climbing, but simply one of going for lower objectives, of being realistic about, but not giving in to, the process of ageing.

And yet, I was not depressed as we made our way back from Sepu Kangri, nor a few months later, while writing this story of an adventure. The quality of the experience as a whole made that ephemeral moment of standing on a mountain top seem less important. There were so many memories, particularly of our reconnaissance in 1996, of the sheer freshness and fun of our adventures, when every bend in the road or track brought a surprise.

I look forward to similar challenges; indeed, I am already planning them. There were new friendships to make and old friendships to be cemented and enjoyed.

For each one of us, these expeditions will hold very personal memories. For myself, Sepu Kangri will always be a very special chapter, and one in which I learnt much about myself and the people around me. I, like Charlie, will always remember Tsini, Karte, the gentle Dorbe, Pasang's wily ways and the exuberant Minchi. Who knows, one day we might return, not to climb the mountain, but to renew those friendships and to see what has happened in the rhythm of the lives of those who helped us beside the Sacred Lake of Sam Tso Taring in the shadow of the Great White Snow God.

Expedition Members

1996 Reconnaisance

Sir Christian Bonington, CBE
Dr Charles Clarke
Pasang Choephel

1997 Sepu Kangri Expedition

Sir Christian Bonington, CBE
Dr Charles Clarke
Dr Jim Fotheringham
Jim Lowther
John Porter
Duncan Sperry
Jim Curran

Pasang Choephel
Dorje Wangdue
Dawa Tshiring Sherpa
Nawang Phurba Sherpa
Pemba Chhiri Sherpa

1998 Sepu Kangri Expedition

Sir Christian Bonington, CBE
Dr Charles Clarke
Victor Saunders
Graham Little
Elliot Robertson
Scott Muir

1998 Film Team

Martin Belderson
Jim Curran
Greig Cubitt (ITN)

Pasang Choephel
Dorje Wangdue
Tachei Tshering
Ram Krishna Tamang
Pemba Chhiri Sherpa

Diary of Events

1982

March	Chris Bonington and Charles Clarke first see Sepu Kangri while flying from Chengdu to Lhasa on their way to the north-east ridge of Everest. At this time they are not aware of its name or significance.
1987	Frank Boothman writes to Chris of a high peak he has identified on maps of north-east Tibet. Chris identifies this as the peak he saw from the plane.
1989	Chris Bonington and Jim Fotheringham apply to climb Sepu Kangri but have permission withdrawn a few days before their departure.
1996	Chris Bonington and Charles Clarke make a reconnaissance of Sepu Kangri.
3 August	Depart Heathrow.
6 August	Reach Lhasa.
8 August	Drive to Nakchu with Pasang, Mingma and Tsering.
9 August	Reach Diru.
11 August	Reach roadhead at Khinda.
12 August	Reach Gyolong, a pleasant meadow with scattered copses of

	juniper by the Chih-chu with three yaks.
13 August	Reach north end of Sam Tso Taring.
14 August	Chris and Charlie camp at south end of Sam Tso Taring.
15 August	They reach and return from Sa La (5600m).
16 August	Return to main campsite at north end of lake and recce slopes on western side to a height of 5700m.
17 August	Reach Bakrong on way back to roadhead.
18 August	Reach Diru.
19 August	Reach Nakchu.
20 August	Drive to road south of Sepu Kangri, camping by roadside.
21 August	Call in at Chali and then backtrack to camp by river on way to Chali-chu.
22 August	Reach southern roadhead.
23 August	Travel on foot and horse some 40 km over Tong La (5180m) camping other side of it.
24 August	Walking down the Yapu valley to look at the south side of Sepu Kangri.
25 August	Return to roadhead.
1 September	Return to UK.

1997

9 April	Charles Clarke and Duncan Sperry fly to Kathmandu with PIA to purchase food and get gear through customs. In the event this was probably unnecessary since Bikrum Pandey's Himalaya Expeditions were both efficient and reliable and could have done all of this.
14 April	Nawang, our Sherpa cook, sets out from Kathmandu with the truck carrying the expedition gear and food to Lhasa. A truck sent by the CTMA transferred the gear at the Friendship Bridge on the frontier.
16 April	The rest of the team – Bonington, Curran, Fotheringham, Lowther and Porter – set out for Kathmandu.
19 April	Team reaches Lhasa to be joined by Dorje, our liaison officer and Pasang, our interpreter.
22 April	The team set out from Lhasa in three Land Cruisers with a

	truck carrying the expedition equipment. Reach Nakchu.
23 April	The team reaches Diru.
24 April	The team reaches the roadhead at Yuchong (4073m).
28 April	Team sets out from roadhead to Gyolong.
29 April	Camped about an hour's walk beyond Samda monastery in Sa nang.
30 April	Reached base camp at the south end of Sam Tso Taring.
2 May	Held *puja* and then made first recce. Porter, Lowther and Clarke climbed 5600m hill to the south-east of base to get views of face, while Bonington and Fotheringham visited the hermit living at the foot of the Thong Wuk Glacier and then followed the glacier to see if there was a possible route behind the north face of Sepu Kangri.
4 May	Start recce of col leading to the western aspect of Sepu Kangri, camping on the northern side of the Thong Wuk Glacier at 5050m.
5 May	The climbing team reach the col to the north of Seamo Uylmitok, the Turquoise Flower, up deep snow and breakable crust and in poor visibility and deteriorating weather, retreating to a hummock three hundred metres below the col. There did not seem to be a reasonable route approaching Sepu Kangri from this aspect.
6 May	Return to base camp.
7 May	Fotheringham, Lowther and Clarke with the Sherpas shift dump of equipment from the north side of the glacier to the other side to below the north-east ridge of Seamo Uylmitok, the Turquoise Flower.
9 May	Camp I established at 5150m.
11 May	Route fixed to site of camp II at 5575m.
14 May	Fotheringham and Porter move up to camp II and push route out about four rope-lengths.
15 May	Bonington and Lowther move up to camp II. Fotheringham and Porter push route on to north face up to 5850m.
16 May	Bonington and Lowther push route up to 6050m, a possible site for camp III, up long snow slopes to the point where it would be possible to traverse left across the face and reach the

	col. It would probably be a three-day push to the summit.
17 May	The team dropped back for a rest at base before final summit push.
18 May	Heavy snow fall – probably almost a metre on the face.
26 May	Camp II cleared of all gear.
27 May	Departure from base camp.
28 May	Reach roadhead and on to Diru.
30 May	Reach Lhasa.
3 June	Flight to Kathmandu.
5 June	Flight to Karachi.
6 June	Flight to Manchester.

1998   The Exploration Party

5 August	Charles Clarke and Elliot Robertson leave Heathrow with Qatar Airways for Kathmandu on their exploratory trip to the eastern approaches of Sepu Kangri.
8 August	Reach Lhasa.
11 August	Leave Lhasa for Nakchu. (They had hoped to approach the eastern part of the Nyenchen Tanglha from the south, but the roads were blocked by a particularly heavy monsoon, so they started by the same route we had used the previous year.)
12 August	Sog Xian.
13 August	Tengchen.
14 August	Riwoche.
15 August	Chamdo.
16 August	At the turning off main road to south towards Lhorong.
17 August	After Dolma Lhakhang monastery, former seat of the Akong Rinpoche, who now presides over the monastery of Samye Ling, Eskdalemuir, Scotland.
18 August	After Lhorong.
19 August	Tsoka (roadhead).
20 August	Tsoka.
21 August	Rainbow Camp, below Shargang La.
22 August	Tsara Sondu, over Shargang La.

1998 (continued)

23 August	Tsara Sondu.
24 August	Po-Lo-Kageh.
25 August	Lu-bu-gna (over three passes, into Nagru valley).
26 August	Dorputang.
27 August	Tashi Lung Valley camp I.
28 August	Tashi Lung Valley camp II.
29 August	Below Sa La.
30 August	Arrive Sepu Kangri base camp.
31 August	Sepu Kangri base camp.
1 September	Over Yam La into Yang valley.
2 September	Yam-Chu valley.
3 September	Samda monastery.
4 September	Khinda.
5 September	Khinda.
6 September	Khinda.
7 September	Khinda: main expedition arrives.

1998   Main Expedition

28 August	Main expedition, Chris Bonington, Graham Little, Scott Muir and Victor Saunders with the media team, Martin Belderson, Jim Curran and Rob Franklin of Northern Films and Greig Cubitt (ITN) leave Heathrow for Lhasa by Qatar Airways via Kathmandu.
1 September	Reach Lhasa.
5 September	Reach Nakchu (Rob Franklin was ill, remained in Lhasa and returned to the UK a few days later).
6 September	Diru.
7 September	Khinda (roadhead) meet Charlie and Elliot.
10 September	All team less Elliot and Tachei, the liaison officer, set out from Khinda with thirty horses to reach Bakrong. Elliot stays behind to look after remainder of loads which are to follow.

11 September	Reach crossing just below Samda monastery and haul all loads across yak-hide rope.
13 September	Reach base camp.
16 September	Victor and Charlie climb *Amchhi Inje-ne* (5850m).
17 September	Elliot arrives at base camp with rear party.
18 September	Graham and Scott set out for Chomo Mangyal, camping at its foot (5300m). Chris, Victor and Elliot set out on recce of western approach, camping at small pasture at 5080m.
19 September	Graham and Scott attempt western face and north ridge of Chomo Mangyal turning back at 5900m because of dangerous snow conditions. Chris, Victor and Elliot reach Moraine Camp (camp I) at 5400m.
20 September	Chris, Victor and Elliot reach crest of Fotheringham's Ridge and follow it to point where it joins the upper Thong Wuk Glacier (5850m).
22 September	Graham and Scott climb Thaga Ri (5930m) to the north of base camp.
24 September	Graham and Scott, with Martin, move up to camp I.
25 September	Chris, Victor and Elliot move up to camp I. Graham and Scott improve the fixed rope just above camp I.
26 September	Chris, Scott and Elliot drop back to base for more provisions and gear. Graham and Victor improve campsite.
27 September	Graham and Victor carry to end Fotheringham's Ridge and Victor improves fixed rope. Chris, Scott and Elliot move back up to camp I.
28 September	All five move to camp II at 6170m.
29 September	All five move to camp III at 6350m.
1 October	All five retreat to base.
3 October	Charlie, Jim and Martin walk down to Samda to attend Devil Dance festival.
6 October	Charlie, Jim and Martin return to base.
8 October	Climbing team of Chris, Victor, Elliot, Graham and Scott move to camp I for second attempt.
9 October	Graham, Victor and Scott move up to camp II in appalling snow conditions with the only three pairs of snowshoes. Chris and Elliot drop back to base.

10 October   Scott and Victor reach the west shoulder of Sepu Kangri (6830m) and then return to camp III. Graham climbs Seamo Uylmitok, the Turquoise Flower, and returns to camp II.

11 October   Scott and Victor make second attempt on main summit but return almost immediately to camp III because of high winds and snow. Graham returns to base.

12 October   Weather remains bad. Scott and Victor return to base.

16 October   Team leave base camp for roadhead.

20 October   All reach Lhasa.

24 October   All reach Kathmandu by air.

25 October   Team return to UK by Qatar Airways.

A Gazetteer

There are considerable difficulties assigning accurate placenames in this region. The mountain and valley names are usually the most reliable of several options used by local people, the map *Immortal Mountains in the Snow Region,* Soviet and other maps (*see* Appendix 4). For main towns we have used the spellings given in the *Tibet Handbook* (*see* Appendix 10.)

Heights and co-ordinates are taken from various sources.
An asterisk indicates Global Positioning System readings en route.

Rivers, Valleys

USUAL NAME	OTHER NAMES
Yangtse	Dri-chu, Di-chu (Tibetan), Jinsha jiang (Chinese)
Salween	Nak-chu (Tib.), Ngul-chu (Tib.), Gyalmo Ngul-chu (Tib.), Black river, Nu jiang (Ch.), Lu jiang (Ch.)
Mekong	Da-chu (Tib.), Lancang jiang (Ch.)
Ngom-chu	Source of Mekong, meets Dza-chu at Chamdo
Dzi-chu	Source of Mekong near Riwoche
Dza-chu	Source of Mekong, meets Ngom-chu at Chamdo
Yu-chu	River at Dolma Lhakhang monastery
Keela Pu	Side valley W of Shargang La

Rivers, Valleys (continued)

USUAL NAME	OTHER NAMES	
Yu-chong nang (valley)	Yak-chu (the main Khinda/Senza valley river)	
Kiru nang (valley)	Chih-chu (the approach valley river)	
Sa nang (valley)	Shanumba Gully (Ch.), base camp valley	
Yapu Valley	Main valley on S side of Sepu Kangri (in *Immortal Mountains . . .*)	
Yang Valley	SW approach to Sepu Kangri	
Reting Tsangpo	Lhasa branch, joins Yarlung	*(main three*
Yarlung Tsangpo	Drains N side of Himalaya	*sources of the*
Yigong Tsangpo	Branch S of Pelbar, joins Yarlung	*Brahmaputra)*
Nagru valley	Valleys approaching Sa La from the east	
Tashi Lung valley		

Cities, Towns, Villages

USUAL NAME	OTHER NAMES	ALTITUDE/CO-ORDINATES
Lhasa	Rasa, Barantola (ancient names)	3600m
Nakchu	Nagchu, Naqchu, Nagqu, Nagchuka	4440m*
Diru	Driru, Biru, Nakchubiru, Naksho Driru, &c	3825m*
Sog Xian	Sok Tsanden Zhol, Sokchian and others)	about 4000m
Sertsa	Sertsa Yongdzong	about 4800m
Tengchen	Denqen, Khyungpo Tengchen, Tengchen Kha, Gyamotang	over 4000m
Riwoche	Rioche, Riwoqe	4338m*
Chamdo	Qamdo, Tsiamdo	about 3200m
Dayak	SE of Chamdo	
Mar-ri		over 4000m

Cities, Towns, Villages (continued)

USUAL NAME	OTHER NAMES	ALTITUDE/CO-ORDINATES
Dolma Lhakhang	(Monastery)	over 4000m
Lhorong		c. 4000m: 30.90N,95.84E*
Lhatse	Lhaze, Lha Dze	over 4000m*
Pelbar	Banbar, Panbar	4025m*: 30.83N,94.84E*
Tsoka	Coka (roadhead)	3815m* 30.91N,94.68E*
Do Martang	also called Pelbar, county capital 4km from Tsoka	
Du Tsuka	Rainbow Camp	over 4400m
Tsara Sondu		4639m*: 30.90N,94.16E*
Dorputang		4309m*: 30.95N,94.18E*
Tashi Lung Camp I		4396m*: 30.95N,94.08E*
Tashi Lung Camp II		4393m*: 30.95N,94.03E*
Tashi Lung Camp III		4576m*: 30.93N,93.54E*
Lu Bug Na		4782m*: 30.90N,94.27E*
Sam Tso Taring	Sem Co, Sacred Lake	4750m*: 30.95N,93.80E*
Base camp		4750m*: 30.95N,93.80E*
Samda monastery	Samdapon *gompa*	4302m*: 31.08N,93.08E*
Bakrong	Bakhirong	4030m*
Khinda	(village across river from expedition roadhead)	c.3900m
Pengar	Pangar, town E of Senza	
Senza	(near Khinda, district centre)	c.3900m
Chali~	(southern recce)	c.4000m
Chali-chu~	(southern recce)	
Jiali, Lharigo or Lhari~	(southern recce)	c.4200m

~ We remain in some confusion about these three placenames.

Passes

Sakta La	4165m*: 30.90N, 96.38E*
Dzeki La	4400m*: 30.75N, 95.90E*
Shargang La	5038m: 30.83N, 94.55E
Gu Gyu La	5265m*: 30.87N, 94.35E
Pemo La	over 5200m: 30.87N, 94.32E
Tang La	over 5200m: 30.87N, 94.33E
Sa La	Se La, c.5600m: 30.95N, 94.85E
Shar La	5100m (between Diru and Senza)
Langlu La	4300m (between Nakchu & Diru)
Janghku La	4700m (between Nakchu & Diru)
Gang La	4800m (between Nakchu & Sok)
Shara La	4700m (between Sok & Chamdo)
Shel La	4800m (between Sok & Chamdo)
Yam La	5430m*: 30.98N, 93.72E*
Tong La	5180m* (southern recce)

Mountain Ranges, Summits, Glaciers

NAME	OTHER NAMES	HEIGHT	
Nyenchen Tanglha	Nyangla Qen Tangla Shan, Tangla Range, Nyainqentanglha	Main range of region; our peaks are in Eastern Section of Nyenchen Tanglha which extends E of Lhasa–Nakchu road	
Sepu Kangri	The White Snow God Sepu Kunglha Karpu/ Karpo, Khamsum, Sa-Pu	6956m, 6995m; 6910m (Soviet 1:200,000 map)	30.91N 93.78E
Seamo Uylmitok	The Turquoise Flower, the Daughter of Sepu	6650m	
Chomo Mangyal	The Wife of Sepu	6236m	

Mountain Ranges, Summits, Glaciers (continued)

NAME	OTHER NAMES	HEIGHT	
Tsoto Takze	The Daughter in Disgrace	6128m	
Gosham Taktso	The Son and Prime Minister of Sepu, Bon Che Dadhul	6296m	
Taktse Dunlhu	The Eldest Son of Sepu, Bon Che Dadhul	6900m, 6956m (on Chinese map)	
Thaga Ri		5930m, 5927m	30.98N, 93.82E
Lhazo Bumla	The Thousand Buddhas	6556m	
Lhallum Tamcho	Mount Sepu	6621m	
Amchhi Inji-ne	The English Doctor	5850m*	30.98N, 93.81E
Maya		6076m	E of Sepu
Mawo Kangri		6619m	SE of Sepu Kangri
Kok-po	Peak SE of Sa La, posssibly Maya of Chinese map	6612m (Soviet)	30.86N, 93.92E
Sem Glacier	NE of Sepu massif		
Thong Wuk Glacier	N side of Sepu Kangri		
Yanglung Glacier	W approach to Sepu Kangri		

Maps

Map of Mountain Peaks on the Qinghai-Xizang Plateau

1:2,500,000 1st edition, 1st impression Tokyo 1989
Published and distributed by China Cartographic Publishing House.

We bought our copy at the CTMA in Lhasa. This map gives an overview of peaks in Tibet (Xizang), without naming many of them. It is of limited value in finding approach routes to the mountains themselves.

Maps in *Immortal Mountains in the Snow Region*

There is a 1:7,500,000 map showing the location of all the peaks described. There are also more detailed maps. The local Sepu Kangri map is at 1:100,000.

References within *Immortal Mountains in the Snow Region* mention other maps, but no large scale series. It seems to us that few detailed maps of Tibet were available to these 'official' authors. Perhaps they had access to the Soviet series.

Soviet Military Map Series 1:1,000,000 and 1:200,000

These sheets have an interesting history. They were published in the 1970s at a time when Sino-Soviet relations were at a low ebb. As far one can gather, they were secret, and it is difficult to know how the detailed information was assembled. Sheets cover the whole of Asia.

1:200,000 Lharigo 08-46-10, H-46-X
1:200,000 Pelbar 08-46-11, H-46-XI
A 1:1,000,000 series also exists.

Sheets of both series are available to view in the Royal Geographical Society, London.

Detailed and highly accurate for geographical features. All names in Cyrillic, some incorrect. Main summits are marked. These were the maps of principal value during our 1998 journey through the Nyenchen Tanglha.

China Tibet Tour Map

ISBN7-80544-291-8/K : 280
Chengdu Map Publishing House, 1993
1:3,000,000

A useful road map, despite scale. This is the usual tourist map available in Lhasa.

Tibet Road Map

1:1,500,000 Berndtson & Berndtson

Another useful road map, available in Britain.

Tangar to Lhasa 1:2,500,000

Incorporating the Surveys of Brigadier-General G. Pereira.
War Office, September 1925. Map No. 2957. In Younghusband, F., *Peking to Lhasa*. London, Constable, 1925.

Of some historical interest.

Sandberg's Maps

Sandberg, G. *The Exploration of Tibet. Its History & Particulars from 1623 to 1904*. Calcutta, Thacker, Spink, 1904.

Two maps are found in the back of the book (the main Tibetan map is missing from the recent Indian reprint available in Nepal). The contemporary street map of the centre of Lhasa is of interest.

Various International Series

e.g. Series 1301 (GSGS 4646). Sheet NH-46. Edition 3-GSGS. 1:1,000,000.

Produced in 1958 from various previous sources this map of central Tibet is of very limited value. No roads are shown, the snow ranges are in general overestimated in lengths and heights. Some useful placenames.

Flight Charts

Series TPC Sheets H-10A and 10B. 1:500,000.

Of very limited value on the ground.

Royal Geographical Society Map & Gazetteer

The Mountains of Central Asia. Edited by Michael Ward. The Royal Geographical Society and Mount Everest Foundation. London, Macmillan, 1987. 1:3,000,000.

Provides an overview of main peaks.

Weather

Some idea of the prevailing weather can be gained from the table below. The information is from the Meteorological Bureau, the Tibet Autonomous Region, No. 1, Linkuo North Road, Lhasa 850000, PRC.

Average Rainfall and Average and Extreme Temperatures: Chali and Sog Xian

	CHALI			SOG XIAN		
Rain/°C	*Av. cm*	*Av. °C*	*Ext. °C*	*Av. cm*	*Av. °C*	*Ext. °C*
Jan	7.4	−12	−37	5.3	−10	−37
Feb	9.9	−9	−26	4.2	−6	−30
March	18.2	−5	−21	7.3	−2	−26
April	30.2	−1	−14	14.5	+2	−27
May	86.3	+3	−8	48.9	+6	−17
June	124.6	+7	−4	130.8	+9	−4
July	141.2	+8	−3	129.5	+11	−4
August	133.7	+8	−4	109	+11	−7
Sept	91.0	+5	−7	89.3	+8	−9
Oct	36.5	0	−14	28.4	+2	−17
Nov	6.3	−5	−27	3.3	−4	−22
Dec	5.9	−10	−31	2.4	−8	−29

TOWN	FIRST SNOWFALL	LAST SNOWFALL
Chali	3rd September 1994	18th July 1995
Sog Xian	2nd October 1994	3rd June 1995

The UK Meteorological Office (Bracknell, RG12 2SY,UK) also supplied free daily reports. These were most helpful, though often in the few hours that had elapsed between compiling a report and its reception, bad weather had already arrived. These reports were compiled from analysis of satellite data, international weather maps and computer models. They were then e-mailed on a daily basis. Sometimes we telephoned Bracknell direct. A typical full report at a critical time in 1998 was as follows:

Meteorological Consultant: Eleanor Crompton. Forecast for Sepu Kangri 30.9°N 93.8°E from 0600GMT on Sun 11 Oct to 0600 on Mon 12 Oct 1998:

General synoptic overview: The latest available satellite picture, 0001GMT, shows the cloud remaining well broken to the west of your area but another significant band of cloud, associated with a major upper level trough, is lying north-east to south-west between 45N 90E and 37N 75E, moving east. The upper trough is expected to continue eastwards through the next twenty-four hours to be situated between 45N 95E and 37N 95E by 0600GMT. As the trough passes to the north, the flow over the Sepu Kangri area appears along parallel contours, due west. However, there are likely to be minor perturbations through the flow, enough to induce shower development.

Position of jetstream relative to Sepu Kangri: The jet is broad and poorly defined but the main core at 0600 GMT Sunday is to the WNW of your area, around 33N 82E, expected to be 33N 89E by 0600GMT Monday, 85 to 90 knots.

Winds (5500m): W to SW 10 to 15 knots increasing 15 to 20 at times.

Temperature (5500m): minus 05 to minus 08°C.

Winds (6500m): W 20 to 25 knots.

Temperature (6500m): minus 08 to minus 16°C.

Weather: Cloud is expected to be well broken through much of the period. The probability of precipitation is only around 10% at first with any showers light. However, the probability is expected to increase through the latter half of the period, nearer 30 to 40%.

Outlook from 0600GMT on Mon 12 Oct to 0600 on Wed 14 Oct 1998

General synoptic overview: The upper level flow appears mainly zonal but the model shows a broad trough over the whole of the region through the period between 30 and 40N, 65 to 95E. The model may not have resolved minor, sharper troughs. There will be a continued risk of showers throughout.

Position of jetstream relative to Sepu Kangri: The jet core is over or just to the north throughout the period, between 32 and 34N, 95 to 95 knots.

Winds (5500m): W to SW 10 to 15 occasionally 20 knots

Temperature (5500m): minus 04 to minus 08°C

Winds (6500m): W 20 to 25 increasing 25 to 30 knots

Temperature (6500m): minus 08 to minus 16°C

Weather: mostly cloudy with a 60% chance of showers or snow.

Communications and Film

CHARLES CLARKE

Telecommunications

The mobile satellite telephone, e-mail, and the ability to transmit digital still and video images has changed one important aspect of mountaineering and exploration in remote areas: communication with the outside world is potentially instant and global. This brings with it advantages, and various possible problems. The age of the mail runner is now long past, but as short a time ago as 1988 we employed one on our trip to Menlungtse. His name was Alan Hinkes; he went on to climb the west summit!

We developed our own communications systems on Sepu Kangri, basing much of the plans for 1998 on experience gained by Duncan Sperry on the 1997 expedition. We relied in part on computers which we already owned; sponsors (principally British Telecom and Apple Computer Company) supplied other equipment. We were helped greatly by Martin Davidson (Skarda International Communications) and Gerry Taylor (GT Associates), both of whom provided advice, technical expertise and many hours of work.

It is important to define the purpose of communications equipment. In our case, the ability to relay information to a wider audience was primarily for our sponsors, via the Sepu Kangri website which was designed, assembled and run by Rupert Bonington in Cumbria, and via ITN news bulletins. These encouraged anyone interested to follow our progress. A secondary very useful role was to provide contact with Lhasa by phone, for example to arrange transport. We were also able to contact our families, and in some cases, work, by phone and e-mail. These latter functions were usually greatly appreciated at home, but also sometimes generated anxiety. Finally, technical, meteorological (and medical) advice could be sought easily by satellite phone.

The notes below outline how our equipment was organised; it will be appreciated that it was assembled piecemeal, from different sources. An expedition starting from scratch with a larger budget might have a more co-ordinated approach. The corollary of our method was that there were, in the event, various back-up systems.

Communications on the march

Elliot Robertson and I travelled some 200 kilometres on foot and horseback through the Nyenchen Tanglha with:
1 a BT Mobiq Satellite Phone.
2 Olympus Camedia C-1400L and 400-L Digital cameras.
3 One Toshiba Libretto 50CT Personal Computer – the smallest PC available.
4 Two Sony PD1P Digital Video Cameras.

We relied exclusively on solar power, provided by:
1 One rigid (but folding) 10 watt 12-volt (dedicated) solar panel for the Mobiq, which would sit on a rucksack.
2 Three linked flexible Uni-Solar solar battery chargers (panels) delivering 25W at 16.5 volts (max). These are tough (could be sat/slept on); we lashed them to a ski pole and carried them on a rucksack (United Solar Systems, Troy, MI, USA).

Power delivery from these panels came via:
1 A direct lead for the Mobiq (from its panel).
2 A Toshiba (in-car) 12-volt Adaptor (for the Libretto PC).
3 A Sony car battery charger DC-V515 battery-charger (for the Sony PD1s – which, oddly, did not have a dedicated 12-volt charger).
4 An RCLINE Multi Plus 12-battery charger for AA cells – an offshoot from model aircraft – (for digital camera AA batteries).

Each lead (we used XLR 4-pin plugs throughout) could also be used in a car cigarette lighter (12V), via an adaptor.

All this equipment (apart from the Mobiq panel) was assembled and adapted by Martin Davidson, of Skarda International Communications. *When the sun shone*, everything worked, reliably.

We maintained satellite telephone communications via the BT Mobiq's throughout the journey and had the luxury of free air time. We transmitted reports and digital (still) images via e-mail. We were able to charge video and AA batteries. Our problem was that the weather was atrocious, and there was often insufficient solar power for the Libretto PC (and hence downloading e-mail and photos). Also, we would have done better to abandon trying to recharge AA cells – it was *so* time-consuming – and to use instead lithium AA cells, despite their cost.

Communications at base camp

The main equipment at base included:
1 A second Mobiq phone
2 Two Apple Powerbook computers (Bonington)
3 One HP Deskjet 340 Printer (Bonington)
4 One Canon Bubblejet 130 Printer (Clarke)
5 One Toshiba 460CDT Laptop PC (Clarke)
6 Multiple cine cameras and batteries (*v.* Film)
7 Four Motorola Visar Radios and chargers (*v.* Radios).
8 An Olympus Camedia colour printer P-300E and additional cameras
9 News packaging and video equipment (*v.* ITN)

We were thus able to make outgoing telephone calls readily, type/print reports and digital images, use e-mail via the Apples and the Libretto, and download (still) digital images.

Power supplies

We relied on several sources of power – solar power via a battery pack ('the Magic Box'), wind generators, and also, as it turned out, petrol generators which had been brought specifically for news packaging, rather than for general expedition use.

Base camp power unit ('the Magic Box')

A simpler version of this system had worked well in 1997.

The Magic Box, a tough plastic case, contained 2 x 12-volt 16Ah Sonnenschein batteries, with, as its designer explained, an 'independent charge control system, and low voltage cut-off'. This weighed some 20kg.

There were, potentially, five power inputs (XLR-4 plugs):

1 A static, rigid, 4 x 25 watt 12-volt solar panel array,
2 The three Uni-Solar Solar Battery Chargers delivering 25W at 16.5 volts (max),
3 An Airwind Generator (3-bladed wind generator) delivering a peak output at MSL of 300 watts (Windsund, Sunderland, SR1 2AG),
4 An Ampair 12V (6-bladed wind generator) delivering a peak output at MSL of 100 watts (Ampair, Poole B12 3L7),
5 One spare input.

Power outputs were:

1 Four 12-volt 4-pin XLR sockets (for general use, with various leads – with particular attention to differing polarities),
2 Two 24-volt inverters to 5-pin XLR sockets (for two Apple Powerbook Computers),
3 One 240-volt 50Hz 200-watt inverter to a standard UK 3-pin socket.

Sadly, it has to be said that the Magic Box was a source of some frustration. The batteries rarely reached their estimated voltage levels despite prolonged charging. In practice, in over a month we were seldom able to use the Box for more than several hours at a time for the Apple computers, or the Toshibas, or for more prolonged charging, e.g. the Mobiqs. There was rarely sufficient power for the printers. We were unable to charge film batteries, or radio batteries from the Box.

Greig Cubitt, as resident technical expert, was unable to fathom an electrical fault, and though Gerry Taylor, the designer and manufacturer, was most helpful on the phone, he was unable to suggest any major remedial actions. Obviously, on any expedition, damage (by yaks, truck and jeep travel, water) can wreck almost anything: we had cared for the Box as best we could and there was no sign of damage.

It is difficult to decide quite why the Box was below par; I suspect it *had* been damaged, and also that our multiple demands were simply too much for it. Its general design, from the 1997 prototype, seemed satisfactory.

In reality we became very largely dependent upon Greig Cubitt's generosity, petrol and the Honda EX500 generators (*v.* ITN). These too failed towards the end of the expedition. Had we not had this source of power, many communications/charging activities would have been greatly restricted.

Wind generators

A generic problem where air density is low, as it is at high altitude, is that windspeeds need to be higher than at sea level (MSL)at to produce a given power output. The variability of windspeed and possible very high windspeeds in storms also need to be taken into account. Firm anchorages are essential. Generator blades must be inaccessible to children, yaks, horses and goats: spinning blades are potentially lethal. We had given thought to the majority of these issues but, oddly, neither generator manufacturer had mentioned the critical issue of air density.

Ampair 100

This six-bladed (usually marine) 12-volt generator has an integral mounting pole and anchor lines. Particular attention in the manual was given to the need for the blades to be well balanced: those supplied were so. The turbine was exceptionally smooth running. Minimum windspeed for operation was under 10 knots at MSL, and in practice around 20 knots at 4700m. Maximum output power was rated at 100 watts.

In the event the blades turned, on average, less than an hour a day. It is difficult to gauge the contribution the Ampair made to battery power, but it must have been small on most days. However, in general terms we would recommend this generator in an expedition setting, if wind generators are to be used at all. It would be worthwhile discussing with the manufacturer whether larger than standard turbine blades could be attached. A voltage regulator was not fitted; this did not appear to be a problem. The bearings had been packed with a low temperature grease before delivery.

Weight (standard pole, with box, packing and spare blades): 15kg.

Airwind module

This 6kg (some 9kg with spare blades and packing) high-output (300 watts) 3-bladed generator had an integral voltage regulator. The unit was supplied with a separate custom-made pole system in a wooden box. This was perhaps heavier than necessary and increased overall weight to over 35kg.

Despite being assembled carefully according to the manufacturers' instructions, when the turbine blades rotated, the generator vibrated excessively, loosening repeatedly the substantial ground anchors. Minimum windspeed required to initiate rotation at MSL was given as around 7mph in the manual (and thus we would expect it would require around 15mph at 4700m). However, in practice, windspeed required for start-up was well over 20mph, always higher than for the Ampair.

We felt that the Airwind generator supplied was potentially dangerous because of the vibration. We had no way of weighing or re-balancing the blades, which appeared to be of slightly different weights. Swapping blades (with spares supplied) did not seem to help.

Radios

We used four Motorola Visar walkie-talkie radios, recharging batteries from the petrol generators. (Had we not had access to the latter, we would barely have been able to use the radios.) The Visars worked excellently, even out of line of sight. One remains in a tributary of the Salween, having slipped from Scott's harness at a river crossing!

Film

(from Jim Curran's notes)
The advent of the mini-digital video camera has changed the concept of expedition filming for ever. The traditional 16mm film documentary, however much one might regret its passing, has already become a rare and costly luxury. For both the 1997 and 1998 Sepu Kangri expeditions we relied on SONY VX1000 cameras, which give TV broadcast quality images, using the small DV video cassettes. The camera bodies were modified to take Sennheiser external microphones. In 1998, over 50 hours of tape were shot, all of which would fit comfortably into a small rucksack – the equivalent in 16mm would barely squeeze into an estate car.

Once on the climb the differences between, say, *Everest the Hard Way*, that milestone in mountain filming, and Sepu Kangri become marked, and readily evident. In the former, *any* moving footage was a bonus, achieved only at considerable cost by a specialist climbing cameraman, who might, if he was lucky, bring home a few minutes of real action. In 1975, cameraman Mick Burke's summit attempt – 16mm camera in hand in Peter Boardman's last photograph of him – ended in tragedy, as Mick died in the storm on the summit ridge. Neither he nor his film were ever recovered. In 1975 these shortfalls of action inevitably meant shooting from extreme telephoto long shots or, worse, panning still photgraphs.

In 1998 all the climbers used DV-CAMS as an extension of their own personal equipment, encouraged perhaps by the possibility of nearly imme-diate exposure on ITN news programmes. SONY PD1-Ps and JVC DVX mini-cameras were used, both for personal video diaries and to make a comprehensive record of the climb and activities in high camps. The climbers became an integral part of the film team.

In the event, hours of excellent footage were shot, often in difficult circumstances. Everyone experienced a rapid learning curve: this was due in part at least to the ease with which they could review their efforts on Greig Cubitt's base camp editing suite. From this, virtually finished news items were transmitted directly to London.

Few technical problems were encountered. One of the two VX1000s was unduly sensitive to damp and cold; it took some coaxing on icy mornings. One of the JVCs developed a similar problem – and a tape jammed which could only be removed on return to Britain. The other JVC used high on the mountain was kept warm in a sleeping bag or jacket at all times and had no similar problems.

The Sony PD1Ps were excellent and gave no trouble.

All the batteries were recharged at base using the Honda EX500 petrol generators. On the final push the team had purpose-made lithium battery packs (made up by Greig Cubitt); each lasted nearly four hours.

The contractual arrangements between Northern Films ITN and Just Radio allowed all parties to have full access to any recorded material, an important point when editing film for the proposed TV and radio programmes, the details of which are still in hand.

For the principal film-makers, Martin Belderson and Jim Curran, the experience of working in this remote area was immensely rewarding.

Independent Television News: news packaging and video transmission

(from Greig Cubitt's notes)
This was the first time ITN had transmitted news items direct from a high altitude mountaineering expedition, with a cameraman/editor as a team member. The ITN equipment consisted of one Sony VX1000 (miniDV) camera with a Panasonic laptop editor for the news reports. News reports were transmitted to the UK via an Inmarsat B satellite phone using a high speed data link.

Tapes from the JVCs and VX1000 could be read directly on the laptop editor; SONY DV CAM tapes from the PD1s could not.

The edited video and audio reports were fed to a TOKO, a specialised computer which stores digital images. These were read at standard ISDN 64K and fed to the high-speed data port of the Inmarsat B, which was also a third satellite phone. Transmission took about thirty minutes for every one minute of real time video/audio – i.e. usually over an hour of continuous transmission for a single two-minute news item.

240 AC mains power (standard UK 3-pin socket) was provided by two Honda EX500 two-stroke generators in tandem. These needed high-altitude jets (and the knowledge of how to fit them). The generators functioned well initially (delivering 50% MSL power at 4700m, as expected). However both seized towards the end of the trip (probably because of inferior fuel, as judged by carbon deposits). There had also been some difficulty obtaining high-octane fuel and two-stroke oil in Lhasa; its quality must remain suspect.

Audio

Following the success of the three Radio 4 Magic Mountain programmes produced by Susan Marling of Just Radio (London WC1N 3QL) in 1997, we made a comprehensive audio collection of personal diaries, communal expedition events, radio calls and local Tibetan scenes. We hope for another series of broadcasts. Audio was also recorded via camera sound tracks. The contractual arrangements mentioned above should be noted.

We used:

     1 A SONY Walkman Professional (standard C-90 tapes);

     2 A SONY TCD-D8 DAT-CORDER (DAT tapes).

The latter was found less easy to use than the standard Walkman Professional, but some form of back-up is clearly essential.

Lessons for the future

1 Substantial power requirements such as our own require detailed planning, and rigorous testing. For a truly portable system, I suspect that individual solar panels for each item are the most effective, and versatile. This is essentially the system Elliot and I used on our journey, and we were pleased with the results, despite the bad weather.

2 For a static system, it is hard to beat a petrol generator, if high-quality fuel can be procured.

3 If solar panels plus batteries are to be used, careful and pessimistic estimates of sunshine hours should be made. Simple and robust equipment is essential.

4 Wind generators require wind! Bear in mind that the minimum windspeeds for operation above 4000m are at least double those at sea level.

We had erected both our generators on a balmy English summer after-noon, when neither rotated at all, and had no other opportunity to test them. Balanced blades are also clearly essential, and a means of re-balancing them if replacements become necessary. Safety is paramount.

5 We experienced no substantial computer hardware problems. However, computers work sluggishly or not at all in cold conditions, below 5°C. We needed to heat the communications tent each morning.

Some computers (e.g. the Libretto) are said to have an altitude limit of 3000m (a fact we discovered in the manual at 4500m!); this seemed not to be a major problem, but sometimes, unaccountably, the Libretto failed. Perhaps altitude was a factor.

The communications tent fabric was black – a little too dark to see a keyboard clearly within it. Conversely, on the march, we carried 2 x 1m of black cotton material, to cover ourselves and computer screen, otherwise it was impossible to see the VDU in bright sunlight.

6 Various software problems were transient, if sometimes very irritating.

7 Running complex communications equipment takes inordinate lengths of time, daily, and requires a dedicated expedition member.

8 We had no easy access to our own website – a lengthy downloading time with a slow (2400) baud rate. It would have been preferable to edit the website at base camp, but again this would have been time-consuming.

9 Finally, it goes without saying that rigorous field testing of everything is desirable, but trying to achieve this at sea level, in Britain, in a city, with a full-time job by day does pose problems.

Overall, we felt that our communications, despite some frustration and various pitfalls, were a success. We hope that our sponsors feel that their generosity has been appreciated publicly and that the exercise, both of a website which was followed regularly by several thousand people, and serial ITN news reports was worthwhile.

Medicine

DR CHARLES CLARKE

This appendix outlines the medical kit we carried in 1998 and the notes I sent to expedition members several months before departure.

Notes to expedition members sent in 1997 and 1998

1 It is important that the team members understand fully the scope of medical support available, and what is likely to happen in the event of a serious accident and illness. It is up to individuals to discuss this with their families. On Sepu Kangri, there was no possibility of helicopter rescue: evacuation would be on foot/horseback to the roadhead, and thence by road. There are hospitals at Diru, Nakchu and Lhasa.

2 We shall not be carrying intravenous infusions, nor bottled oxygen.

3 Medical insurance must be completed through the British Mountaineering Council. I must have a copy of your policy.

4 Immunisation can be carried out through local general practioners or by arrangement with Charles Clarke. Up to date immunisation against tetanus, diphtheria, polio, typhoid, hepatitis A and rabies is recommended (there are fierce dogs on the Tibetan plateau). These immunisations were provided free by Pasteur Mérieux Ltd.

BRITISH SEPU KANGRI EXPEDITION 1998
MAIN MEDICAL KIT

Note for Customs Authorities

These drugs are for the personal use of the ten members of the expedition during August–November 1998.

All are labelled and listed, with instructions for use.

Any unused drugs will be re-exported from Tibet/Nepal.

Painkillers

Paracetamol 500mg tablets	Pain: two every 4hrs	100
Codeine phosphate 30mg tablets	Pain/diarrhoea: two every 4hrs	200
Diclofenac 50mg tablets	Pain: one three times daily	100
Diamorphine 10mg tablets	Severe pain: one every 6hrs	50
Diamorphine 5mg injection	Very severe pain one every 6hrs	10

Altitude sickness

Acetazolamide 250mg tablets	One tablet twice daily	50
Nifedipine 10mg tablets	Two tablets three times daily	100
Dexamethasone 2mg tablets	Two tablets four times daily	100
Dexamethasone 8mg injection (2ml vials)	Give one 4mg injection four times daily i.e. 1ml	10

Gastrointestinal

Loperamide 2mg tablets	Diarrhoea: two, then one four times daily	100
Ranitidine 150mg tablets	Severe indigestion: one twice daily	40
Gaviscon tablets	Indigestion: 1–2, 4 hourly	100

Eyes, ears, skin, throat &c

Chloramphenicol eye ointment 4g	Apply three times daily	3 tubes
Anusol cream	For piles: three times daily	2 tubes
Betnovate ointment 100g	For severe sunburn: apply twice only	2 tubes
Malathion 50ml	Lice, scabies, bugs: see bottle	2 bottles
Piriton 4mg tabs	Itching: one 3 times daily	20
Various throat lozenges	Fisherman's Friend, Strepsils	28 pkts
Otosporin ear drops 5ml	Itchy ears etc. three times daily	2 bottles
Calamine lotion	Skin soothing	100ml
Sunblock cream	RoC UK	30 tubes
Sunblock lipsalve	RoC UK	50 sticks

Instruments &c

Stethoscope	1
Ophthalmoscope	1
Sphygmomanometer	1
Auriscope	1
Foley urinary catheter	1
BM stix	1
Syringes 2ml	10
Needles	15
Scalpel + blades	1 + 3
Scissors	2
Tweezers	2
Potassium permanganate	30 tabs
Lignocaine 2% inj. 5ml	10 vials
Water for injection 5ml	20 vials

Infections (continued)

Empty labelled pill bottles	15
Dental forceps &c	1 set
Spencer-Wells forceps	1

Dressings &c

Crepe bandages 3"	20
Adhesive bandages 2" & 3"	20 mixed
Melonin 4 × 4" NADD	30
Tulle dressings	20
Elastoplasts	60
Steristrips	20
Sutures	10
Alcohol swabs	50

Infections

Amoxycillin 500mg caps	Antibiotic: one capsule 3 times daily	60 caps
Ciprofloxacin 500mg tabs	Antibiotic: one twice daily	20 tabs
Oxtetracycline 250mg tablets	Antibiotic: one four times daily	50 tabs
Cefotaxime 2g injection	antibiotic: give one 2g injection four times daily	12 inj
Metronidazole 400mg tablets	Antibiotic: one tablet three times daily	50 tabs
Tinidazole 500mg tablets	Amoebic dysentery: four tablets then 1 twice daily	28 tabs

Infections (continued)

Quinine 600mg tablets	Malaria: one 8 hourly for seven days	21 tabs
Mebendazole 100mg tablets	Worms: one twice daily for three days	12 tabs
Rabies vaccine Read instructions	Dogbites: give one i.m. injection in arm	3 injs

EXPEDITION MEDICAL KIT: LONDON TO LHASA

Paracetamol 500mg tablets	Two four hourly	50
Loperamide 2mg tablets	Diarrhoea: two, then one 4 × daily	100
Throat lozenges	Fishermans Friend	50
Various dressings		
Steristrips	Various	10
Acetazolamide 250mg tablets	One tablet twice daily	50

Severe altitude sickness

Each climbing team carried bandages and a single bottle of:

Dexamethasone 2mg tablets & Nifedipine 10mg tablets	Two of each three times daily

The drugs were dispensed by the Pharmacy, the National Hospital for Neurology and Neurosurgery, London. Particular attention was paid to clear labelling, as shown above. We also bought a small supply of homeopathic drugs on the way through Tibet prior to the main 1998 expedition, to supplement dwindling supplies. In addition various expedition members brought their own medicines.

A signed copy of the medical kit list accompanied it while it was being freighted.

Appendix 8
Acknowledgements

We could not have mounted our two expeditions to Tibet without a great deal of financial help and other support. We are all deeply grateful to the organisations and individuals who have made our two attempts on this wonderful mountain possible. We list below the sponsors who provided us with financial support, the suppliers who gave or loaned equipment, and the people who have helped us:

Main Sponsor
1998 National Express Group plc

Sponsors

1997
Claris (UK) Ltd
Coleman (UK) plc
Cumbria TEC
International Powered Access
   Federation
Sealy UK Ltd
Silva (UK) Ltd

1998
Barclays Bank PLC
Burton McCall Ltd
William Hill Ltd

Grant aid

1997 and 1998
Mount Everest Foundation
British Mountaineering Council
National Hospital Development
   Foundation
Anonymous donor
Duncan Sperry
Eric Parkin
Sue Skinner
David Ward

Suppliers

Climbing, trekking and camping gear

Beal *Fixed and dynamic rope*
Berghaus *All clothing, rucksacks, Yeti gaiters and walking boots*
Black Diamond *Snow shovels and ice screws*
Bollé *Sunglasses and goggles*
Cascade Designs *Therm-a-Rests and seats*
Coleman *X-Treme High Performance Gas stoves and lights, Globe Trotter Lightweight cooking sets*
Charlet *Karabiners, ice tools, crampons and ice screws*
DMM *Friends, rocks and deadmen*
Gaber *Ski-poles*
Fire Jet *Wind-shield*
Inoxal *Double layer cooker sets*
Lyon Equipment *Non-stretch rope*
Maglite *Torches*
Petzel *Crash hats, harnesses and headtorches*
Sigg *Water bottles*
Terra Nova *Loan of tents*
Victorinox *Swiss Army knives, tools and watches*
Yale *Padlocks*

Travel

Qatar Airways *Air travel and airfreight*

Communications, Technical and Electronic Equipment

Apple Computer Inc. *PowerBook G3 & 1400 plus Newton 2000*
Agfa (1997) *Loan of Digital Cameras*
British Telecom *Loan of BT Mobiqs and satellite air time*
Findhorn (1997) *Communication integration*
Garmin *Loan of Global Positioning Systems*
Gerry Taylor Associates *Design and supply of solar panels and power suite*
LakesNet *Internet service provider*
Logica (1997) *Design of communications system software*
Olympus Optical Co (UK) *Camedia 400, 800, 1400 Digital cameras & printer*
South Midland Communications (1997) *Loan of walkie-talkie radios*
Skarda International Communications (1998) *Loan of VHF Radios and expertise*
Sony Broadcaster & Professional *PD1 P DV Cams*
The Met Office (1998) *Daily weather forecasts*
Vicom *Software*

Food and Drink

Highland Distillers *Black Bottle Whisky*
Jordans *Fruesli Bars & breakfast cereals*
Lanes *Tartex Paté & Natex Spread*

Medical

Pasteur Mérieux MSD *Immunisations*
The Pharmacy – National Hospital, London *Drug Supplies*
RoC UK *Sun Protection*

Travel

Qatar Airways
Himalayan Kingdoms, UK
Himalaya Expeditions, Inc.,
 Kathmandu
China Tibet Mountaineering
 Association
Tibet International Sports
 Travel

Support

Jim Lowther *Packing, insurance, air
 freight*
Louise Wilson, Margaret
 Trinder *Secretarial for Chris
 Bonington*
Frances Daltrey *Pictures*
Rupert Bonington, Paul Batey *Web
 design & Administration*
Ann Tilley *Secretarial for Charles
 Clarke*

A Tibetan and Chinese Glossary

tsampa – ground roasted barley, staple diet

chura – hard dried yak cheese, faintly like Parmesan

chuba – long-sleeved sheepskin gown

chorten – traditional, monumental shrine at entrance to monastery

gompa – monastery

mani stones – prayer stones

O mane padme hum – 'Hail to the Jewel in the Lotus', written on *mani* stones

katak – white (usually) ceremonial silk scarf

lhakhang – shrine

dukhang – prayer hall

tangkha – religious (or medical, or other) paintings on cloth

yuan – currency $1~8 *yuan*; £1~14 *yuan*

Bon – original animistic religion of Tibet

Bod, or Bod-Kham – indigenous name for Tibet (Mongolian: *Thubet.* Old Chinese: *Tufan.* Arabic: *Tubbat*)

Xizang – Chinese name of Tibetan Autonomous Region

Kham – general term for eastern Tibet

shan – mountains, mountain range

tashi de le – traditional Tibetan greeting, used little outside Lhasa

chu(Tib.), *jiang(Ch.)* – river, also spelt *qu (Ch.)*; or water, generally

moutai – a Chinese distilled liquor, very strong, an acquired taste

nee ha, nee ha . . . – Chinese greeting, usually repeated several times

ba – yak-hair tent for long-term residence – a lighter canvas tent, a *ma* is used on the move

Appendix 10
Bibliography

Bonington, C.J.S and Clarke, C.R.A. *Everest the Unclimbed Ridge.* London, Hodder & Stoughton, 1983.

Curran, J. *K2, Triumph and Tragedy.* London, Hodder & Stoughton, 1987.

Curran, J. *K2, The Story of the Savage Mountain.* London, Hodder & Stoughton, 1995.

Fleming, P. *Bayonets to Lhasa.* London, Rupert Hart-Davis, 1961.

Fowler M. *Vertical Pleasure. The Secret Life of a Taxman.* London, Hodder & Stoughton, 1995.

Guibaut, A. *Tibetan Venture.* London, John Murray, 1947 (+ Oxford University Press Paperback, 1987).

Hanbury-Tracy, J. *Black River of Tibet.* London, Frederick Muller, 1938.

Huc, R-E. *Lamas of the Western Heavens.* London, Folio Society, 1982.

Immortal Mountains in the Snow Region. Edited by Yu Liangpu, Chen Qun and Xue Yun. 1995, Tibet People's Publishing House. ISBN 7–223–00880–6/J.26.

Kaulback, R. *Salween.* London, Hodder & Stoughton, 1938.

Kingdon Ward, F. *The Mystery Rivers of Tibet.* London, Seeley Service, 1923.

Ma Lihua. *Glimpses of Northern Tibet.* Beijing, Chinese Literature Press, 1991. ISBN 7–5071–0800–4/I.74 and 0–8351–2090–2.

Mountains of Central Asia. Edited by Michael Ward. The Royal Geographical Society and Mount Everest Foundation. London, Macmillan, 1987.

Rinjhard, Dr S.C. *With the Tibetans in Tent and Temple.* Edinburgh & London, Oliphant, Anderson & Ferrier, 1901.

Salisbury, Harrison E. *The New Emperors. Mao and Deng, a dual biography.* London, Harper Collins, 1992 (Paperback 1993).

Sandberg, G. *The Exploration of Tibet. Its History & Particulars from 1623 to 1904.* Calcutta, Thacker, Spink, 1904.

Saunders, A.V. *Elusive Summits.* London, Hodder & Stoughton, 1990.

Smythe F.S. *Kamet Conquered.* London, Gollancz, 1932.

Tibet Handbook, edited by Gyurme Dorje, 1996. Trade and Travel Publications Ltd, Bath BA2 3DZ, England. ISBN 0 900751 69X.

Tibetan Medical Tangkhas of the Four Medical Tantras. People's Publishing House
    of Tibet, 1987.

Turner, S. *An Account of an Embassy the Court of the Teshoo Lama, in Tibet.*
    London, Nicol, 1800.

Younghusband F. *Peking to Lhasa.* London, Constable, 1925.

Index

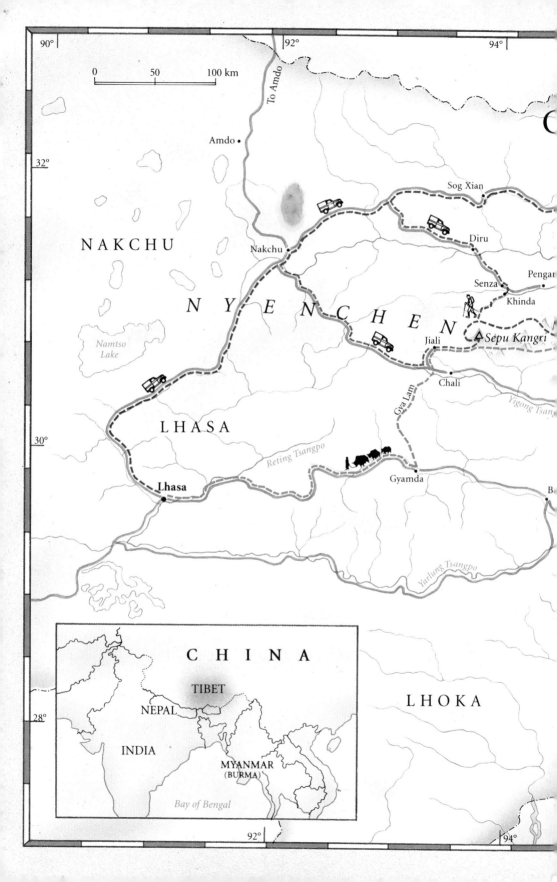